*Stick Together and Come Back Home*

The publisher and the University of California Press
Foundation gratefully acknowledge the generous support
of the Anne G. Lipow Endowment Fund in
Social Justice and Human Rights.

# Stick Together and Come Back Home

## Racial Sorting and the Spillover of Carceral Identity

PATRICK LOPEZ-AGUADO

University of California Press

University of California Press, one of the most distinguished university presses in the United States, enriches lives around the world by advancing scholarship in the humanities, social sciences, and natural sciences. Its activities are supported by the UC Press Foundation and by philanthropic contributions from individuals and institutions. For more information, visit www.ucpress.edu.

University of California Press
Oakland, California

Library of Congress Cataloging-in-Publication Data

Names: Lopez-Aguado, Patrick, author.
Title: Stick together and come back home : racial sorting and
   the spillover of carceral identity / Patrick Lopez-Aguado.
Description: Oakland, California : University of California Press, [2018] |
   Includes bibliographical references and index. |
Identifiers: LCCN 2017033396 (print) | LCCN 2017038082 (ebook) |
   ISBN 9780520963450 (ebook) | ISBN 9780520288584 (cloth : alk. paper)
   | ISBN 9780520288591 (pbk. : alk. paper)
Subjects: LCSH: Prison administration—California. | Social
   control—California. | Race discrimination—California. | Prison
   gangs—California. | Prisoners—Violence against—California.
   | Prisoners—California—Social conditions.
Classification: LCC HV8756 (ebook) | LCC HV8756 .L67 2018 (print)
   | DDC 365/.609794—dc23
LC record available at https://lccn.loc.gov/2017033396

Manufactured in the United States of America

26   25   24   23   22   21   20   19   18   17
10   9   8   7   6   5   4   3   2   1

*For Emma, Jorge, and Melissa.*
*And for Fresno.*

# Contents

# Acknowledgments

A lot of people contributed to this book, putting their time, energy, expertise, and goodwill into its completion. I have to first thank everyone in Fresno who helped me conduct this research, especially all of the high school students and returning community members who were brave and generous enough to share their stories with me. Doing justice to your experiences pushed me to do my best every time I sat down to write. In one of my earliest interviews, one of you told me that "it's not that [many] people who make it. When they come off of parole, it's not a lot, you know? So when you doin' your research, it's a good thing because you got a lot of people tellin' you different things, and it's up to you to put it into words." More than anything, I hope I have at least been an accurate and effective voice for some of the things you all have been through, and for some of the things that should change. I especially want to thank Richard, Chuy, Eddie, Anthony, Diana, Michelle, David, Sammy, Jose, AJ, CT, Daren, Victor, John, Mark, Darryn, Yasmin, Ricardo, Andrew, Steven, Felipe, and all the other young people who let me get to know them over the course of this research, and who made sure I knew what it was like for them at the school and the hall.

Obviously I could never undertake a project this extensive completely on my own, and there are several people who deserve recognition for helping me actually get into these research sites and bring my findings to this finished product. I want to extend my appreciation to the administrators, outreach workers, and teachers—especially Mrs. Diaz, Mrs. Damon, Mr. Cruz, and Mr. Martinez—who helped me gain access to institutions that are typically very difficult to research. Cid Martinez was an invaluable role model and authority on all things Fresno—a fellow ethnographer who was always down to talk about current events in town, and who put me in touch with a number of insightful community members. Thank you to Javier Guzman and the Chicano Youth Center for welcoming me to Fresno, tapping me into the city's distinctive history of community organizing, and giving me the opportunity to get involved. Thank you as well to Grandpa Bill, Uncle Bill, and Aunt Lia for always being around for support, and for inviting Meli and I over whenever we needed a break. I am grateful for the support of the University of California Institute for Mexico and the United States (UC Mexus) and UC Santa Barbara's Chicano Studies Institute, which made this research financially possible, and for the help provided by Valeria, Gaby, Doug, Jenna, McKenzie, Juliet, Gianna, Alec, and everyone else who assisted with transcribing so many interviews. And finally, I am tremendously appreciative for Maura, Sabrina, and everyone at UC Press who recognized the importance of this story, and gave me the opportunity to put it into print.

I owe much to the many mentors I have been blessed with, who have given me the perspective, curiosity, analytical skills, and endurance to take on this project. My earliest mentors and connection to Fresno, my parents Liz and Herb, are the ones responsible for making me a writer and for teaching me the importance of trying to understand others' experiences. In graduate school, my advisors George Lipsitz, Victor Rios, Reginald Daniel, and Nikki Jones were the first to guide me on this specific project, and remained consistent voices of support and clarity throughout. You helped me build this research through its many stages, teaching me how to discuss the important social problems I was finding in an approachable way while still developing my analysis in scope and nuance. Through your mentorship, you have taught me how to be a professional scholar and a critical writer, and your lessons will stay with me throughout my career.

I also want to thank the many established scholars who went out of their way to read earlier drafts or versions of this research, and contributed to making it better. Particularly deserving of my appreciation are Ruth Peterson, Laurie Krivo, Aaron Kupchik, Cheryl Maxson, and everyone else involved with the RDCJN network. I would also like to thank Manuel Pastor, Timothy Matovina, the University of Notre Dame's Institute for Latino Studies, and everyone involved with the Young Scholars Symposium for their valuable input. Finally, I want to extend a special recognition to Anthony Peguero and Robert Durán—not only for providing their own feedback on earlier drafts of this research, but also for laying the groundwork for a community of Latina/o criminologists that has provided me and so many others with a professional space to grow into. You have all not only helped me tremendously in developing this book, but have also welcomed me into the academy and made sure I knew that the scholarship I had to offer was valued.

Throughout the process of planning and writing this work, I have been lucky to be surrounded by a talented group of peers and colleagues who have always helped me immensely and pushed me to keep up with their own brilliance. Thank you everyone from the 2014 cohort of the SRI—Daniel Gascón, Reuben Miller, Michael Walker, Nicole Gonzalez Van Cleve, Evelyn Patterson, Lallen Johnson, and Valerie Wright—for your feedback, ongoing friendship and encouragement, and memories of racist dots and cracking the ground. Thanks to Jerry Flores and Adrían Félix for being motivating writing partners I could always rely on to meet up at the library or coffee shop and actually write. Equally important were Katie, Scott, Armando, and Danny, who kept me sane by getting me out of the house during this process, congratulating me when it went well, and encouraging when it got dicey.

Most of all, I need to thank my partner and colleague Melissa Guzman. You have been there for me the entire time and never let me give up—when I couldn't find a research site, when I didn't think I could afford to stay in the field, or when I hit a wall while writing and didn't think that I could finish it. You always keep me sharp and challenge me to think about my research in new ways. You have made me a better writer, teacher, and scholar. But most importantly you always believed in me, even when I didn't believe in myself, and not only reminded me that this was an important project but convinced me that I was capable of doing it. I love you, and can never thank you enough for the support you gave to me during this research. You influenced this work more than anyone.

Finally, I would like to dedicate this work to my grandparents Jorge and Emma Lopez-Aguado. The entire time I was conducting this research, you opened your home to me and gave me a place to stay and recover from long days of traveling, volunteering, and interviewing. You have always shared everything you have and done everything you could to help and take care of me. It was a personal blessing to me to be able to spend this time with you, to share meals and desserts with you, and to get to know the two of you again as an adult, and I will never forget it. I owe finishing this book to you, because without you this entire project would have never been possible. Thank you grandma and grandpa, for everything.

# Introduction

*The Carceral Social Order*

Frank went to prison the first time when he was twenty-one years old. Coming of age on the predominantly Chicana/o Eastside of Fresno in the early 1990s, he became active in its drug trade as a young man—he started rolling with Crips at fourteen, selling crack at sixteen, and by nineteen had moved on to robbing drug dealers. Then his daughter was born. Frank decided to quit gangbanging, leave the drug game, and make an effort to straighten his life out. "[I] started slowing down everything. Stopped hanging around with my cousins, just started working. Just doing the right thing." But working in the formal economy was not making him enough money to get by and support his new family. As times got more desperate Frank turned back to what he knew made money—drug robberies. After one robbery his victims report him to police, and when the police come to investigate they find stolen property in his home. Frank is arrested and eventually sentenced to three years in prison.

As his bus pulls up in front of the Sierra Conservation Center in Jamestown, he sees a collection of armed guards waiting. They pull him off the bus and march him and the others into the facility like cattle, past the large barking dogs that lunge and sniff at him as he passes by. His eyes catch hostile glances from everyone around him, both the prison staff and the other inmates. Once inside, nobody will talk to him. He gets nervous seeing everyone else around him start to clique up into small groups, but he stays by himself on a bench waiting to see what is going to happen to him. A corrections officer finally comes for him and escorts him to a large gymnasium lined with rows of double bunks and filled with hundreds of inmates. Not sure why he's been brought here or who else is here, he sits on a bed feeling alone and unsure of what he is going to do. But hearing someone yelling behind him, Frank turns around and realizes something.

He already knows a lot of the men in here.

"[I hear] hey Frank! And I look. My heart was like thank you! I was like thank you God!" So many years later Frank would laugh as he remembers how relieved he felt in that moment, and how surprised he was to see so many familiar faces in the prison with him. "[W]hen I got there, to Jamestown, I knew practically everybody in there. From all the years I was growing up, all from the Eastside. [I knew a] lotta guys there." Soon he hears more and more calls of "Frank!" "Hey man, what's going on?!" "Frank!" "What's up?!" Many remember him from high school as one of the students who always got good grades. "Man what are you doing here?" All he can think to tell them is "I got caught up."

Frank finds several of the guys he grew up with in his neighborhood are already here, meaning that he won't have to face the prison alone. Their presence helps him feel much less fearful about how the next three years are going to unfold. But with the unexpected support Frank finds with this group, being associated with them also exposes him to new tensions and conflicts, and in some cases violence.

> Then I didn't roll with the Crips. I told him I don't wanna be gang-banging no more, I was just from Fresno. And so they just put me with the Fresno people but they were all Bulldogs in there, but they didn't know me. I was just running with Fresno. Everybody asked me "Where you from?" "Fresno." "Oh you a Bulldog?" "No, I'm just from Fresno," but they would get it twisted sometimes. "Oh you from Fresno so you have to be a 'dog!" but I was like "Naw, naw." I had some problems with that, [had to] fight a few people over that.

Frank's ability to find some support with the others from Fresno also subjects him to being associated with Bulldog gang members from Fresno. As Frank begins doing his time and acclimating to the prison, he starts to face challenges from other groups of inmates, some of which escalate into fistfights. But these do not start just because others suspect he is a rival gang member. Instead, he gets into fights for breaking the rules.

Not long after arriving at Jamestown, Frank joins a basketball game with a group of Black inmates one afternoon on the yard. He thinks nothing of it, but afterwards other Latino prisoners confront him about it. Latino inmates from Southern California flex their authority on the yard and tell him he can't be hanging around with the Blacks. Frank reacts angrily to people he doesn't know telling him who he can or cannot hang out with, but his friends quickly intervene. They tell him that even though the Fresno group doesn't care about socializing across races, he should abide by the Southerners' rules in order to keep the peace because they drastically outnumber them. Frank can't believe it and protests: "You got me messed up dude. I don't even know these people! I ain't playing that!" But the others insist.

"No man, you just can't. You gotta follow prison rules."

The rules surrounding race that Frank has to learn to navigate are determined by a complex history of conflict between the powerful prison gangs in California's system. In the late 1950s a group of Los Angeles-based Chicanos form La Eme, ostensibly to protect the few Mexicans inmates held in the then mostly White system. However, over time they begin preying on Latino prisoners from rural territories in Northern California, who some ten years later respond with their own group, La Nuestra Familia. Around this same time, shifting racial demographics in state prisons push White inmates to form the Aryan Brotherhood in response to losing their majority status to a growing population of Black and Latino prisoners, and compel George Jackson to form the Black Guerilla Family as a prison-based faction of the broader Black Power movement. For the next several decades these four groups compete with each other for control of the prison's drug trade. Eventually the Aryan Brotherhood and La Eme create an alliance to help each other battle the Black Guerilla Family and La Nuestra Familia respectively. These latter powers create their own pact soon, thus establishing the racial politics that still govern prison life in California.

The "prison rules" Frank collides with following his basketball game are based in these same conflicts. Because La Eme is allied with the Aryan Brotherhood against the Black Guerilla Family, Southern California Latinos cannot socialize, trade, or share items with Blacks in the prison. When Frank is at Jamestown the Southerners are also able to impose these restrictions on his group from Fresno because of their fairly small presence there. Frank gradually learns these tenets, which he explains "was more jailhouse rules than [they] are actual guidelines that the prison sets." However, the prison does have a hand in this; while the institution may not define the particular rules for each group, it does determine who is subjected to them. Prison authorities intervene in the conflicts between prison gangs through the implementation of racial sorting, following a logic that they can separate prison gangs by separating the racially defined populations that contribute members. But in institutionally grouping inmates by race and hometown, these officials have essentially established the system's major prison gangs (and their rivalries) as not only the basis for segregation, but also for the identities that prisoners are now pushed to adopt in order to fit into this segregated system. Frank is sent to the housing unit he is precisely because correctional staff suspect that he would fit with the other men there. Despite never being a Bulldog—and not even Chicano like most of them are, but Puerto Rican—the fact that he is Latino and from Fresno is enough to categorize him with them. Now, regardless of if he bangs or not, because Frank is with the Bulldogs he is held accountable to their role in the racial politics of the prison.

Some inmates first learn of these politics once they get to prison as Frank did, but many others are familiar with them long before ever going to prison. Throughout years of researching, volunteering, and working with criminalized youth, I have consistently met young people who were intricately aware of the racial politics at work in the prison and even identified with the same groups that inmates are categorized into by correctional staff. In this book I propose expanding discussions of the collateral consequences of mass incarceration—the cumulative costs and penalties individuals and their families incur as a result of a prison term (Mauer and Chesney-Lind 2002)—to consider how high-incarceration communities are impacted by socializing processes instilled in the prison. I argue that in their attempts to control gang violence, punitive facilities construct a "carceral social order" that divides the entire institutional population into a handful of conflicting gang-associated groups. Within this social order, one's race, home community, and peer networks are interpreted as signs of potential gang affiliation. These criteria are then used to sort individuals into criminalized collective identities that are continually socialized and reinforced as they acclimate to the institution. Youth hear about these identities from loved ones who have been imprisoned, but also encounter the same social order within juvenile facilities that similarly give gangs the same power to determine who youth can socialize with. This social order consequently contextualizes some of the unanticipated consequences mass incarceration has for the communities targeted for imprisonment: the transmission of prison culture to the street, and the extension of the prison's ability to define and construct criminality.

## CONCENTRATED INCARCERATION, CONCENTRATED CONSEQUENCES

As the era of mass incarceration has made imprisonment a prominent feature of the American justice system, its implementation has closely followed race and class power structures.[1] Blacks and Latina/os are significantly more likely to be incarcerated than are Whites (Mauer and King 2007), but prison admission rates are most inflated among *poor* Blacks and Latina/os (Pettit and Western 2004). Because patterns of residential segregation effectively contain poor people of color to high-poverty, racially defined neighborhoods (Massey, Gross, and Shibuya 1994; Lipsitz 2012)—spaces in which residents are exposed to targeted policing and subsequently more likely to become ensnared in the justice system—incarceration rates are also spatially concentrated. For example, in mapping the geographical distribution of incarceration rates in Tallahassee, Florida, sociologist Todd Clear found that imprisonment was overwhelmingly concentrated in low-income Black neighborhoods (2007). Subsequent studies in New York City, Phoenix, New Orleans, and Wichita similarly found that the neighborhoods in these cities from which prison inmates are disproportionately drawn are those with the highest concentrations of poor Blacks and Latina/os (Spatial Information Design Lab 2008). Within these poor communities of color, a significant portion of young male residents experience imprisonment at some point in their lives (Pettit and Western 2004; Braman 2004; Simon 2007).

Mass incarceration is then something that predominantly and most severely affects specific neighborhoods: the residents of poor communities of color are disproportionately subjected to imprisonment (Clear 2007; Parenti 2000; Gilmore 2007; Mauer 2006) but are also overly exposed to its aftereffects, particularly the pains of prisoner reentry. Of the approximately 640,000 individuals released from prison every year (Carson and Golinelli 2014), most return to the same communities from which they were incarcerated (Petersilia 2003). Concentrated incarceration then subsequently also creates "central-city neighborhoods and inner suburban ring communities—where much of urban poverty is situated—[that] are playing host to the majority of inmates leaving jails, prisons, and detention centers" (Venkatesh et al. 2007, 9). Once released, parolees often struggle to find stable employment (Pager 2007) and housing (Lipsitz 2012), which can jeopardize their efforts to avoid reoffending. For former inmates with limited mobility, returning to neighborhoods with already high poverty and unemployment rates offers little opportunity for successful reentry (Sharkey 2013; Sampson 2012), which sends most parolees back to prison fairly quickly, most commonly within six months of release (Petersilia 2003).

But high rates of imprisonment and release also aggravate the structural inequalities these marginalized communities already experience (Lipsitz 2012; Clear 2007). Incarceration severely limits the employment options of former prisoners after release (Western 2006; Pager 2007), and the influx of workers with poor job prospects further strain weak labor markets (Hagan and Dinovitzer 1999). The consistent removal and return of neighborhood residents also deteriorates informal social controls in the community

(Lynch and Sabol 2004), producing a "tipping point" at which high incarceration rates actually raise crime rates rather than reducing them (Clear 2007). After this tipping point incarceration erodes the neighborhood's collective efficacy (Sampson, Raudenbush, and Earls 1997), and may even create a vacuum effect in destabilized drug markets in which many candidates compete to replace dealers who have been sent to prison. Additionally, the political disenfranchisement of convicted felons diminishes the voice of high-incarceration communities in electoral outcomes and reduces access to political representation (Marza and Uggen 2006).

But while mass incarceration magnifies the structural disadvantage of poor communities of color, the transmission of prison cultures into these communities also represents a significant but little-understood outcome of mass imprisonment. As concentrated incarceration establishes imprisonment as a frighteningly common experience in affected neighborhoods (Simon 2007; Western 2006), prison-based cultural styles or practices find their way into criminalized communities through a "growing hybridization and cultural interpenetration of prison and street" (Brotherton 2008, 63). This transmission is similar to how high rates of recruitment and participation in the military influence its cultural presence in rural communities (Krier, Stockner, and Lasley 2011), and even synchronize local understandings of masculinity with those constructed and valued in military training (Woodward 2000). Recognizing that inmates are socialized to take on the worldviews, values, and behaviors of the prison (Clemmer 1958), the cycling of so many community residents through the penal system may carry some of this socialization into the neighborhood. Within the emerging literature on the collateral consequences of mass incarceration, the impact that identities socialized inside the prison may have on life outside the facility remains a largely unexamined area.

## CRIMINALIZATION AS COLLATERAL CONSEQUENCE

Criminologists have long argued that as individuals enter the prison and begin to serve their sentences, they experience a process of prisonization (Clemmer 1958) in which they learn to adjust to prison life and are assimilated into an inmate subculture. But learning to fill this prisoner role is not a benign or uncostly socialization process. Michel Foucault (1977) argues that it is through such socialization that the prison ultimately defines and constructs criminality. Socializing people to *be* prisoners distinguishes prisonization as a criminalizing process, one that entrenches a criminal status by teaching the individual to embody it. This criminalization is often described as prisoners learning to refine criminal participation from other inmates (Foucault 1977), or being compelled to become gang members (Hunt et al. 1993; Skarbek 2014). But we must consider how criminality is shaped by the social status produced by incarceration—former inmates are not only readily recognized as criminal, making their deviance more visible (Chambliss 1973), but are also less able to access legitimate means of self-sufficiency precisely because they are former prisoners (Travis 2004). Foucault argues that this identification of former inmates as a criminal class is the central accomplishment of the prison (1977).[2]

Most important to Foucault's point is that this status lingers even after release, so that it is in free society where one is identifiable as previously incarcerated and therefore criminal. The expansion of mass incarceration not only structures the consistent return of such-labeled "criminals" to poor communities of color in large numbers (Clear 2007), but also funnels them into a fairly small number of urban neighborhoods (Sharkey 2013). Concentrated incarceration effectively raises crime rates in subsequent years (Clear 2007), but the concentration of prisoner releases also reinforces the identification and subsequent policing of targeted neighborhoods as criminal. For example, when California's prison realignment called for the release of many low-level offenders, law enforcement agencies across the state expressed concern that this would elevate local crime rates and that they would need more resources to combat the inevitable crime wave (Petersilia and Snyder 2013).

Intensified policing of poor communities of color is closely tied to the growing role of the prison in the management of social problems (Wacquant 2009; Gilmore 2007), but also to the close connection this reliance structures between the prison and "problem" communities. Loic Wacquant (2001) frames this as a meshing of prison and neighborhood in which the two increasingly resemble each other in terms of both form and function; while the prison takes on the ghetto's task of racial confinement, the ghetto begins to resemble the prison in terms of everyday experiences with surveillance and social control. Within criminalized neighborhoods, law enforcement agencies increasingly embed themselves within local institutions such as schools and community centers, appropriating these sites as segments of a punitive justice system (Rios 2011; Kupchik 2010). But Wacquant (2001) goes on to argue that the prison and the ghetto essentially become extensions of each other; these sites collaborate to form a "carceral continuum" that effectively contains poor people of color and isolates them from socioeconomic mobility.[3] The school-to-prison pipeline—a frequently traveled trajectory in which punitive school policies push poor youth of color into the criminal justice system (Wald and Losen 2003)—represents a dramatic manifestation of this relationship between penal and community institutions. Within this system, schools in poor Black and Latina/o neighborhoods treat students as criminal suspects by criminalizing their behavior (Hirschfield 2008; Nolan and Anyon 2004). Simultaneously, local governments establish systems of "alternative" or "continuation" schools that effectively exclude students from public school districts while keeping them under justice system supervision (Wald and Losen 2003). Youth growing up in the ghetto are resultantly more likely to enter the prison as young adults, only to return as felons to criminalized communities that continue their exclusion from civic and socioeconomic participation.

The reliance on crime control to address social problems (Gilmore 2007; Wacquant 2009) also presumes the prison as a place to which the perpetrators of social disorder can be sent following removal from the community. Youth criminalization is then the process of identifying who is to be sent—a personification of social disorder (Feldman 1991). Mass incarceration therefore structures the criminalization of poor communities of color in ways that situate young peoples' experiences with criminal labeling. Sociologist Victor Rios (2011) contends that the era of mass incarceration intensifies both the scale and consequences of criminal labeling—as increased law enforcement involvement in community institutions drags more youth into the juvenile justice system, it tags them with stronger and more enduring labels that ensure an ongoing cycle of surveillance and punishment. But while mass incarceration intensifies the consequences of youth labeling, its concentration in poor neighborhoods of color also establishes a certain continuity between how residents are managed in the prison and criminalized in the neighborhood. For example, school-to-prison pipeline scholars have argued that poor students are already socialized for incarceration in prison-like school settings that feature metal detectors, security fencing, surveillance equipment, pat-downs and searches, in-school suspensions, and a constant presence of law enforcement that collaborate to define students as criminal suspects (Hirschfield 2008; Nolan and Anyon 2004). Furthermore, social theorists have argued that the prevalence of incarceration in Black and Latina/o neighborhoods has established it as a new stage in the life course of poor young men of color (Pettit and Western 2004; Comfort 2012), making the prison "a normal socializing institution for whole segments of American society" (Simon 2007, 472). In this sense, the prison's connectedness to the neighborhood may then lead the prisonization process that acculturates inmates to the penal institution to appear in other criminalizing environments. But as I address in the next section, prisonization is also characterized by the construction of specific identities that are read as criminal, some of which now appear in poor and heavily-policed communities of color. Consequently, the cultural "meshing" or "hybridization" of prison and neighborhood (Wacquant 2001; Brotherton 2008) that results from the consistent churning of residents between these sites may align how community members are criminalized both inside and outside of the penal facility.

## CONSTRUCTING CARCERAL IDENTITIES

Racial segregation and conflict is a significant aspect of the prison social order inmates acclimate to (Wacquant 2001), but in California this is directly structured by the state. Since the 1970s state facilities have divided entire institutional populations by race (Parenti 2000; Robertson 2006), ostensibly to control escalating violence between the Aryan Brotherhood, Black Guerilla Family, La Eme, and La Nuestra Familia (Irwin 2005; Spiegel 2007). California Department of Corrections (CDC)[4] officials separated these prison gangs by racially categorizing all inmates as they entered the prison system (Irwin 2005; Goodman 2008) and sending them to facilities with clear spatial boundaries between groups.[5] For male prisoners, being categorized as Black, White, Latino, or "Other" (Asians and Pacific Islanders) by correctional staff (Goodman 2008) not only shapes who they can bunk and socialize with (Lindsey 2009), but also exposes them to conflict with other racial groups (Parenti 2000; Robertson 2006; Spiegel 2007). These social dynamics push prisoners to internalize the race- and place-based identities created by this process.

But these identities are also legitimized by facility staff members who implement this sorting. Sociologist Michael Walker found that officers also learn to rely on racial segregation to manage and control imprisoned populations (2016). Consequently, correctional officers maintain this segregation by encouraging incoming inmates to see themselves as members of the groups they are sorted into, and by consistently presenting race as an important divide that organizes institutional conflict (Goodman 2008). Sociologist Phillip Goodman (2008) argues that this practice represents a race-making process that institutionalizes narrow and incompatible racial identities. But there is also an aspect of "place-making" work in prison sorting (Gupta and Ferguson 1997) that shapes how inmates learn to articulate local identities. After being separated from other racial groups, Latino inmates are also geographically categorized as Norteños (Northerners), Sureños (Southerners), and Bulldogs depending on if they are from Northern, Southern, or Central California respectively. This context established important regional identities and even allowed place to shape one's racial identity, such that Chicanos from different parts of the state are recognized as distinct races in the prison. For example, in his study of a medium-security prison criminologist John Irwin (2005) found that Northern and Southern Latinos generally avoided interacting with each other and recognized institutional boundaries between them as they would with other racial groups.

Importation theories argue that prisoners bring street, neighborhood, or gang identities into the prison with them (Irwin and Cressey 1962). Similarly, Joan Moore (1978) argued that for Chicano gang members, barrio gang ties shape their identities in the prison just as they would in the neighborhood. However, the social order structured by racial sorting imposes new identities on inmates that are prioritized in this context. In this sense, many gang-involved prisoners see a disruption of street gang identities when they are incarcerated—neighborhood loyalties and feuds become secondary to the prison's racial politics, and former gang rivals often must put their conflicts aside while imprisoned in the interest of cultivating a united racial group identity (Skarbek 2014). Inmates have a difficult time claiming identities that fall outside of the narrow framework presented to them in sorting (Goodman 2008) because their classification structures so much of their experience in the prison (Robertson 2006; Lindsey 2009), making it an essential situational identity in this space (Goffman 1961).

Finally, we must acknowledge the role that prison sorting has in ascribing criminal labels (Lindsey 2009; Parenti 2000). Social organization in the prison is defined by race, place, and the sorting process that uses these identifiers to categorize inmates (Robertson 2006; Spiegel 2007). But because this system is based in institutional efforts to control gangs (Irwin 2005; Goodman 2008), the resulting groups are themselves commonly framed as gangs (or extensions of gang) that dominate the prison's social order (Hunt et al. 1993; Skarbek 2014). For example, researchers studying the racialized social order in California's prisons in the early 1990s explained that "where previously prisoners made choices about joining a gang, membership has now become more automatic, especially for Chicanos. Today . . . if [an inmate] comes from south of Fresno, he is automatically a Sureño, if he is from north of Fresno, he becomes a Norteño" (Hunt et al. 1993, 404–5). Assuming that everyone who goes to prison is a gang member—or becomes one while incarcerated—fails to recognize the institution's influence in shaping its own social order. What Hunt and his colleagues overlook is that while not all inmates are gang affiliated, they are all subjected to a sorting process that essentially marks them as such.

To be clear, the groups Hunt and colleagues refer to as "gangs" here (Norteños and Sureños) are not the same groups as prison gangs like La Nuestra Familia and La Eme. Rather, Norteños and Sureños are groups born from the prison's efforts to control La Nuestra Familia and La Eme by separating Latinos into Northerners and Southerners. It is important to conceptualize the collectivities discussed here differently from gangs for two main reasons: first, many prisoners simply do not consider themselves to be gang members or see the groups they associate with as gangs (Irwin 2005; Parenti 2000). Second, these groups are fundamentally based in and maintained by processes that label individuals as gang affiliated—both in the prison through sorting practices that use race and place as proxies for gang membership (Lindsey 2009), and in the neighborhood through the expansion of criminalizing practices in community institutions (Rios 2011).

## PARALLEL CRIMINALIZATION

Their similar function in isolating people of color generates a relationship between the prison and the neighborhood that fosters a cultural bridging between the two (Wacquant 2001). Within this cultural meshing, the identities constructed in the prison find their way back into the neighborhoods from which prisoners are disproportionately drawn. Sociologist Megan Comfort's work on the families and partners of incarcerated men helps us conceptualize this by introducing "secondary prisonization" (2008). She uses this concept to explain how inmates' partners are themselves subject to the restrictions and culture of the prison as "quasi inmates" (2008, 15). In California, secondary prisonization makes the racialized conflict and discipline that structure inmates' day-to-day lives consequential for the families and communities of the incarcerated. For example, until 2014 California state prisons used race-based lockdowns (Spiegel 2007) that restricted all inmates of a given race to their cells anytime there was a security threat in a facility. These lockdowns in turn affected the ability of inmates' families to visit them; when Black inmates were locked down and restricted from leaving their cells, Black families were simultaneously separated and restricted from coming into the visitation room (Comfort 2008). Prisoners' families are therefore affected by the same race- and place-based sorting practices that categorize their incarcerated loved ones, as these families' relationships with incarcerated members tie them to the identities institutionalized inside the facility.

These connections to the incarcerated expose prisoners' families and high-imprisonment neighborhoods to prison socialization processes that mark their recipients as criminal. The appearance of Norteña/o, Sureña/o, and Bulldog identities in California's poor Latina/o communities offers a compelling testament to this. In the neighborhood these identities exist as umbrella terms that several Latina/o street gangs claim simultaneously (Skarbek 2011), and that may also articulate ethnic, linguistic, and/or class divides within the community (Katz 1996; Mendoza-Denton 2008). But there is some debate as to why barrio youth have been appropriating these prison-based identities for the past several decades.

One common discourse claims that these identities mark communities in which prison gangs have recruited local street gangs into an expansion of their criminal enterprises outside the prison (Rafael 2007). Political scientist David Skarbek offers a more nuanced take of this argument, explaining that these identities function to indicate which prison gangs have the authority to mediate local drug trades (2014). Just as segregation allows prison gangs to dictate the racial politics for the entire car,[6] it also gives them broad authority over any street gangs whose members are locked up and segregated alongside them. Imprisoned street gang members may be used by prison gangs to attack rivals or maintain order inside, but they are perhaps most valuable as collateral for extorting drug revenue from gangs in the neighborhood. Prison gangs are able to impose "taxes" on street gangs by threatening to hurt incarcerated street gang members if they are not paid. Therefore, if gang-involved dealers (or gangs who themselves extort local dealers) want to protect their incarcerated homeboys—and recognize that they may be incarcerated themselves someday—then it becomes in their best interest to appease the prison gang (Skarbek 2014).

However, it is important to consider the institutional role in this relationship. For example, the ability of Chicano prison gangs to extort Chicano street gangs in this way is in the least facilitated by—if not outright dependent on—penal policies that force all Chicano prisoners to be housed together by positioning them against other racial groups. Additionally, these ties between prison and street gangs may also have their limits. La Eme and La Nuestra Familia have conspired with street gangs in a handful of well-publicized drug trafficking cases (Rafael 2007; Blatchford 2008; Skarbek 2014), but it is impossible to know if similar arrangements exist with all such affiliated neighborhood cliques. Consider that not all neighborhood gangs who claim Norteña/o or Sureña/o identities necessarily sell drugs or have access to sizeable drug markets; some are in towns with barely a few hundred residents. If there is little drug money to offer, how then are these identities distributed? Differing from this top-down view is Robert Durán's (2013) explanation of how Sureña/o identities reached the states of Utah and Colorado. In his account, Mexican youth excluded from the existing Chicana/o gangs in their communities simply adopted Sureña/o identities they saw sensationalized in antigang media as an act of oppositional resistance against the racist social order they lived in. Not coincidentally, Southern California's Sureña/o identities came to be a locally recognized form of criminality as LAPD-based gang experts consulted local police on how to identify gang youth (Durán 2013).

In recognizing law enforcement's ability to name and identify criminality, it is important to remember the increasing role the prison has in this process. In California, the state in whose prisons these identities were originally born and where they first appeared in Latina/o communities, the neighborhoods they appear in generally correlate with how residents are sorted inside the prison.[7] Within the prison these identities are ascribed in a mandatory sorting process and encouraged as legitimate identity categories around which social life is organized (Lindsey 2009; Goodman 2008). But within the poor communities of color that host parolees released from detention (Clear 2007), law enforcement agencies read these same identities as evidence of criminal gang membership (Katz 1996; Mendoza-Denton 2008). As such, parolees are often sent back to prison for violating gang stipulations of their parole based on actions such as socializing with similarly labeled peers or possessing anything that officers see as promoting this "gang" identity.

Criminalizing the very identities that the prison demands of its inmates never lets parolees shake their criminal status; this is the essence of Foucault's (1977) delinquency. But these Norteño, Sureño, and Bulldog identities also come to inform how criminality is articulated in the neighborhood; they comprise the labels law enforcement ascribe to youth in gang validation processes (Rios 2011), as well as the identities neighborhood youth subsequently embrace to signal their resistance to local social hierarchies (Durán 2013; Mendoza-Denton 2008; Rios and Lopez-Aguado 2012). The policing of prison-based identities in neighborhood contexts represents an important extension of the prison's ability to designate criminal status to the families and communities of the incarcerated. In these identities we can see how the prison produces meanings of criminality that increasingly define poor people of color and their neighborhoods as the appropriate targets of mass incarceration by labeling them as gang affiliated. This production by prisons pushes us to consider how "gangs" operate as a social construct—one that is part of a hegemonic master narrative of crime (Brotherton 2008; Ewick & Sibley 1995) that rationalizes not only perpetuating mass incarceration but also concentrating it almost completely in poor communities of color (Clear 2007).

## WHERE PRISON AND FRESNO MEET AND MESH

The details are blurry, as they usually are with these kinds of stories, but people seem to agree that it happened sometime in the mid-1980s. Fresno was already an important dividing line in the prison for corrections officers separating Northern and Southern Hispanics; it was the southern frontier of Norteña/o street culture and one of largest cities from which La Nuestra Familia could extort drug market revenue. For at least the previous decade local street cliques on Fresno's expansive Eastside had acknowledged this affiliation through the shared name of Fresno 14 (or F-14). But in the mid-1980s, members of F-14 incarcerated in San Quentin convened and decided that they would no longer "follow orders" from La Nuestra Familia. Some say that they were tired being used to attack La Nuestra Familia's rivals, but most importantly this signaled that F-14ers active in the drug trade were now refusing to pay the prison gang any shares from local drug market earnings, instead now keeping all profits for themselves. These homeboys subsequently broke rank with other Norteña/o gangs and began calling themselves Bulldogs, a regional designation emanating from the marketing strategy to represent Fresno State University's sports teams as being from "the Valley." Word of this split soon spread through to the state's other prisons, the California Youth Authority facilities, and back to the streets of Fresno where F-14 was soon "retired" and many young people began claiming Bulldogs for themselves. Decades later, young teenagers calling themselves Bulldogs still vaguely reference this event in local street mythology through regular proclamations of "We don't take any orders!"

The story of the Fresno Bulldogs is generally understood as one of gang formation, or perhaps secession. But this story has had consequences for scores of local youth and adults who don't consider themselves to be gang involved, and in many cases have explicitly avoided gangbanging throughout their lives. Gang politics affects what happens to everybody inside the prison, but this influence eventually trickles out to impact the "quasi-inmates" back home too. Part of why word spread so quickly and effectively is because the CDC began removing everyone from Fresno from Northern yards and segregated them into different housing assignments. Over time Fresno County Latinos came to be segregated as their own racial group in the prison, and for the most part even sent to the same facilities.[8] Now people in Eastside Fresno knew that if they got locked up they were doing their time with Bulldogs, regardless of if they banged or not. What started as a dispute between a handful of Fresno-based gang members and the prison gang they formerly paid tribute to soon changed not only how all

Fresno Latinos are categorized but consequently also the collective identities that traveled back home.

Fresno is a city of about a half million people, over a quarter of whom (28.9%) fall below the federal poverty line (Census 2015). Additionally, over half of the city's poor residents (50.9%) live in high-poverty neighborhoods, giving Fresno the fourth highest rate of concentrated poverty in the nation (Kneebone 2014). These neighborhoods with poverty rates exceeding 40 percent are mostly confined to the communities south of McKinley Avenue[9] in which 75 percent to 99 percent of residents are people of color. These are the same communities we see disproportionately affected by mass incarceration. Fresno's problems with poverty and unemployment, coupled with a notoriously aggressive police department (see Parenti 2000), have left its communities of color particularly vulnerable to criminalization; while people of color represent 57 percent of all county residents, they account for 69 percent of all arrests (Benjamin 2015). But the disproportionate investment of public funds in crime control over community support also pushes poor criminal suspects into confinement. For example, despite California State Bar guidelines recommending parity in the resources available to prosecutors and public defenders, in 2009 the Fresno County Board of Supervisors adopted a resolution to finance the Public Defender's Office at 61 percent of the funding made available to the District Attorney.[10] This disparity has led to a Public Defender's Office that is grossly unequipped to meet the local demand for its services; individual public defender attorneys average 612 felony cases and 1,462 misdemeanor cases every year, over four times what the American Bar Association recommends. Faced with such overwhelming caseloads, public defenders can do little more than advise their clients to plead guilty so as to avoid more serious charges or longer sentences. As a result, only 0.19 percent of the cases brought to the Fresno County Public Defender's Office ever actually go to trial.

Fresno's place as a borderland between regions of the state dominated by rival prison-based subcultures, and a county with higher incarceration rates than the Bay Area or Los Angeles (California Sentencing Institute 2017), make it an important site to examine how the prison's social order spills into the community. In this work I focus on three points of contact at which the neighborhood intersects the carceral system, sites where residents pass from one to the other at different points in the life course—the juvenile hall, a continuation high school for youth on juvenile probation, and the prisoner reentry center. By incorporating multiple sites that impact criminalized youth into my analysis, I was able to track youth across institutional settings and observe how the social orders they encountered in each were related. In the reentry center I sat in on group meetings with parolees and interviewed them individually about their experiences both in the prison and the community.[11] This ethnography includes seventy-nine in-depth, semistructured interviews conducted with parolees and probation youth in Fresno. While I collected this data I lived on the Eastside for over fifteen months, blocks away from many of the participants that I would get to know during this time.

## Juvenile Detention Facility

Just south of the city limits, where the railyards and industrial warehouses finally give way to the surrounding farmlands, a large complex of two-story gray cement boxes with color-coded doors and paneling sits alongside the highway. Rather than being built up as one monolith structure, Fresno County's Juvenile Detention Facility (JDF) is sprawled out across a large property. It actually includes two separate campuses—each capable of incarcerating up to 240 youth—that span out on either side from a central courthouse; one is for "detention housing" for youth awaiting trial or transfer to a state facility, the other for "commitment housing" for youth already sentenced by a juvenile court. JDF opened in 2006 at a cost of $145 million, making it the largest capital project in the county's history. But this facility is actually just the first stage in Fresno County's original master plan for the site; at the time of this research planned future additions included three more 240-bed confined housing wings, a boot camp, group homes, a continuation school, a reporting center, and more law enforcement offices to fill the 220-acre site that the county has already purchased. These additions would bring the total capacity of JDF to over 1,440 youth by 2040, making it the largest planned juvenile justice facility in the nation. In a county that currently has a population of less than one million, only the tenth largest in the state.

When JDF opened, the county boasted of it as the future of youth corrections, and it became an explicit representation of the county's investment in punitive justice. By 2008, two years after the facility's opening, the number of youth booked into juvenile hall rose by over a thousand to 5,331 juveniles. By far the largest increase was in the number of youth brought in for simple probation violations (VOPs)—citations given to youth who are already on probation for minor offenses such as truancy or tardiness at school, failed drug tests, or possession of "gang paraphernalia."[12] The expanded space afforded by the new facility made it possible to detain far more young people, resulting in a doubling of the number of youth booked for VOP to over 1,200. In the years since the county has struggled to finance the large facility, even closing pods and losing almost 20 percent of its juvenile corrections officers (JCOs). The unviable costs of funding such a large facility combined with dropping juvenile crime rates have now put some of the county's ambitious plans for the site in question. Still, JDF currently provides the necessary infrastructure to incarcerate a great number of local youth.

I came to JDF through the Fresno Youth Network (FYN), an outside agency who helped me find my way in, both figuratively and literally. Exiting from the freeway, a manicured, tree-lined road leads around the courthouse to the "commitment side" of the facility where FYN has a clubhouse for the youth inside. Standing alone in the dry, hot openness of the San Joaquin Valley, JDF is surrounded in each direction by flat fields that stretch out to the horizon, filled only with the noise of the highway and warm, unmitigated winds that carry the smell of tilled soil. It just makes coming in or out of the facility feel that much more dramatic. The glass door at the entrance is locked, as it often is. There's a reception desk just inside, but when they're short-staffed you have to just wait for someone free to come let you in. Sometimes it can take a while. I push the button on the metal intercom next to the door and a voice comes in asking "Can I help you?" I glance up to the round black camera bulging from the overhang ceiling and explain that I volunteer with FYN inside. They have hundreds of the same camera throughout the facility, above every doorway and down every hall. "Alright someone will be there in a few minutes." While I wait for them to let me in a pair of rabbits chase each other around nearby, in the field between the parking lot and the cement wall of one of the pods.

After about ten minutes one of the JCOs finally gets to the door and lets me in once I show them the ID card the agency gave me. I store my wallet and cell phone in one of the lockers built into the opposite door, pass through the metal detector next to the reception desk, then wait until I hear the door buzz and the handle click open before going into the waiting room on the other side. I turn left in the waiting room and pass through a double set of security doors, the kind with a small room between them where the second won't open until the first one is closed again. I push the same metal intercom button to open the second door and wait for the staff controlling the door remotely to inspect me over the camera again. This is why I keep my ID out. Eventually the thick steel bar locking the second door begins to slide open and I proceed into the visit room. I pass by the rows of lunch tables to another set of double security doors on the other side. These doors open into a long gray hallway with a concrete floor and walls, and more black camera bulbs every so many feet along the ceiling. The sound of the door closing echoes down the hall, and I walk to the end through one more door, this one leading to the grass quad outside. Outside is a soccer field with all the pods built into a circle surrounding it. I walk along the outside wall of the gym until I reach the door to the rec room, where I knock so the FYN staff will let me in.

The recreation room FYN runs inside JDF is a stark contrast to the rest of the facility. The white walls are covered in posters and artwork created by the youth who come in. The room features a pair of TVs with Xboxes; some beanbag chairs and a couch; ping pong, foosball, and air hockey tables; and a stereo for them to play music. Ten youth from each pod are allowed to come into the rec room for one or two hours every two to three days. The pods use a point system developed to monitor behavior to determine which ten get to come. FYN brought me in to facilitate a violence prevention program in which I asked youth a great deal about their communities, their ambitions, and their perceptions and experiences with the justice system. But more than anything the room serves as a place that just lets them get out of the pod for a little bit, which they greatly appreciate. Consequently much of my time here was spent hanging out with the youth as someone to play cards, video games, or just chat with. I jotted notes on their conversations and interactions during break periods between pods. Additionally, many of these youth were required to report to the San Joaquin Educational Academy (SJEA) upon their release from custody, which gave me the unique opportunity of stay in touch with them as they moved between these settings.

### San Joaquin Educational Academy

Hidden from the main streets among rows of apartment and office buildings, few people know that SJEA is there, or even exists at all. The county runs the small continuation high school out of a converted AT&T call center that is surrounded by barbed wire fencing, the only opening a gate with a metal detector and stationed guard who searches students as they enter, confiscating keys and cell phones they forgot to leave at home or hide in the surrounding shrubbery. There are about 100 to 150 students enrolled at any given time, most of them (usually about 85%) boys. The racial makeup of the school was fluid during my twelve months there, but most of the time about two-thirds of the students were Mexican or Chicana/o, about a quarter of them were Black, and the remainder comprised of a mix of White, Native American, and Asian students. All of SJEA's students are on juvenile probation, and most are ordered to attend the school upon their release from JDF. The drug treatment and mental health programs that many of the youth are required to complete as conditions of their probation also have their offices on campus, as do five probation officers (POs) who supervise most of the students at the school.

The county established SJEA to provide transitional education for probationary youth that would allow them to catch up on the credits missed during incarceration and transfer back into the public school district. Students earn credits faster here than they would in public school, which helps make up for lost time and catch up to their grade level, but surveillance at the school keeps most of the youth on probation. Few students actually transfer back to public school from here, as only a small number complete their minimum stay at SJEA before violating probation, and even those who do stay on track may see their transfers denied by a district that refuses to take them back. Instead, SJEA essentially functions as part of a system of continuation schools throughout Fresno that isolates criminalized youth from the rest of the district. While the school's faculty and staff work well with the students and are genuine in their desire to help them graduate high school, the way SJEA is structured "helps" students through punitive discipline, pushing them deeper into the justice system and making it difficult for them to attain a standard education. Most students have their PO on site, and can be incarcerated for violating their probation based on discipline problems at the school. Even excessive absences can be enough to send them back to juvenile hall. Most of the students I met in my time here were at some point reincarcerated, many based on something that happened while they were being monitored at the school.

I originally came to SJEA as an intern shadowing a counselor who worked onsite, but was fairly quickly asked to contribute as a tutor for disruptive students, which came to be how I spent most of my year. Three days a week I would pull students out of class and help them with assignments, either individually or in small groups. Teachers often gave me the students who gave them the most trouble, but these students were usually able to focus and complete their work once they were taken out of class. Oftentimes they simply acted out because they didn't like their teacher, but usually enjoyed getting out of class and were willing to do their work once I took them. Taking four to five students out at a time gave me the opportunity to get to know many of the students at the school, to hear their stories, and to listen to them talk with each other about the school, their weekends, their neighborhoods, who had been arrested or released, and other topics relevant to their daily lives. These conversations also gave me a chance to explain my research and recruit students for interviews after school. I also frequently sat out with students in the hallways and outside of offices when they got in trouble, which helped me learn more about conflicts at the school and hear students' concerns about violating probation or returning to juvenile hall. Some students initially suspected that I worked with law enforcement, but sharing so much time with them and most importantly not "snitching" on them for minor things like tagging in schoolbooks helped them trust me as someone at the school they could speak candidly with without getting into trouble. At times this created some tension with a few faculty members and administrators who expected me to cooperate with their surveillance and discipline of students, and I had to negotiate this so as to maintain access to the school while also protecting the students' trust. However, most staff respected that helping them monitor and discipline students was not my role at the school.

I conducted interviews with thirty-six of the students from the continuation school that I had gotten to know in my time volunteering at the school as a tutor, as well as with two security guards and the school principal. These interviews focused on youths' experiences with street cultures in Fresno and how they felt the justice system impacted their lives and communities. These interviews provide a deeper context for the observation fieldnotes, particularly regarding the identities the youth perform and how they interpret the roles street culture and incarceration play in their day-to-day experiences. Participants were recruited for interviews from the groups of students I pulled out for tutoring,[13] as well as through snowball sampling. Youth were asked if they would be interested in being interviewed and contributing their stories after I explained the focus of my research.[14] Although I was unable to conduct any interviews at JDF, many of the students I met there eventually attended SJEA and participated in interviews once they were enrolled there. Interviews were conducted and digitally recorded in private offices on the school grounds at the end of the school day.

Attempting to make my sample of student interviewees roughly representative of the racial demographics of the school, I interviewed twenty-four students who were Mexican or Chicana/o, eight Black students, five White students, two Native American students, and one Asian student. Four of the students I interviewed identified with more than one racial group when asked about their background, but at the school primarily socialized with one racial group of students. Student interviewees ranged in age from fifteen to eighteen, and of these thirty-six participants, ten were girls and fifteen self-identified as gang members.[15] Finally, in approaching students for interviews I also made an attempt to be inclusive of the different cliques present at the school[16] and more or less mirror their share of the overall student body.

## Fresno Job Placement Center

On a wide but quiet street in downtown Fresno, among buildings for city bureaucracies and public utility companies, a small office building houses a prisoner reentry center. The Fresno Job Placement Center (FJPC) is a non-profit agency in which counselors help people returning from prison find housing and job opportunities. Outside, a small group of parolees gather for a smoke before heading in. After wrapping up they go in through the center's computer lab and past the whiteboard that announces this morning's meeting. They continue into a room with about a dozen folding chairs arranged in a circle, grabbing a cup of coffee from a table in the corner before sitting down.

Every Friday morning, the FJPC hosts mentoring meetings for all new clients entering the program. These meetings last for about an hour and average about ten to twelve people in attendance. In these meetings parolees discuss their experiences returning to Fresno, offer each other support and encouragement, and share strategies for searching for and applying for work. The agency's staff invites me to attend each week, allowing me to introduce myself to those in attendance and explain why I am interested in their stories. After the meeting, I conduct and record interviews with anyone interested in contributing their story in a private office.

Thirty-one of these formerly incarcerated men and women eventually volunteer to be interviewed for this research. In these interviews participants talked about their personal histories with the justice system, and discussed how they learned of and navigated the prison's social order. The parolees interviewed in this work described being categorized as Blacks, Whites, Northern Hispanics, Southern Hispanics, Bulldogs, and Others. All but one of the participants were on parole or probation at the time of the interview. Most had been released from custody in 2010 or early 2011. Interviewees ranged in age from twenty-seven to forty-nine. A small number of participants were also contacted through an inpatient drug treatment center near downtown Fresno.[17]

## OUTLINE OF THE BOOK

The first half of this book primarily takes place inside the punitive institution, focusing on how the carceral social order is created and understood in these settings. In chapter 1 I describe how punitive facilities structure, socialize, and reinforce the carceral social order within the institution. I argue that in their efforts to prevent institutional violence by separating rival gangs, the prison, the juvenile detention facility, and the continuation high school instead construct a consistent social order that is based in gang rivalries—one in which everyone in the facility is compelled to participate. Within these facilities, staff members construct this social order by using race, home community, and peer networks to categorize entire institutional populations into gang-associated groups. Staff members then routinely maintain these categories as distinct peer groups by policing the spatial boundaries between them, as keeping rival groups separated is perceived as necessary for ensuring institutional security. I conclude this chapter by discussing how the relationships and conflicts that are structured by these sorting and segregation practices ultimately socialize this carceral social order as a dominant, "common sense" logic for both managing and navigating punitive facilities.

Chapter 2 discusses the identities that are constructed by and instilled within the segregated carceral facility, as well as how the parolees and probation youth learn to understand them. Racial and neighborhood identities come to be rearticulated as carceral affiliations inside the institution, and incarcerated residents learn to see these affiliations as valuable resources for protecting themselves while navigating the punitive facility. But while carceral affiliations are often framed as criminal gangs by authority figures, participants used and understood these identities differently, and I argue that developing a critical analysis of the carceral system's socializing power requires recognizing this difference. Additionally, I use this chapter to examine how the sorting process not only creates carceral affiliations as collective identities but also influences how individuals understand aspects of their own personal identities. As participants are socialized to identify with carceral affiliations, this process also shapes how they learn to understand their own racial, gang, and gender identities, as these are each molded to help one fit within the social order of the punitive institution.

In chapter 3, I examine how affiliated identities are performed within a context in which individuals must read each other's position in the carceral social order. Specifically, I examine how participants use space and style to signal one's ties to the racialized groups institutionalized in the facility, and to interpret who others are affiliated with as well. I also use this chapter to explore how individuals attempt to negotiate and resist the prevailing carceral social order when they do not fit neatly into the system's organizational schema; participants who were mixed race, had family members in rival gangs, or who affiliated with a different racial group had to figure out how they would navigate a divisive environment in which their position was not immediately clear. In these instances, individuals had to choose one affiliation over another, or in some cases, attempt to resist the carceral social order entirely by refusing to affiliate with anyone. In this chapter I explore these participants' experiences, outline how and why they came to occupy the positions they did, and describe what obstacles they faced.

Chapter 4 begins the second half of the book, which focuses on how the carceral social order ties high-incarceration neighborhoods to the prison, and details some of the implications that this has for local residents. This chapter specifically looks at how prison-based affiliations come to appear in local communities, where they are learned and reproduced among criminalized youth. I argue that this spread of carceral identities is shaped not only by the institutional appropriation of penal sorting practices, but also by the effects of concentrated incarceration. For incarcerated residents, affiliations serve as important ties to home and as sources of support while confined in unpredictable settings. When these community members return home with little formal or material reentry support, many hold on to these identities—both because they may supply the only help that parolees do find, but also because these residents could never be certain that they would not be locked up again. At the same time, young people in the community first learn about these same affiliations from previously or currently imprisoned friends, relatives, and neighbors, informing how they imagine they would survive their own potential experiences in the prison. This close relationship between carceral affiliations and neighborhood identities shapes residents' experiences with criminalization and violence, but it also contributes to a public perception of poor Black and Latina/o neighborhoods as pathological spaces, one that many local youth internalize.

Chapter 5 explores how the carceral social order structures the parolees' and probation youths' experiences with violence, both inside and outside of the punitive facility. The need for strong group identities controlled some forms of gang and interpersonal violence in the institution, but it also dictated when violence was appropriate, or even demanded. The socialized perception that racialized groups were threats to one another compelled participants to use violence to themselves police the social order that the institution established—lashing out when group boundaries were threatened, or to force authorities to relocate them when they felt outnumbered. In turn, institutional staff generally used these instances to confirm their perspectives that probation youth and prisoners needed to be separated. This chapter also examines how penal violence spreads into the neighborhood through secondary prisonization and the institutional reproduction of the carceral social order, influencing the local conflicts that young residents must learn to navigate. Finally, I use this chapter to discuss how the expansion of carceral affiliations into local spaces also shapes young peoples' exposure to police violence that is carried out in the name of gang suppression.

In chapter 6, I explore how the carceral social order has become an authoritative framework for labeling poor youth of color as criminal gang members. The affiliations that the prison institutionalizes through the systematic separation of inmates are socially constructed as ties to criminal gangs. As juvenile facilities rely on this same separation to organize the institution, it structures a prevailing assumption that youth are gang involved, and that the forms of creative expression that they practice are examples of gang activity. But this system also shapes how police label youth as gang members in the neighborhood; similar to correctional officers sorting incoming prisoners, local police deploy a process I term "polarized labeling" in which young people are racially categorized, then assumed to be loyal to one side or the other of a rivalry between criminalized affiliations. In such instances, the sorting process essentially begins the first time youth are stopped in the street by police, long before ever reaching a prison. The extension of this sorting process from the punitive facility to the community represents a frightening capacity for the prison to produce criminality far beyond its own walls. But within the context of a neoliberal California, this criminalization also functions to frame youth, their families, and communities as economic burdens and social threats who need to be punitively managed rather than supported. I argue that this rationalizes the mass incarceration of poor communities of color by defining these spaces as "gang-infested" neighborhoods that require aggressive policing and surveillance, subsequently marking residents as appropriate targets for imprisonment.

Finally, in the conclusion I outline the implications of the book and make recommendations for future research and policy considerations. I argue that relying on identifying and separating gang members not only fails to prevent violence in carceral institutions but also has serious consequences for those who are processed through these facilities. Namely, this practice positions individuals into rivalries between criminalized affiliations—exposing them to confrontation and violence, and ultimately ascribing them with criminal labels that keep them cycling through the justice system. I also use this chapter to explore alternative models, discussing instances both in this research and in previous studies in which criminal justice facilities desegregated their institutions, and argue that establishing a more just and effective criminal justice system requires reducing the emphasis institutions place on identifying and controlling gang membership.

# PART I

# Inside the Facility

# 1. Constructing and Institutionalizing the Carceral Social Order

"Aw you suck sir. Next!"

Aaron just decimated my Batman. When we play boxing I can usually hold my own, but when they want to play this fighting game with Mortal Kombat characters battling comic book superheroes I usually just mash the controller buttons and hope for the best. Aaron actually knows the special moves and combinations though, so I don't last long. I pass the Xbox controller to the next person in the rotation, then look over my shoulder to see what else is happening. Jordan is at his usual spot managing the playlist for the afternoon, arm resting on the stereo speaker ready to pick the next song. Adrian and Mike play ping pong while Eddie and Julian are playing dominoes on the table next to us. All things considered it is a pretty good place for them to forget for an hour that they are locked up. The boys here today certainly seem to be enjoying that opportunity. All of them except one.

A boy I haven't seen before sits by himself on one of the benches that line the wall with his head in his hands. Every few minutes someone else from the pod comes up to him and says a few words before going back to what he was doing. But still he stays on the bench. After a while I come over and sit next to him to introduce myself and to see what is troubling him. He introduces himself as Javier and explains that this morning he was sentenced to six months in the Fresno County Juvenile Detention Facility (JDF). He just transferred into this pod a few hours ago. He was brought in two weeks ago on a probation violation for a minor drug charge, and since then had been held in JDF's detention wing while waiting for his court date. This was his first time in juvenile hall, so he thought he would receive a much shorter sentence or maybe even be released. Instead, because he was unable to demonstrate that he would receive treatment on his own, he found out that he was being sent to JDF's substance abuse program for a mandatory six-month term. He tells me that his mom took the news pretty hard, and while he talks to me he still seems to be in shock himself.

He speaks slowly, struggling to push his words out onto the floor while he stares down and shakes his head. "I really want to change my life. Maybe some of the programs in here can help me a little, but I dunno." He pauses and looks up, staring into space while he tries to find how to describe what he is feeling. "I feel like when I get out of here I might be like a whole 'nother person. Like worse, causing more problems. Cuz normally I don't cause many problems, I'm a pretty calm person. But after being in here, I feel like I'm gonna be more, just, gang life." He looks to me to see if I understand, perhaps unsure how else to explain it.

"Why do you think that?" I ask him.

"Because everyone I associate with in here are all gang members. When you're locked up, gangs become like your family, cuz they understand what you're going through cuz they're there with you."

Javier feared his incarceration would strengthen the role gangs played in his life, in large part because the peers that youth come to depend on for basic contact when locked up likely include gang affiliates. Even in the few minutes we talk, other boys from the pod come by and try to help him feel better, telling him "I know how you feel man, this is my first time being locked up too!" But Javier's fear is also shaped by the social dynamics at work in the pod. Most of his time at JDF will be spent in a divided housing pod, or more accurately on one side of it depending on which gang members in the pod staff think Javier is most likely to side with. Even though he doesn't bang, it will be easy for others to assume that he does based on which side he is celled on and who they see him talking to. Now every day when his pod leaves the unit for class he will have to line up with the others, interlocking his fingers in front of him and leaving his back exposed to anyone behind him—a prime opportunity for anyone who might have a problem with him to "snake" or sucker-punch him in the back of the head. Other youth here have reported this occurring at least a few times a week. It would help Javier to have others in the pod who will back him up in these instances, or better yet to surround him so as to diminish the likelihood of such a brazen assault. Javier's perception that everyone he interacts with here is gang involved is not quite accurate, but it is understandable because it is informed by the potential for everyone in the pod to be drawn into gang conflicts in this way—in large part due to how his pod is institutionally divided and managed.

It is tempting to frame Javier's dilemma—as he does—in terms of how youth become involved with gangs while incarcerated. But focusing on gang conflict would miss how institutionally organizing young people around gang conflict—in Javier's case dividing everyone in the pod by presumed affiliations—has a lasting impact on those who need to adjust to being categorized in this way. In this chapter I examine the origins of the criminalized affiliations that come to bridge prison and community. Within Fresno's communities of color, understanding the neighborhood's relationship with carceral institutions has to begin with looking at what happens when residents are incarcerated in these facilities. In both state prison and local juvenile justice facilities, incorporating residents into punitive institutions relies on classifying them as gang affiliates. Staff members categorize and separate the individuals in their charge by potential affiliations into racialized, gang-associated groups, then police the boundaries between these groups as part of the everyday management of the facility. The identities and conflicts that are constructed in this process comprise a carceral social order that directs day-to-day life in the institution, and that establishes it's residents' and workers' common sense understandings of identity and criminality.

CATEGORIZING THE INCARCERATED

Within punitive facilities, the carceral social order operates as a dominant lens for understanding the incarcerated, but this framework is largely structured by the process of categorizing those in the institution by their potential gang ties. Race, home community, and peer networks are used to sort people into criminalized groups and situate them into separate segregated spaces under the presumption that they represent threats to each other. In doing so, the institution establishes a social context in which these collective identities not only define inmates' everyday experiences in the facility, but also label them as associates of criminal gangs. In examining both penal and juvenile justice institutions, we can identify parallel processes that construct this same social order—one based in beliefs about racial incompatibility and gang rivalry—in both settings. In the Wasco State Prison (WSP) and in Fresno's juvenile justice facilities, we can see how this social order is created at two ends of the criminal justice system, and how the consistent experiences across these institutions in turn produce consistent identities across generations.

## Wasco State Prison Reception Center, Wasco, California

Throughout the week dozens of men recently released from state prison— many of them residing in nearby halfway houses—congregate at a reentry center in downtown Fresno to attend workshops and counseling sessions, or to use the center's computers to look for jobs or write résumés. Most of these men grew up within a few miles of this center and lived in Fresno until they were finally sent to prison. In their stories, going to prison usually starts with a 100-mile bus trip south from the Fresno County Jail to the Reception Center at WSP, a trip that is repeated by the approximately 1,500 male residents the county sends to prison each year (CDCR 2014). Reception centers like Wasco serve as points of entry into the prison system for both newly convicted felons and parolees returning on violations. Here, California Department of Corrections and Rehabilitation (CDCR) officials hold incoming prisoners for 120 days while they "process, classify, and evaluate new inmates physically and mentally, and determine their security level, program requirements and appropriate institutional placement."[1] In this screening, men will receive a housing assignment that will dictate which of the state's thirty-four prisons they will serve their sentence in, where they will be celled in that facility, and whom they will be housed with.

Wasco is the largest reception center in the state, receiving inmate transfers from jails throughout Southern and Central California. WSP is designed to process 2,334 inmates at a time through its reception center, but as of the time of this research Wasco was housing some 5,500 inmates in reception on any given day. As groups of men are bused in from the surrounding county jails, they are funneled into the facility, stripped, searched, identified, fingerprinted, and photographed. Here David, a twenty-eight-year-old Latino parolee, describes what it is like to step off the bus and pass through this process at Wasco:

> Yeah, so going in there, You talk to the front desk, they'll ask you your name, your CDC number. You walk off, you go through a metal detector, take off all your clothes, from the county [jail]. So you're butt-naked, barefooted. They got you searched, know what I mean, check your hair, your ears, turn around, spread your buttcheeks, squat and cough, pick up your nuts, flush under the nuts, your mouth. Then they give you your pants, and oranges [prison jumpsuit], and a pair of shoes, like the slip-on shoes. . . . You get uh, five sets of shirts, white shirts, two oranges, top and bottom, five pairs of socks, five pairs of boxers. You don't get no shower shoes, you have to wait 'til you buy 'em. Understand what I mean? You get a bar of soap a week, a roll of toilet paper a week. . . . And [then you] go ahead, get your lunch and go. It's kinda like a herding thing, they herd you, know what I mean, 'til they can get you situated into a room.

We can understand this process by following one such group of arrivals. When a busload of men from Fresno arrives at Wasco, one by one their personal information is recorded or updated, they are searched for contraband,

and some basic supplies are distributed to them before they are finally assigned to a cell or dorm bunk. But being "situated into a room" is based in many factors, and is determined by how an inmate is categorized across a number of fields. In this process, the large crowd of men who come in together from the county are divided and subdivided down until they are all individually reorganized into the prison's classificatory system. Low-custody-level inmates in Wasco are sent to C yard where they stay in less restrictive, open dormitories before being sent to minimum security facilities. Inmates who may be vulnerable to assault in general population, either due to their offense or because of conflicts from a previous prison term, are isolated in B5, the protective custody unit on B yard. Similarly, anybody with a history of violence is likely sent to the administrative segregation (or "ad seg") unit on D yard. Any prisoners coming in with an admitted or documented Norteño affiliation is immediately sent to D3 since they may be vulnerable on other yards. Everybody else is placed in one of the "mainline" buildings on B or D yard.

Even after these groups of men have been assigned to a building they are divided down still, this time paired with cellmates depending on how they are racially classified. During this sorting process incoming prisoners are categorized as Whites, Blacks, Hispanics, or "Others" (Asians and Pacific Islanders), and housed with other men in the same racial group. Latino inmates, the largest racial group in the prison, are also divided by where in the state they were committed from; Latinos from Southern California are sorted simply as "Southern Hispanics," but most of our group from Fresno will be kept together as "Bulldogs." The result is that prisoners find themselves slotted into an environment that is defined by race- and place-based divides, as Francisco, a thirty-five-year-old Latino parolee describes:

> Going into prison, they already had like a modified program. Like uh, if you're a certain group, you can't be around this [other] group. So like when you go in to R&R, they have big [signs] like "Fresno," "San Bernardino County," "LA County," you know from the counties where you're from right? And they have doors already open for people in Fresno, they just rush us in, close it, and that's how they did it. They just uh, it was already, it was already a modified, there was segregated kind of like in a way . . . it was like it was split. Um, they modified Bulldogs, Blacks, um Others, on top, and then on the bottom it'll be Whites and Southsiders. All bottom tier. So it was already there.

In Francisco's words we can see that after incoming prisoners are divided across the different buildings at WSP depending on their individual status or needs, inmates are still separated even within the same building. Important to note here is which racial groups are housed apart from each other on different tiers—Whites are housed away from Blacks, and "Southsiders" are kept on a separate tier than "Bulldogs."

From an institutional perspective, this segregation is implemented because of the potential for gang violence between these racial groups. CDCR has always justified racially sorting inmates as necessary to prevent racial violence, and more specifically to separate rival race-based prison gangs. However, the number of validated prison gang members is actually quite small, and these inmates are already removed from general population and isolated in SHU units. But despite this, *all* incoming inmates are still segregated in this manner anyway. Racial sorting then operates as a process of identifying and separating pools of inmates who may become extensions of gang rivalries. For example, Blacks and Whites are separated out of fear that conflict between the Aryan Brotherhood and the Black Guerilla Family may lead White and Black inmates to fight each other. Similarly, Latinos are split as Northerners or Southerners due to the belief that they may support the prison gangs that draw members from these respective regions of the state.

Framing racial groups as extensions of prison gang conflicts makes segregated spaces seem necessary because it marks individual prisoners as assumed gang associates. Within this system one's presumed gang ties are determined by race, but also by one's home community. In Francisco's excerpt he illustrates that inmates are first tagged by the county they come in from, and for Latino prisoners this is consequential. The counties that Latino inmates come from affect the housing assignments that they receive because each county is classified as a Northern or Southern county; Kern and San Luis Obispo Counties on south are considered Southern counties, whereas most Latinos north of this (with the exception of Fresno) will be counted as Northern Hispanics. The *Norteño* (Spanish for "Northerner") and *Sureño* ("Southerner") identity categories that stem from this schism are commonly interpreted as gang affiliations by correctional staff and law enforcement, although not necessarily by prisoners. Here Martín explains how Latino prisoners are labeled as gang affiliated in the sorting process based on where they are from:

> Well basically see, when a person don't bang it's either because they're in church, or they're just trying to do their time. See, nobody really puts 'em on any[thing], [or] categorizes them. But when you get booked in, in the reception or so forth, when you get to prison, they gonna tell you "you from Fresno, you from LA, or where you from? What hood you from?" Say "I don't bang." But then what they always do anyways, police themselves categorizes you as being from Fresno. So

either way, whether you're out there gangbanging, whether you go in the prison being a gangbanger or not, the police are gonna categorize you anyways. Know what I mean? Every time, wherever you're from. Whether you're from Bakersfield, LA, Sacramento, whatever. They're still gonna categorize you as Northern or Southern, regardless.

Martín says that nobody forces prisoners to join gangs ("nobody puts them on"), and that gang-involved inmates generally do not mistake or confront those who "don't bang" as gang rivals. Instead, he claims that new inmates are often labeled as gang affiliated by correctional staff. Many of the Latino parolees similarly described being labeled as gang members because of where they came from and how they were sorted. Because the purpose of racially sorting inmates is to separate gang rivals, this process inescapably associates individual prisoners with one gang or another by virtue of categorizing them as potential supporters. This process conflates race and gang association in a way that gives the criminalized identity categories ascribed to inmates the same kind of permanence and inescapability as race within the institution. It comes to define one's role within a segregated social system, and stays with the individual throughout their term.

Even within protective custody (PC)—a unit explicitly inaccessible to active gang members—incarcerated men still struggle to get away from the gang-associated identities ascribed to them. Javier, a Latino parolee originally from Northern California, was sent to a PC unit when he went through reception at Wasco because he had previously renounced his Norteño affiliation. In this quote Javier describes how his history with the Northerners was made known to the entire unit:

> They knew I was from San Jose because there's like a big ole board, like a bulletin board where you have to write your name and where you're from in San Jose, like the COs [corrections officers] put it out there on purpose. . . . It's like right in the front in like in the dayroom area, with like benches and everything right there for you to watch TV but at the same time the bulletin board's right there. They put everyone's name up there, and what cell you're in, and where you came from and if you're a Northerner or a Southerner.

Javier's experience gives us an idea about how pervasively the identity categories created in sorting permeate the prison, and how stubbornly they attach themselves to individual inmates. Despite the fact that he is in protective custody precisely because he wants to distance himself from the group he was sorted into, he is still identified to everyone in his unit by this gang-associated label.

Institutionalizing a segregated environment is at the heart of how the prison constructs the carceral social order. Prison authorities define the handful of identity categories that the institution will recognize and divide inmates into this rigid schema as they are processed through reception. How one is classified in this process has spatial consequences, as it defines the spaces (and therefore people) that one does or does not have access to. The institution distributes and distinguishes spaces for different groups, such that space in the facility—yards, buildings, cells, or even the different corners or tables of shared rooms—then come to be defined by who is there or who *can* be there. But this classification also comes to determine one's relationship to other inmates, as the resulting segregation becomes a way to define who you and "your people" are, who you are not, and who you are in conflict with. In treating sorted groups as extensions of prison gangs, prisoners are positioned into a preexisting set of relationships and conflicts that consequently shape the environment they must adapt to while incarcerated. But back in the communities that inmates come from, a similar process is institutionalizing some of the same groups among young residents.

## San Joaquin Educational Academy, Fresno, California

As the Fresno Sheriff's "grey goose" bus makes its way down the Central Valley to Wasco, its passengers can see the rows of crops whip by like the pages of a flipbook, and some perhaps think of the homes they are leaving behind. Most would remember home as somewhere among the Latina/o and Black neighborhoods that straddle downtown Fresno, within the old regions of the city known simply as the Eastside and the Westside. Left behind by the residential and commercial development that pushes ever northward, the neighborhoods here are home to some of the highest rates of concentrated poverty in the nation (Kneebone 2014). Complementing this economic desertion has been the subsequent mass perception of these communities as dangerous parts of the city, and the ensuing declarations by public officials to wage war against the criminalized residents living there. During the 1990s and early 2000s, units of masked SWAT officers equipped with body armor, armored vehicles, and military weapons—not unlike the riot police used to suppress 2014's Black Lives Matter protests in Ferguson, Missouri—were deployed on a *daily basis* in these neighborhoods for routine patrols. Black and Latino youth in particular were targeted by these units as violent gang members, as one such officer claimed that "if you're 21, male, living in one of these neighborhoods, and you're not in our computer,[2] then there's something definitely wrong."[3] However, this intimidating criminalization and legal violence directed against Fresno's youth of color did not begin with the militarized policing of the 1990s; my own father lived on the Eastside in the 1970s until he was twenty-two, and decades later would still caution me as a young man to never make eye contact with police officers.

The long-term criminalization of Fresno's communities of color has led to multiple generations of local residents simultaneously navigating the criminal justice system. While the incarcerated men from these communities are sorted into the prison's segregated social order in Wasco, local youth are exposed to juvenile justice institutions that classify and separate them in much the same manner as their older neighbors.

When young people are arrested in Fresno, they are sent to booking in JDF, the county's new and expanded juvenile justice campus. After an officer drops a teenager off here, they are fingerprinted, have their picture taken by a camera mounted to the ceiling, and are interviewed at one of the desk stations before being put into one of the holding cells that line the walls. Some youth may be released to their parents if it is their first arrest or if they were brought in on a minor offense. Otherwise they are sent to the detention side of the facility. Within the detention wing of JDF, youth are sent to different pods depending on individual needs—girls are sent to their own pod, youth aged fourteen and younger are sent to another, and youth who may be violent or mentally ill are also in a special pod. On JDF's commitment side some pods are similarly designated for specific populations such as girls, high security youth, teens sentenced for drug offenses, and those sentenced to a full year (the longest sentence one can serve at JDF without being transferred to state custody) for a serious felony. But much like at Wasco, within each pod young people are also split up by their potential affiliations. Again youth are labeled by their race, neighborhood, and peers into categories that staff members use to determine where in the facility they should be housed, rooming youth from rivaling affiliations on opposite ends of their assigned pods. Diego explains this to Edgar, one of the few students at the San Joaquin Educational Academy (SJEA) who had not been "locked up," when describing to him what juvenile hall is like:

E: Do they ask you where you're from?
D: Well yeah, but if you're down then they'll already know.
E: But what if you aren't labeled down?
D: Well then yeah, they'll ask you. Cuz they need to know before they put you in, cuz in the pod all the Sureños, Norteños, and taggers are all on that side (gesturing his hand away from his body) and [on] this side it's all Bulldogs.

While describing incarceration to one of his peers, Diego explains that it is important for the institution to properly identify young people in order to appropriately divide them. Juvenile Probation makes files on youth while they are at JDF that document their suspected affiliations (which may or may not be accurate) and send these to any facility youth may transfer to after their release, including SJEA.

However, as these files are passed to different institutions, the gang labels generated by how youth are categorized simultaneously follow them into new spaces. When Joey was sent to JDF for drug charges, they housed him alongside Bulldog gang members, despite the fact that he had no history of gang involvement. This assignment set into motion a criminal label that has persistently shadowed him ever since:

JOEY: [In JDF] I told them I didn't bang, because on one side they had the nortes and the Sureños, and [on] the left side were the dogs. So I guess there was an opening and they put me there and it stuck.

AUTHOR: You ever feel like you've been labeled?

J: Yeah, I do! Cuz I was reading a sheet and it said I affiliate with Bulldogs. Fuck, they're labeling me as a gang banger! Just cuz I hang on the east side, like I hang out with Bulldogs doesn't mean I bang! [It] just means I get along better with the Bulldogs!

A: When did you see that you were labeled?

J: When I got out of my fuckin [appointment for drug treatment]! It said uhhh, "He doesn't bang but does affiliate with Bulldogs occasionally." Like what the fuck! That's fucked up! Now I'm labeled as a Bulldog and I don't even bang! So [now] people call out "So wassup dog? You a mutt or what?" Fuck! Are you serious? I don't even bang and now you wanna disrespect? Yeah, starting a fight for no reason!

When Joey was housed with the Bulldogs in JDF, he befriended one of the other boys housed with him, and continued to socialize with him at SJEA. Joey "gets along better with the Bulldogs" in large part because this is who he was housed with in JDF and who he came to develop friendships with. But this housing assignment, which he had no control over, is recorded in his file as a gang affiliation, framing him in subsequent settings as criminal and exposing him to confrontations from other youth.

At SJEA staff members note any affiliations already recorded in students' probation files, but also make their own assessments in student orientation sessions, either confirming or updating the file. Each Thursday, new students transferring into the school come in for an orientation session, usually within a week of their release from juvenile hall. Here they meet with various counselors and school staff members, who explain things they need to know about the school like the dress code, daily schedule, and what is expected of them as students. These staff members also attempt to determine new students' gang affiliations from police reports and juvenile probation files, as well as questions about what other students they know at the school. These orientation sessions provided the school staff with an opportunity to categorize new students into the criminalized affiliations they recognized. For example, one week a school counselor recaps one of these orientation meetings to me shortly after finishing: "We have six new Bulldogs, and we have one who affiliates with Bulldogs, but he hasn't been labeled yet. I asked him who he knows here and he said 'Oh I know him and him.' So I said 'OK, so you affiliate with Bulldogs' and he said 'No, I'm not in no gang! I just talk to those guys!' but I told him 'OK, but that's still affiliating.'"

Much like the racialized housing assignments in Wasco, youth are categorized as they enter juvenile facilities so that they can be separated. After determining students' affiliations the staff then direct them one side or the other of the divided blacktop, structuring a physical split between students. Students resultantly experienced the identity categories ascribed in this process through the division of youth into separate spaces, particularly visible when students came outside for lunch and recess breaks. During these breaks, SJEA students were contained to a small portion of the school's asphalt parking lot—two rows of parking spots for about a dozen cars with a lane between them. Bracketing one end of this long and narrow space were a set of unused basketball hoops and a ping-pong table, and on the other a small trailer serving as a snack bar that sold chips and cups of instant ramen during lunch. Between them, twenty picnic tables were spread out across the blacktop, divided by a thirty-foot gap that split the entire space into two sides. Probation officers, security guards, and teacher's aides would form a tight perimeter around this space that students were not permitted to venture beyond.

At the lunch tables, youth sat with their friends (who they usually already knew from their communities) and others they felt were most like themselves. However, at SJEA students' peer networks were often interpreted as ties to neighborhood gangs, and consequently sections of the blacktop were seen by both students and staff as designated for different gang-associated groups, with rival groups positioned at opposite ends. Students dismissed for lunch would exit the school's side door to the blacktop and first see the "Bulldog tables" clustered to their left, although most of the students sitting here were Latina/o kids from Fresno's Eastside who

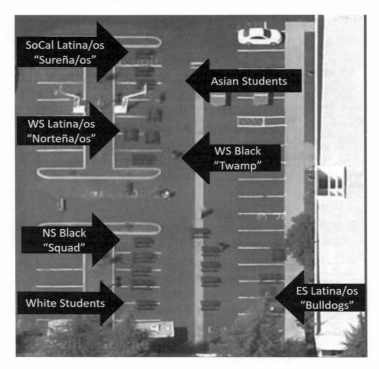

FIGURE 1.    The segregated blacktop at San Joaquin Educational Academy.
Patrick Lopez-Aguado

didn't gangbang. In the far left corner by the trailer is a table with all the White kids, most of whom are from the middle-class neighborhoods in North Fresno or Fresno's more affluent suburb, Clovis. Next to them is a table with a multicultural group of students, most of them also from the Northside, who dress like skaters and hang out with the Whites. Continuing to scan the blacktop clockwise, to the right of them are most of SJEA's Black students; first the teens from the Northside (although not as far north as the White neighborhoods) associated with Murder Squad, then the thirty-foot gap, then the Westside youth categorized with Twamp Gang. Next down the line is the table with all the Norteñas/os and all the Latina/o students from the Westside, then a table with a few Asian kids. Finally at the far right was the "Sureña/o table," mostly filled with Latina/o youth whose families had recently moved to Fresno from Southern California.

The size of these groups and the dynamics between them could shift with the demographics of the students enrolled at any given time because student turnover was very high, but even groups that were absent for a time still had a space that was recognized as theirs. When I first came to SJEA, one of the staff members pointed out each of the groups on the blacktop before pointing to an empty space and telling me "there aren't any Sureños here right now, but when there are they stay over there." The division of space was fundamental to the daily operation of the school to the point that it was recognized even if the isolated group was not even present—illustrating how the presumed need to categorize youth is engrained as a dominant logic, such that the categories ascribed in this process hold meaning even when there is nobody to fill them. The consistent emphasis placed on identity categories defines group boundaries by constructing the collective threat of an "other," even when this other is an imagined enemy. This othering is accomplished through the designation of group space, and space is only divided among gang collectives. In this arrangement there is no space for unaffiliated youth of color, meaning that nonwhite youth are always imagined as gang members.

## BOUNDARY MAINTENANCE

Fresno's criminalized residents encounter a consistent social order in both the state prison and local juvenile justice facilities, one in which they are put into race- and place-based groups that are then separated from each other in relation to gang rivalries. Also consistent across these sites is the institution's direct role in designing and enforcing this system. Facility staff members not only classify incoming inmates/students into racially defined groups and separate them spatially, but they then also police the boundaries between these groups. This reinforcement of spatial boundaries in turn reifies carceral affiliations as cohesive groups with powerful collective identities. By encouraging people to stick with "their own" and structuring an environment in which it is hard not to do this, the institution engrains into individuals the rationale that segregation is an important means of protecting themselves from violence.

It is not hard to see how inmates quickly understand this logic in reception. Reception centers are overcrowded facilities with high rates of turnover and reputations for being unstable and dangerous institutions. Facilities like Wasco have relatively high rates of inmate violence, and a 2006 report found that Wasco had the highest rate of improperly placing violent inmates (who should be in ad seg) in general population among nonviolent offenders (Cate 2006). For the parolees reception was intimidating and unpredictable. Nobody in reception knows each other because everyone is just passing through, so none of the relationships, reputations, or general stability that might otherwise shield one from violence in a more permanent setting are present. Instead, COs tell incoming prisoners to find and turn to their "people" to keep themselves safe and assess which inmates to look out for (Goodman 2008), communicating to inmates that their safety relies on their ability to foster protective bonds with others based in common racial identities and hometowns.

Within the segregated facility, sticking close to the people one is safe around then shapes the space one has access to. In this context, parolees understood space as racially divided, and that transgressing racial boundaries could easily lead to violence. Prisoners are already kept to racially determined housing assignments or cells, but in shared spaces such as the yard, day room, or open dorm housing units, physical boundaries between racialized groups become very important. Inmates make meaning of this segregation in terms of safe and unsafe spaces, as Mark, a forty-seven-year-old White parolee explains:

> Everything is territorial there. Like the Northerners will have their spot. The Blacks will have their spots, their tables where they sit on the yard and play their games you know, [just like] the Northerners have their spot. The Others, which is you know, are your Asians or your Samoans, you know just a mix. Like they have their designated area. And the Whites have their designated area. And if you wanna play some card games, or dominoes, or whatever on the yard, you sit in your designated area. Ok, you can't go to no other designated areas. [Nor] are you supposed to walk through someone else's designated area. That's off limits. You gotta walk around . . . you can't just walk on through, you gotta walk around. Walking through their area is like a disrespect issue. You know, you're like saying "F-you."

Parolees learned to only see their own group's spaces as safe and others' as dangerous, and understood that entering such areas could easily lead to confrontation and violence. This presumed threat also shapes why some would take seriously outsiders who violate group space, as this would challenge the safety of that space.

No matter what facility parolees ultimately went to after reception, they always found similarly segregated institutions. The housing assignments they received in reception still kept them away from other racial groups, and continued to shape their perceptions of who was safe or dangerous. But this segregation was also so consistent because COs throughout the system learned to keep facilities secure by maintaining physical distance between sorted groups. The institutional perspective that different racial groups will fight if they are not separated then leaves it to COs to control the prison by actively enforcing the carceral social order. Here Mark, a former CO from Calipatria State Prison, describes how learning to be a correctional officer entails familiarizing oneself with the carceral social order: "The number one tool you could have in working in [the prison], being a correctional officer and so forth, is knowing who's who. Part of the training that they give you when you're going to go into corrections is 'know your inmates.' Know who hangs with who, who doesn't like who, where the certain races [are], where they divide themselves, where they sit, where they play, where they shower, all that comes into play." Mark explains that a fundamental part of being a CO is knowing which groups inmates are "supposed" to be in, who their enemies are because they're in that group, and where they should be within the segregated space of the facility. Most interesting is that he mentions this as part of how individuals are officially trained to be corrections officers, revealing how the carceral social order is embraced at the institutional level as a lens for understanding—and therefore as a means of managing—prison inmates.

Racial segregation in the prison is regularly rationalized as something inmates want, demand, or do on their own. Some parolees even pointed to this characterization as evidence that inmates, not the guards, in fact control the prison. But while prisoners may to some extent choose who they affiliate with and find some empowerment in this, they are limited by the parameters that the institution makes available to them. Correctional staff enforce racial segregation in multiple ways, in large part because it offers them a manageable way to maintain order in carceral facilities when they have too many people to supervise. Sociologist Michael Walker found that racial segregation makes correctional work much easier for staff members who learn to delegate many of their managerial tasks to the informal leaders of racial cliques (2016). But rarely discussed is how protective custody contributes to the enforcement of prison segregation.

PC is a separate unit in the prison reserved for removing inmates who staff think would be particularly vulnerable—primarily sex offenders, informants, and gang "dropouts"—from general population. While PC is supposed to be a safer alternative to being in general population for these inmates, most parolees actually saw being in PC as *more* dangerous in terms of making oneself a target for assault,[4] because one of the few ways someone can get into PC is by offering incriminating information on other inmates to prison authorities. Even "dropouts" who want to leave a gang cannot get into PC without first going through a process called "debriefing" in which they offer COs information on other active members. PC ultimately enforces the carceral social order by acting as a deterrent; prisoners can either go along with their role in the dominant social order or they can go into protective custody, be seen as a snitch, and receive a stigma that puts them at consistent risk of assault. Because of this risk, many of the parolees adamantly stated that they would never consider going into PC. Consequently, one of the most effective mechanisms for enforcing segregation in the prison is referring inmates who refuse to abide by the carceral social order to PC.

Expecting prisoners to belong on one side of a segregated space leaves little room for ambiguity, and frames inmates trying to do their time outside of racial boundaries as signs of imminent trouble. Assuming that inmates needed to be on a side also dismissed the possibility of doing time on the mainline without identifying or "running" with one's sorted group. Resultantly, anyone who was not accepted by the other inmates in their racial group was seen as vulnerable and consequently removed from general population and sent to PC. For example, Steven was originally housed with the Northerners until a rumor spread that he had incriminated a friend while talking to police. When staff learned that the other Northerners wouldn't accept him anymore, they told him they were going to transfer him to the Special Needs Yard (or SNY, another term for PC), but Steven didn't want to do that. He wanted to stay in general population by himself rather than go to PC, but for staff that was not an option:

STEVEN:   I'm not gonna lie to you, even doing my own thing, as I went my own way, I got harassed big-time. I got harassed more by staff going off and doing my own thing than I ever got harassed belonging as a whole, you know?

AUTHOR:   Really? Why?

S:   Yeah. I don't know. They fucked with me big time, because they felt that I needed to be uh, [either one of the] dudes that are active (clique up with racial group), [or one of the] dudes that SNY [go to PC]. Me, I choose to do my own thing. Just because one group says that I'm not worthy of what they're doing, doesn't mean I have to go over here and kick it on the yard with a bunch of pieces of shit, you know? So I'm gonna do my own thing. I consider myself independent, so I got myself in a lot of trouble to the point to where they wouldn't even put me with no one else. They kept me single celled. I caught SHU [Secure Housing Unit] time, and thank God I never had to hit a yard full of garbage. . . . I did cages, single celled cages, single celled living for three years five months, and it, to me it fucked me up, you know? What happened is, like I said, I didn't mess with these people [the Northerners], didn't mess with these people [the PC yard], didn't mess with administration, so what they tried to do

> was kinda like socially isolate me, you know? So I was by
> myself, know what I mean? Nobody talked to me, nobody gave
> me no genuine conversation, none of that shit, you know?

Steven claims that the COs gave him a hard time when he tried to defy the
social order of the prison and exist outside of his sorted group. They would
not let him stay in general population, and the only way he could avoid PC
was by getting himself into enough trouble that they would send him to
administrative segregation in the SHU. Consequently, Steven spent the
remaining three and a half years of his sentence in solitary confinement in
the SHU, where he feels he was punished with social isolation for trying to
do his time outside of his assigned category.

In Steven's story, we can see how thoroughly the logic of the carceral
social order guides the management of inmate populations; because staff
see it as impossible for inmates to live in the prison without a racial group,
they end up enforcing this social order by isolating "independent" inmates
in either protective custody or solitary confinement. This removal of independent prisoners contributed to the institutionalization of the carceral
social order by keeping space divided and making it impossible to do time
without abiding by the racial division of the population. While the COs'
concerns for Steven's safety are certainly not groundless, they are the direct
result of a constructed environment that demands everyone be classified.

Inside punitive institutions like the prison, the carceral social order is
implemented not only by categorizing and separating people, but also by
socializing and maintaining the resulting segregation. But while prison
staff structure and facilitate this segregation through housing assignments,
race-based punishments (Spiegel 2007), recognizing informal racial leaders
(Walker 2016), and racially dividing shared spaces, much of the enforcement of racial boundaries is carried out by inmates themselves. By the time
they are adults, prisoners effectively enforce much the carceral social order
themselves by monitoring spatial borders and confronting nonconformists.
Most of the parolees were already well familiar with the divides and expectations of this social order before they ever reached the prison. Probation
youth, however, are still being socialized into this. In their facilities, institutional staff members take on a much more direct role in maintaining the
separation between sorted groups.

## Policing Space

SJEA's influence in shaping the carceral social order became clear through
the ongoing policing of students' physical space. During student breaks six
to eight staff members are typically on duty to supervise, making sure that

students stay at their designated tables and sending them to the bathrooms in separate waves depending on which side of the gap their table is on. As the weather began to warm it revealed an underlying emphasis the school placed on maintaining physical distance between groups of students. Fresno is known for intense summers where long stretches of triple-digit heat are not uncommon, and by early April it was already becoming uncomfortable for students and staff alike to stay in the sun during lunchtime. The students' lunch area was in the center of an asphalt blacktop that absorbed much of the heat while offering little in the way of shade. Two trees by the side of the school building offer the only protection from the sun, shading a small area of the parking lot immediately adjacent to the "Bulldog tables," and because of how the lunch area is divided the students sitting here are the only ones able to access it.

One day the heat prompts SJEA staff to reevaluate this configuration. As the students finish eating their lunches most stay at their tables, barely talking as they try to shade their faces with their hands, but the Bulldog students all stand up and position themselves under the shade of the trees. After about forty minutes of sitting in the heat, the sun becomes too much for the half dozen Black students in attendance,[5] and they collectively walk across the blacktop and stand with the Bulldogs in the shade. The staff members supervising lunch seem stunned and look at each other in confusion, unsure of what to do. The Black students and Bulldogs don't generally have problems with each other and it quickly becomes clear that neither group is interested in fighting, so even though the Probation Officers (POs) seem alarmed by this boundary crossing, they don't do anything to correct it. Soon the rest of the students follow suit, joining them under the trees and in any pockets of shade they can find along the wall. The only students still in the sun are two Norteño boys who stay by their table and look sadly over at everyone else in the shade—as uncomfortable as they are, they know crossing over will likely start a fight with rival gang members and get them in trouble with the staff, so they stay put.

When I come back the next week I find that the tables have been rearranged into two parallel rows spaced about 25 feet apart. Each row has 7 tables, stretching about 60 feet from the trailer through the space between the planters. Most interesting is that while still divided, all of the tables are now centered in the middle of the blacktop, intentionally positioned away from the wall and the shade provided by the trees. When I ask her about it, Mrs. Rodriguez, a youth outreach worker at the school, explains: "We did that to move that group that thinks they run everything around here. We moved them out of the shade cuz if this side has to be in the sun, then they can in the sun too!" The school changed the setup of the students' lunch area because they wanted to make it fair for all of the students, arguing that it was unfair for the "Bulldog-affiliated" students to have the only tables in the shade. However, because staff members fear that students will fight if they are allowed to simply share the shade, they decide to keep everyone in the sun, addressing the disparity while still enforcing the separation between groups and keeping students on their appropriate sides. The emphasis the school placed on dividing students even while reorganizing the tables highlights how important they considered it for preserving institutional security and student safety, and during the summer months policing the students' access to shade served as an important means for preventing them from crossing group boundaries.

After rearranging the tables outside, the staff wouldn't let any of the students stand or sit in the shade during break or lunchtime, even when they were talking with me. When the students were out on break I usually sat on one of the side benches under a tree by the building so that I could observe what happened during break without imposing on students while they socialized with their friends. When I was outside some of the students I worked with or had gotten to know would often come up to me and talk for a while before going back in for class. However, now when they did this one of the probation officers or staff members would step in and tell them to move along, sending them back to their table. Consequently, policing the students' access to the shade became a way for staff to keep students at their appropriate tables and on their designated side of the divided blacktop.

During one of these lunch breaks, I sat with Ben, one of my regular students, while he complained that he had to stay after school to help clean up the yard as punishment for getting to school late this morning. He explained, "It's not even hard work or anything, it's just hella hot."

"Yeah, and they won't even let you guys in the shade anymore huh?" I responded, referring to the staff moving the tables away from the trees.

"Naw, it was cuz we were all chillin' here, and kids from the other side started coming over, started sitting in the shade."

"Were they scared something was gonna happen?"

"I dunno, probably. They probably thought there'd be fights, like different gangs would both be in the shade and they'd get into a fight, cuz this is like the only place there's shade."

One of the POs supervising lunch spots us and walks over. She says hi to me and walks around the bench to stand directly behind Ben, putting her hands on the top of the seatback and leaning forward over him. "Get off the bench."

"What?" Ben asks incredulously, looking back up at her.

She replies calmly: "You know you're not supposed to be sitting here. I'm not calling you out, it looks like you got up on your own." Ben rolls his eyes, stands up, and goes back to sitting with his friends. I ask her why students can't sit here, and she answers: "They can stop and talk for a few minutes, but then they try to play it off like 'Oh I'm just talking to him.' So just so no one gets hurt feelings, just move them along."

As Ben's comments indicate, students understood that the school's attempts to restrict their access to shade intended to keep them separated. Probation officers shooed students out of shade anytime they tried to linger under the trees, arguing that if some of the youth could not have access to shade then none of them should. While staff members felt this kept things fair between students, it functioned to maintain divisions between youth because kicking them out of the shade inevitably entailed sending them back to their designated tables.

The school's staff also reinforced divisions between students by policing the boundaries between groups and directing youth who crossed these boundaries to "stay with their side." Probation and security staff members restricted students to one side of the blacktop in order to prevent gang members from crossing sides and starting fights with rivals. However, uncertainty about which students were actually gang members exposed almost all of the students to these same restrictions. When Rafael, an unaffiliated tagger, went to talk with a friend of his who had just come to the school, he sat with her on one of the tables furthest from the building. The security guard calls for these tables to use the restroom if they need to and Rafael, who usually sits with the Bulldogs on the tables closest to the school building, gets up from the table and starts walking inside. One of the probation officers supervising the break calls after him:

"Rafael! Where are you going?"

"They called bathroom."

"Aren't you on this side?" She asks, pointing to the tables closest to the school building.

"I was sitting over there." He counters, pointing back to the opposite side.

"Don't be switching sides! If you're gonna be on that side, you stay on that side!"

"Seriously?"

"Yeah, serious. If you gonna go to the bathroom you go when your side is called."

The probation officer scolds Rafael for not remaining on the side that he usually sits on because his presence on the far tables violates the strict division of physical space. Even though Rafael is not a gang member, staff sees his presence on the "Norteña/o side" as a potential security threat because they associate him with the Bulldogs he usually sits with. To avoid this risk they reprimand him and tell him to "stay on his side," enforcing the division of students into gang-associated groups. In doing so, the school ascribes gang labels onto students and blurs its ability to distinguish between gang members who may start fights and unaffiliated students.[6]

The restrooms the students used during breaks were seen as especially vulnerable sites for fighting, making it particularly important for the staff to keep students separated as they came inside to go to the bathroom. Later in the week I sit with Ben again during break, and we watch another student try to head in to use the bathroom out of turn, only to be sent back when the PO yells at him "I didn't call your side!" We laugh and I say to Ben, "Damn they're serious about the sides huh?"

Ben smirks and nods, "Yeah." I tell him about the PO scolding Rafael for switching sides a few days ago, and he explains why they're so strict about keeping students separated during bathroom breaks: "It's cuz they don't want someone sneakin' over here and then goin' into the bathroom where they can fight, cuz out here it'll probably get broken up quick, but in there you could probably fight for longer."

These efforts to keep students separated in the name of preventing fights extended into where they did their schoolwork as well. Students were not divided in the classroom or split into different classes, but some staff members were concerned about keeping the students that I took out away from potential rivals. The school's RSP (Resource Specialist Program) teacher and I both pulled students out of their regular classes and worked with them in small groups at the opposite ends of a large room. One day the vice principal, Mrs. Garcia, calls us both into her office. I come in and sit down, and while waiting for the RSP teacher to join us I ask Mrs. Garcia "Is something wrong?"

"Well there's some concern about you taking out kids from different gangs."

"Oh, did something happen?"

"This morning there was an incident that was an extension of something [that happened] yesterday after school, so I've already suspended 3 students this morning over that. So things are a little tense right now. Our staff has noticed it and asked that I talk with you, because you tend to pull out more Bulldog affiliates, and she gets the few Norteño and Sureño students, and they're too close to each other. There hasn't been a problem yet, but the looks have started. It's all in the body language. And cuz you're way in the front [of the building], I'm concerned that if there was a problem it would take security a minute to get there, and by then someone could really get hurt."

As Mrs. Ruiz, the RSP teacher, comes in Mrs. Garcia repeats her concerns to her and goes on to say that she wants us to start working with our students in separate rooms, telling me to use the conference room from now on. Mrs. Ruiz and I look at each other with some confusion, and she turns back to Mrs. Garcia and counters that neither of us have had any problems with our students sharing a room. Indeed, I had never seen either Mrs. Ruiz's or my own students do anything to try to start a fight while we had them out, and none of our students were involved in the shouting match/verbal provocations that resulted in that morning's three suspensions. Mrs. Garcia simply responds: "Our staff knows who these kids are and they've seen the stares and the looks starting. It may not be swearing or yelling but it's all in the body language."

Mrs. Garcia's concerns articulate an underlying assumption of the prevailing logic at SJEA—differently affiliated youth are bound to fight unless they are separated, so it's important to properly identify students' affiliations in order to keep them away from any potential rivals. Even though the students I took out had never given me any problems and had not been involved in any fights at the school, they were still seen as likely to attack others based on which side of the divided student body they associated with. However, the criminalizing associations that supposedly made these students likely to fight were structured, in some cases even forced, by the divisive context imposed by the school—one in which students' race and class identities, and where in Fresno they were from, shaped how they were subsequently divided and categorized in the institution. Much like the juvenile hall and the prison, the school then relied on the labels it institutionalized to establish a social frame for understanding the young people it managed, creating a "knowledge" of youth criminality that was removed from the actual threat posed by these individuals. The school's systematic division of students and the relationships it imposed between them actually generated the very threats staff were scared of, as it reinforced students' identifications with particular affiliations, their fears of other groups, and the institutionalization of the carceral social order.

## THE CARCERAL SOCIAL ORDER AS COMMON SENSE

At the beginning of this chapter Javier describes his fear that his incarceration could embroil him in "gang life." Because he sees most of those around him in JDF as gang affiliated, he worries that acclimating to being locked up will require him to become part of the gang conflicts that shape everyday life in the pod. Javier feels that this is especially true because he sees these gang-involved peers as a surrogate family within a context in which he is removed from his real family. But his real concern is that the consequence of his inability to access substance abuse treatment could keep him cycling though punitive facilities for a long time:

> If my mom could have found a rehab that was in-patient, but was out there, she would have sent me to that, but they couldn't find one. The judge said I needed rehab for my addiction, so he sent me to [JDF's substance abuse program]. . . . I dunno, I feel like instead of helping me they're just punishing me by putting me in here. I know I need help with my addiction but I don't know if the programs in here can really help, I mean taking everyone away from their families, everybody's always all depressed in there. I wouldn't care so much if it was just me and I didn't have a family, but I do have a family, so I don't belong in here. I feel like I'm just gonna get used to being locked up, like I'll probably be back in here.

The dearth of resources for poor youth in Fresno and the role of punishment in managing local social problems make the only drug treatment option accessible to Javier one inside the juvenile hall. But in addition to feeling that he is being punished rather than helped, he also senses that this may expose him to a far more permanent penalty; Javier's adjustment to what is supposed to be a temporary circumstance entails a much more persistent criminalization. Said another way, he knows that adapting to being locked up could very well lead him to continue to get locked up.

Positioning oneself within the carceral social order is a big part of the adjustment and socialization Javier is describing. But it is important to recognize that beyond a set of institutionally defined collective identities, this social order also becomes a common sense framework for understanding who one does and does not get along with within punitive settings. The assumption that different racial groups represented threats to each other was a fundamental underpinning in the day-to-day management of WSP, JDF, and SJEA, and the subsequent segregation of prisoners and students engrained this belief into the individuals held in these facilities. Consequently, the groups that individuals are divided into become strong identities inside the institution that individuals are socialized to appropriate; the policing of spatial boundaries and the constructed threat of the other teach incarcerated residents to see these identities as necessary, ultimately conditioning individuals to position themselves into this social order. In this context, the carceral social order provides a logic for how individuals navigating these institutions come to see themselves, their peers, and what is best for them while incarcerated.

But as Javier realizes, learning where one fits in this system also risks exposure to long-term criminal labeling, because just as the carceral social order becomes the guiding logic concerning rivalry and affiliation in the prison, it also serves as a dominant way of thinking about criminality and "criminals." Specifically, it frames the criminalized groups and conflicts institutionalized in punitive facilities as naturally occurring. Among institutional staff, the sorting of inmates and students provided a basis for seeing them as members of criminal organizations. As individuals adapt to the structure of the environment they are thrust into, this adaptation in itself is interpreted as criminal. Placing people into a segregated system makes them appear as "naturally" racist, violent, territorial, or irrationally invested in gangs. Consequently, probation youth and paroled inmates become subject to ongoing surveillance and punishment.

# 2. Carceral Affiliation and Identity Construction

Ben was the first student I met at the San Joaquin Educational Academy (SJEA). On my first day at the school I was supposed to shadow a youth outreach counselor, but by midmorning a special-ed teacher pulls me aside and asks if I would be willing to help Ben with his classwork. She explains that he doesn't really struggle with the work itself, but that he is one of their most disruptive students. She hopes that by working with him individually, I will help his teacher get through her lesson in peace and he will stay out of trouble. I find him waiting outside the classroom, sitting at one of the cafeteria tables that fill a large multipurpose room, with his shoulders slouched, his face serious and a bit annoyed, and his leg strapped with an ankle monitor just above his black Chuck Taylors. I sit across from him and introduce myself. He asks if I'm a new teaching assistant, so I tell him about the research project I am beginning here. His first response is simply "This school sets you up to get locked up." He scans his book and quickly fills in the rudimentary worksheet assigned to him, but doesn't want to go back to the classroom when he's done. When I ask him how this compares to other schools he's been to, he says he's never been to a "regular high school," but that he can't go to the county's other continuation school because the principal there has a restraining order against him. Most of the rest of our time is quiet except for some small talk, but the next day he asks his teacher if I can come get him again.

From then on I work with Ben almost every day I'm there. Before long his standard sullen expression grows into a steady sly smirk and even the occasional grin when something cracks him up. After a couple weeks he asks if his friends from class can come out too. The first to join us is Juan, the young tagger with excellent grades; he is followed by Edgar, the affable if not knuckleheaded tagger-turned-gang-member; then Mario, the laid-back homeboy who was always on teachers' bad side for reasons I could never really understand. I cap it at taking four students out at a time, but other regulars alternate with those who are absent, transfer out, or get locked up; when they leave we are joined by Ramon, who almost never talks and uses the time outside of the classroom to practice his cursive; Anthony, whose childlike hyperactivity always makes him speak in excited half sentences that trail off into laughter; and Vincent, who spent a year in Fresno's Juvenile Detention Facility (JDF) after narrowly avoiding going into state custody for an armed robbery. Over the year this rotating group of friends features a constant mix of boys with a range of reputations, temperaments, convicted offenses, and levels of gang involvement. They tease and joke with each other as friends, advise each other on how to approach new facilities, places, or cases, back each other up in confrontations during or after school, and hang out, smoke weed, and drink at each other's homes in the evenings.

Allowing Ben and other students to bring their friends out for tutoring helped me meet more of the student body, but it also showed me something about how relationships developed in this place. Like several of the boys in this group, many of the youth who come into SJEA already know several other students when they arrive because juvenile probation, like imprisonment, is geographically concentrated into Fresno's poorest communities of color. Young people in these neighborhoods are stopped, arrested, and sent into the juvenile justice system at a rate that youth in other parts of the city are not. Consequently, many students coming into SJEA already know each other as neighbors, classmates from previous schools, or members of their own families. Those who don't have these local ties coming in soon develop them, as most students live fairly close to each other and begin socializing after school. This concentration enables the institution to easily categorize its charges geographically (and therefore racially due to how segregated these neighborhoods are), but it also strengthens the bonds between the people in these sorted groups because their relationships are not limited to the facility. This pattern effectively disguises as organic the institutional rearticulation of local peer networks as criminal affiliations, obscuring the structural and multigenerational labeling process that reframes the relationships between neighbors and families as criminal associations. By virtue of knowing each other and other youth already labeled, Ben and his friends are categorized with Bulldogs within the juvenile justice system. Not coincidentally, they all also have parents, siblings, or uncles who have been to prison and were categorized the same way while incarcerated.

In addition to labeling peer networks, the institutionalization of criminalized affiliations also emphasizes gendered and racialized identity performances that are designed for surviving the carceral social order. In this chapter I focus on how young people and adults in punitive facilities understand this social order, and examine the meanings that they give to the identities socialized in these settings. The punitive institution constructs and instills carceral affiliations through a sorting process that compels individuals to reframe how they see and present themselves. The parolees and probation youth understood that surviving the carceral institution required aligning themselves with groups they felt could protect them from threats of physical violence. However, accomplishing this required not only learning to properly claim and perform appropriate racial, geographic, gender, and/or gang identities, but also understanding where one stood within institutional feuds. The carceral social order came to define a context within which people made decisions about their own safety, typically not by joining a gang (as few actually did so) but by crafting an identity that would fit within the affiliation that would help them navigate this setting.

## CLIQUING UP AS SURVIVAL STRATEGY

The potential of encountering violence and victimization consistently informs the choices, identities, and loyalties of those ensnared in the justice system. Because of the heavy emphasis the sorting process placed on identifying prisoners' and students' supposed gang affiliations, participants often could not avoid being positioned into gang-based conflicts while in the prison or juvenile system. For many, this process of being categorized as particular types of gang members led to confrontations with others in the facility who viewed them as rivals because of whom they were associated with. However, although their ties to peer groups were the basis for many confrontations and fights, individuals also needed these peer groups to protect them from the threats of violence they faced while in the institution. Regardless of their own level of gang involvement or whom they aligned themselves with, participants were criminalized and faced confrontation from others in the punitive facility based on their peer group. In this context, it then made sense for them to affiliate with peers who would accept them and who could best protect them during their term or sentence. Both the parolees and probation youth expressed that there was safety in numbers in the unpredictable environment of the carceral institution, and most therefore used the race- and place-based groups they were sorted into to find and develop supportive and protective peer networks.

## Safety in Numbers

As inmates enter the prison, racial sorting confronts them with a labeling process that they cannot avoid; everyone who passes through reception is racially categorized based on whom they will be housed with, so inmates have to decide (if given a choice) which racial group they want to be associated with. State prison authorities have long argued that racial sorting is designed and even necessary to keep rival gang members separated (Robertson 2006), yet impose this categorization on everyone who enters the prison, regardless of their personal racial politics or level of involvement with street or prison gangs. For the parolees in this research there was really no way around making this choice, and any choice they made established them as supporting one group of inmates and opposed to others. Because this process positioned them into rivalries, relying on peers and knowing how they fit into the carceral social order became important survival strategies for navigating the institution and remaining as safe as possible.

Because sorting is built around the premise of separating rival gang members, the racial groupings inmates were sorted into were often conflated with gangs and implicated individual prisoners in gang conflicts. While prison officials contend that sorting reduces conflict within the prison by keeping rivals separated, in the parolees' experiences it established a framework for group conflict and violence. In this system, gang rivalries served as a dominant frame for understanding and organizing prisoners. For the Latino parolees, this meant that peer groups were contextualized through a divisive Norteño/Sureño/Bulldog rubric while they were incarcerated, which extended the conflicts between Norteño, Sureño, and Bulldog gangs to all Latino inmates from Northern, Southern, and Central California. Violence between racially defined prison gangs not only exposes inmates to the persistent threat of confrontation and race riots, but also forces them to rely on peer networks that are generally distrustful of other racial groups in order to survive the institution. Parolees felt that they could not escape the conflicts of racial "politics" while in the prison because these divisive relationships between racialized groups effectively shaped day-to-day life, as Darren, a forty-three-year-old Black parolee, explains: "You can't help but be in politics, because that's the way that whole level is ran."

Racial sorting structured the threats of violence that prisoners had to be wary of, even for those who were not involved in gangs, because it still labeled them as a rival to others groups in the prison. However, parolees also valued the groups they were sorted into because they gave them a sense of having "safety in numbers," and that as part of a large collective they were protected from threats posed by other groups in the prison. Robert, a forty-four-year-old Black parolee, explains that Black inmates protected each other from aggressive White prisoners by sticking together as one group: "Your safety [is] in numbers. That's where your safety come at. But like when I was in Wasco, I mean you know, all the Blacks, regardless of if we Cuz (Crips) or Bloods or whatever, we all come together. You know, because of the Whites, because the Whites always trying to run shit. And if we have to take off on them [fight them], we all be as one unit, you know what I mean? So that's where your safety come in at."

In discussing his experiences in Wasco, Robert describes the danger posed by White prisoners as a defining reason Black inmates need to clique up. He argues that the risk of being bullied by White inmates, and the resulting need to potentially defend themselves against or even attack these prisoners, requires racial solidarity to ensure a strong collective force—regardless of any ongoing gang rivalry therein. Like many of the parolees, Robert sees the presence of other consolidated, united groups of inmates as what prompts his own need to be part of a larger group. In this context, affiliating with the racialized groups inmates are sorted into becomes recognized as a vital survival strategy.

The parolees overwhelmingly described this kind of grouping together as necessary for surviving the prison, explaining that everybody needs supporters available to back them up and protect them from being victimized by other inmates. Trying to keep to oneself on the other hand was seen as much more dangerous, as prisoners who did not align themselves with their race were seen as particularly vulnerable. Here Henry, a Latino parolee from Fresno, articulates the common understanding the parolees had of the risks involved in not affiliating with anybody: "If you don't run with anybody, then that person's gonna have a lot more problems. You know what I'm saying? A *lot* more problems, you know? Because they see you as a private individual, and you're not, you know, you're on your own, nobody to help you. So you'll get uh [clears throat], you'll be more susceptible to the, you know, to the harassment in there."

What Henry may be hinting at here in terms of the "harassment" unaffiliated inmates face is the potential of sexual assault. Indeed, the possibility of being raped was one of the most common fears the parolees recalled from when they first went to prison. However, most parolees also explained that prison rape was far less common than they originally feared, primarily because they believed that their affiliations to their racial group protected them from this risk. Such ties allowed the parolees to access protective relationships with cellmates, respected older inmates, and incarcerated friends and relatives who watched their backs and taught them what to look out for, and this is what most felt protected them from victimization during their terms. For example, when I asked Javier, a Latino parolee who affiliated with Northerners while incarcerated, about how common rape was in the prison, he responded that it wasn't very common and mainly happened when inmates "put [themselves] in that predicament" by "hanging out with guys who like doing that stuff." When I asked him about how new prisoners learn about who they need to stay away from, he explained: "Somebody would come up to you and let you know. They'll come up to you and ask you if you're a Northerner or a Southerner. Then if you're a Northerner, a Northerner will go up to you and tell you how it is, how it'll program, who's who and where, who to hang out with, what not to do, a lot of the dos and don'ts. Somebody will let you know."

In Javier's explanation, being a Northerner or a Southerner becomes necessary for keeping oneself away from potential rape because it is this identity that connects the prisoner to others who can advise them on how to stay safe and avoid predatory inmates. In this way, the parolees' racialized affiliations helped them manage some of the fears and anxieties of imprisonment by giving them a sense of security. Similarly, many of the youth navigating Fresno's juvenile justice system learn to see the race- and place-based groups that they are divided into in much the same way.

## "A Lot of Kids are Scared When They Come Here"

Most of the young people in Fresno's juvenile justice system come from neighborhoods in which they already face a consistent threat of violence. In Fresno's poor communities of color on the Eastside and in West Fresno, neighborhood rivalries significantly influence the lives of young residents, restricting where they can go and shaping whom they interact with, avoid, or perceive as a threat. Because youth could be confronted with these feuds at school, while socializing with friends and family, or when going to any of the few places around town accessible to teenagers to hang out, these conflicts were difficult for many to stay away from or keep themselves safe from, and soon came to structure much of their peer networks. Here Curtis explains that youth eventually have to commit their loyalties to one side of the fight or the other because it is almost impossible to stay out of it:

> Eventually you're gonna have to pick and choose right? Like say you just moved down here and you meet somebody nice that's real cool and you kicking it with him. Then your mom call your cousin or somebody come over, and they be like "Oh don't kick it with him," and now you gotta pick and choose. You either pick your friend or you're gonna pick

your family member. Half of the time you can only pick your family member, that's your blood. Then now that you did that, now your friend like "Oh damn, they are my enemies." Basically that's what he's saying: "They my enemies, so you gonna come kick it with me or you gonna pick him?" And once you do pick him, that's basically labeling yourself. You're basically saying "Oh I'm not gonna kick it with you no more, I'm gonna go kick it with them," and they look [at] it like now, basically in their eyes they think you in a gang now.

Curtis sees becoming entangled in neighborhood feuds as inevitable; because conflicts between neighborhood cliques are so ubiquitous, it is almost impossible to find friends who are uninvolved or who all get along, forcing one to eventually pick sides. But he points out that choosing to socialize with one group of friends over another—be they friends one grew up with or met at school, or even one's own cousins and siblings—essentially labels oneself as a supporter of their side of any conflict they may already be involved in. The subsequent perception of being gang involved puts one in considerable danger, making the peers one has chosen all the more important as a source of protection. But inside the punitive institution it becomes even more difficult to stay out of such conflicts because the facility focuses on keeping gangs separated without offering much if any space for those uninvolved in these rivalries. In this context there is no room for ambivalence in terms of how youth align themselves—rivals come into immediate and consistent contact, and young people face a high potential for confrontation from anyone who doesn't like their friends or other youth from their neighborhood.

Because of the heavy emphasis the institution placed on affiliations, many of the conflicts probation youth had to navigate in juvenile facilities stemmed from challenges over which peers they were associated with. In addition to having labels ascribed to them by authority figures during the juvenile hall booking and school orientation processes, youth were also frequently labeled as gang members by other young people in the institution. Students at SJEA and JDF were routinely confronted as members of particular gangs based on whom they associated with and what their suspected affiliations were. Here Brandon explains that although he is not in a gang, in the hall he learned to anticipate confrontations from other probation youth who feuded with his friends:

AUTHOR: What's drama in [JDF] about?

BRANDON: Like some people come in, they already know who I am. Like "Oh, you kick it with them," so I'm like automatically gonna have problems with these dudes. I remember one time,

[chuckles] this one time this dude comes in there, his name is
Ray. I was like playing dominos and he comes in there like
"Oh you a bitch" or something. Like bruh, what's good bruh?
You gonna prove I'm a bitch? Like out of nowhere, I'm just
minding my own business and just cuz I kick it with these
people, they already know like "Damn, this nigga kick it
with them," so there's gonna automatically be problems.
Just cuz I kick it with them people. So even though I didn't
start nothing, they still know who I am. So there still gonna
be problems.

Brandon indicates that confrontations over associating with one group or
another commonly led to fights or assaults in the juvenile hall. In facilities
like JDF, young peoples' friendships were often defined through the lens of
the carceral social order as affiliations to neighborhood gangs—meaning
that one's relationships to their peers often positioned youth onto one side
of a rivalry or the other. Consequently, the fact that Brandon socializes
with one set of people automatically establishes him as an enemy to youth
like Ray who don't get along with his friends. Because their friendships—
both past and present—could position them into such conflicts, youth like
Brandon learned to realize that in JDF or SJEA they may already be seen as
somebody's rival based on where they were from and whom they knew.

Even though Brandon has no interest in gangbanging, he still finds himself caught in feuds between local cliques because of whom he is perceived
to affiliate with. Yet while peer groups were a source for many conflicts that
got students into fights, the resulting threat of violence also ironically made
such groups an important protective resource. This was particularly the
case when one's neighborhood or friends were enough to associate them
with one side of a rivalry, and consequently identify them as enemies to
other youth in the facility. In this context peer groups not only offered
young people a sense of protection but also support during imprisonment.
Here sixteen-year-old Eric, a Bulldog gang member, explains that cliquing
up with other Bulldogs helps make the time spent detained in juvenile hall
much more stable and manageable:

AUTHOR: Do you think it's easier having homeboys with you [in JDF]?
   ERIC: Yeah, it kinda relieves you off the other things, you know?
         You don't really have to worry about a lot of things. You know
         there's always gonna be someone watching [out for] you. So
         you ain't gonna worry about anything. Just keep to them.

A: Like worry about enemies you mean?

E: Yeah, like basically you ain't gotta worry about them. Same thing with like, you know you're not gonna be bored, you know? You're always gonna have someone to talk to.

Like Eric, many youth cycling through the system rely on the networks developed within the racialized neighborhood groups they are categorized into to navigate the institution, access supportive peers, and protect themselves from violence. Here we can also see that the groups young people identify with in this context are not entirely self-generated, but are also shaped by the boundaries drawn by the institution itself.

For many youth this grouping together functions to manage the fear and uncertainty associated with coming to juvenile justice institutions, as fifteen-year-old Carlos explains that many youth uninvolved with gangs tend to stay with the largest groups at SJEA: "I think a lot of kids are scared when they come here. That's why you have like forty kids at the Bulldogs tables." SJEA's reputation as a school for probation youth and its strong emphasis on gang conflicts informs students' perceptions of it as a space in which they need to be ready for confrontation and need to rely on their friends for support and protection. Sociologist David Harding argues that young people learn to manage such confrontations by developing and valuing neighborhood-based collective identities that offer bonds of mutual protection with other residents in their community (2010). In JDF and SJEA, these neighborhood identities are contextualized by how the concentration of policing in Fresno's poor Black and Latina/o communities virtually ensures that youth find other people they already know from their neighborhoods in the institution with them. Because it is so easy to get drawn into violent rivalries in juvenile justice facilities, students stick with those they grew up with regardless of gang status, fostering protective relationships between both gang members and nonmembers. For example, one day when I was scheduled to interview Mario, a sixteen-year-old self-identified gang member, he cancelled at the last minute. The next day I found out it was because he chose to walk home a friend of his who didn't bang, because Mario had heard that another group of kids at the school were planning to jump him.

Young people in JDF and SJEA chose to stay with the peers who helped them feel safe in these uncertain environments, even though this often marked them as gang members and got them into additional legal trouble. These choices worked in conjunction with how youth were categorized by staff, reflecting the "negotiated settlement" (Goodman 2008) at work in prison sorting in that youth use their personal agency to influence how they are classified along the rigid template of affiliations recognized by institutional staff. Probation youth entering juvenile facilities understand that these environments are segregated and that how they are labeled will affect whom they can be around, so they make the decisions that they feel will best protect them.

## Differentiating Affiliations and Gangs

I would like to take a moment here to make a clearer distinction between affiliations and street or prison gangs. Groups like Norteñas/os, Sureñas/os, and Bulldogs (and in Fresno Twamp and Squad) are commonly referred to as large criminal gangs by media, law enforcement, and scholars. However, in this work I argue that this characterization is not quite accurate, and that it would benefit our understanding of how young people navigate the justice system to conceptualize these groupings in a new way. Participants saw street and prison gangs as neighborhood-based cliques and exclusive criminal organizations respectively, but the groups I focus on in this chapter are something different. These affiliations are racialized, place-based collective identities that are established in how individuals are categorized and separated in the punitive facility. Because the sorting process is unavoidable, any affiliated group is going to include several members of local gangs as well as many more individuals who are uninvolved in gangs. Affiliated persons are often as a whole labeled as gang members or associates,[1] but this mass labeling overlooks how gang involvement may be assumed or even imposed by justice system institutions themselves. Recognizing this problem reminds us that it is important to consider how the individuals navigating and appropriating these identities actually understand them themselves.

The parolees referred to these affiliations as "cars" that structured much of their day-to-day experience and helped them navigate and survive the institution. The parolees recognized these cars as simply a collective of everyone who was sorted into the same racialized group. The cars helped the parolees address the "pains of imprisonment" (Sykes 1958) while they were incarcerated by providing some of the material needs, emotional support, and physical protection that the institution cannot or will not supply themselves. Because these groups are based in shared racial and geographic identities, the car for many became a powerful identifier that signified connections to other prisoners. In their interviews, several parolees credited their cars with helping them adjust to prison life and "showing them love" at low points in their lives. Many claimed that friends in the car offered them support when they needed help, or showed them how they could get practical resources that they needed for day-to-day living like food, clothes, hygiene supplies, or small luxuries that the prison did not adequately provide. Addressing these needs significantly helped the parolees adjust to prison life, and this was a crucial factor that established the car as part of participants' personal identities—one that shaped how they saw themselves and their relationships to others.

The importance of the car in day-to-day life for prisoners makes it a significant factor in establishing the carceral social order as a dominant logic in the prison, one that follows the structure of racial sorting and prison gang rivalries. Within these groups inmates hold each other accountable to informal behavioral codes—not unlike the convict code (Weider 1974)—that function to uphold the segregation structured in the facility, particularly as prisoners learn to perceive these divisions as beneficial. It is important to note, however, that cars are not the same as prison gangs—the parolees recognized these groups as distinct from prison gangs and did not see themselves as prison gang members. Additionally, the parolees' cars do not match the predominant academic definition of prison gangs.[2] Instead, the cars were groups established in the sorting process that framed the parolees' peer networks and relationships along racial and geographic boundaries; parolees understood the peers they were housed with, shared resources with, and fought alongside as being "inside the car." These cars, and the divisions between them, are continually maintained through the security measures that prison authorities insist are necessary to keep rival gangs separated. This structure can foster a perception that a majority of those in the prison are gang involved, although this is inaccurate.

In JDF and SJEA, young people understood these affiliations in regional terms. Norteñas/os, Sureñas/os, Bulldogs, Twamp, and Squad existed here as racialized groups that were largely determined by where students lived.[3] These identities highlight how the carceral institution functions as a place-making (Gupta and Ferguson 1997) site that redefines what local identities mean to people. Regional identities are very important in the prison because it draws people in from all over the state, so being from the same hometown commonly became a bond between people that situated an expectation to support and protect each other.[4] In the county-level juvenile facilities that I observed, regional bonds and collective identities centered on broad districts of urban Fresno (being from the Eastside or Westside, for example) or the smaller rural communities that dot the county. In poor communities of color such as these, high levels of violence make neighborhoods a central form of identity for young people that entails bonds of mutual protection with peers (Harding 2010). However, I argue that because these communities are overrepresented in punitive institutions and grouped together in the sorting process, neighborhood-based identities are reframed as affiliations such as the Bulldogs.

In their conversation comparing affiliations in Fresno's Black and Chicana/o neighborhoods, Brandon, Mario, and Vincent describe these affiliations' relationships with communities and individual neighborhood gangs. One afternoon when I have the three of them out of history class, they finish their assignment quickly and begin flipping through their heavily worn and vandalized textbooks. Mario and Vincent start crossing out Sureño tags they find throughout the pages and write Bulldog tags in their place. Brandon watches them for a few minutes, then writes "WSTG" on his paper and points to it with his pencil while addressing Mario:

BRANDON: I bet you can't guess what that means.

MARIO: (looks at it for a few seconds and guesses) West Side Thug Gang?

B: Ah man, if you can't even guess it I ain't fittin' to tell you!

M: Ah come on, what is it?

B: (points at the letter T with his pencil) What's the "T"?

M: I don't know, what is it?

B: Think of different hoods on the Westside.

M: Fink White Gang?

B: Ain't no "F" in there!

M: Twamp Gang!

B: Yeah.

M: But you don't bang though right?

B: Naw I don't, but everyone I [hang out] with is Twamp Gang.

M: But I don't get it, what is Twamp?

B: It's like a bunch of hoods all cliqued up.

M: Oh, kinda like the Bulldogs in the Eastside.

B: Yeah, but like you all just say "Eastside."

VINCENT: Yeah, like we got McKenzie [Street], Calwa . . .

M: College Street, Bond Street . . .

V: Lewis Street, Floradora . . .

In this conversation Brandon, Mario, and Vincent begin to recognize similarities in how affiliations are structured in Fresno's Black and Chicana/o communities—Brandon explains that Twamp Gang consists of "a bunch of hoods all cliqued up," a pattern Mario and Vincent recognize when they start listing all the neighborhoods in Eastside Fresno that identify as Bulldogs. The boys do not describe Twamp Gang or Bulldogs as gangs per se, but rather as collections of similarly affiliated neighborhood-based gangs. Gangs from the same racially segregated parts of the city associate with each other in these larger affiliations. Most Black neighborhoods on the Westside side affiliate with Twamp, and rival neighborhoods in West and North Fresno run with Murder Squad. Similarly, Latina/o sets from the Eastside affiliate with Bulldogs, and those from the Westside often identify as Norteña/os. Barrio gangs from Fresno's surrounding rural communities are more likely to identify as Sureños.[5]

While groups like Twamp Gang and Bulldogs include neighboring street gangs, we should consider how they reflect the broader criminalization of Black and Latina/o communities in Fresno. They are identities that are shared among many of the youth in these neighborhoods who have been affected by the justice system, not just gang members. As Brandon points out to Mario and Vincent, he doesn't gangbang "but everyone I [hang out] with is Twamp Gang." Similarly, most of the youth at SJEA did not identify as gang members or support individual neighborhood gangs, but did side with one of these broader affiliations based on where they were from and whom they hung out with. This informal gang affiliation is partly due to how being sorted and divided socialized these affiliations, but also because it reframed neighborhood identities and networks that were already mean-ingful to students. Most of SJEA's students came from the same handful of neighborhoods in Fresno, and often knew many of the other students from their communities, schools they previously attended, and even their own families. When students began attending SJEA they generally hung out with other youth they already knew, and for most Black and Latina/o stu-dents this tied them to affiliations like Twamp Gang and Bulldogs.

To the students, supporting or identifying with one of these affiliations did not indicate gang membership or an aspiration to be part of gang life. Young people make an important distinction between banging a neighbor-hood (being a gang member) and backing up or running with groups like Twamp or Bulldogs (identifying with a broader affiliation). When youth talked about joining a gang or friends of theirs who were gang members, they recognized gangs as small, neighborhood-based groups. Many young people identified with criminalized affiliations like Bulldogs, but being "from a neighborhood" was central to identifying and being recognized as a gang member—one couldn't be a Bulldog gang member without banging a specific neighborhood like College Street or Parkside. Therefore, the affil-iations between neighborhood gangs do not indicate the existence of larger gangs, as some law enforcement personnel and scholars commonly assume.[6] The affiliations youth identified with in this research did not have any kind of initiation rituals or clear distinctions between members and nonmembers, and had little if any formal organization or hierarchy. Most importantly, many of the youth who identified with these affiliations did not see themselves as gang members.

While youth certainly recognize and identify with these affiliations in the community, much of this cliquing up is accomplished inside punitive facilities. These institutions are sites in which youth come into contact with other affiliations, are identified as associates of particular groups, and are confronted by rivals. As such, affiliations become important for support and protection in these places. However, these facilities are also sites in which institutional authorities use these broader affiliations as a basis for managing populations of criminalized youth, and where youth are ascribed with criminal identities based on how they are categorized.

## LEARNING TO IDENTIFY WITH AFFILIATIONS

Much like the placemaking influence described in the previous section, the punitive institution constructs specific identities in the process of socializing carceral affiliations. The shared experiences of navigating the facility and being sorted together rearticulates the relevant peer networks into a shared, institutionalized affiliation. Claiming this affiliation allows individuals to access protective networks while they are in the institution, but positioning oneself within such a group also requires learning how to properly identify or constitute oneself as part of the group. To accomplish this association, participants needed to redefine aspects of their identity to fit the affiliation they were claiming, as the institution not only reinforced ties to affiliations but also molded them into particular understandings of race, gangs, and masculinity that fit the carceral social order's template. Learning to successfully position oneself within the carceral social order was instrumental for safely navigating the punitive institution.

### Gangs as Secondary

Contrary to the popular assumption that gangs become more important when one is locked up, most participants' gang ties (if they were gang involved) became secondary to broader affiliations while they were in the facility. For individuals who identify with street gangs in their home communities, being in the punitive institution commonly forces them to redefine whom they recognize as allies and enemies. Individual gang members may not have anyone else from their clique or neighborhood incarcerated with them, but place-based identities enabled them to band together with people from other neighborhoods to form a larger protective unit. As the conversation between Brandon, Mario, and Vincent indicated, affiliations developed between neighborhood gangs from racialized communities in the same districts of the city. For example, if someone in JDF banged Calwa Bulldogs but was the only person from their neighborhood in the pod, they might spend most their time with other youth banging College Street or Bond Street—other Bulldog neighborhoods in Eastside Fresno—while they were locked up. Similar to how Robert, one of our parolees in the previous section, explained that Black prisoners needed to stay together regardless of if they were "Cuz or Bloods," gang youth in JDF and SJEA cliqued up with their counterparts from similarly affiliated neighborhoods—even those they didn't otherwise get along with—to develop protective groups large enough to contest rival affiliations in the facility.

In many cases this need to form larger groups pushed gang-involved youth to affiliate with people they normally fought with outside the institution. For example, young people from rival Bulldog street cliques suspended their feuds to socialize with each other and form a united group while they were in JDF and SJEA together. Here Eric, a sixteen-year-old Bulldog gang member, explains that bickering street cliques need to band together around their shared affiliations because it is important to unify in the face of other groups in the institution:

> ERIC: It's like whether in JDF or in county or prison, you know Bulldogs are gonna be Bulldogs. You guys are gonna be together. You guys ain't gonna go keep yourselves apart, take each other out when you guys know the enemies are just right there. Cuz that's what they probably want you to do, you know? Cuz they probably know how it is out here, how we take each other out. So you know it's better for us to stay together than just to go against each other.
>
> AUTHOR: So the school's kind of the same thing where you have other enemies?
>
> E: Yeah like when we're at school or something, we're all together, cuz we know there's enemies here. But like if it was just all of us here, no other enemies, we'll probably end up having problems with each other.

Eric lists the juvenile hall alongside the county jail and the prison in a telling comparison of sites that call for Bulldogs to clique up and stick together. He explains that many neighborhoods affiliated with Bulldogs frequently fight with each other outside of the institution, but in the hall and at the continuation school these conflicts are put on hold because these are places where rival Norteña/o and Sureña/o affiliations are present. He notes that in these facilities "we're all together cuz we know there's enemies here," but in the absence of these rival groups, Bulldogs would likely continue feuding among themselves.

Many of the gang-involved parolees described a similar reframing of gang identities in which gang-based loyalties and conflicts were redrawn and became secondary to racial identity. In the prison being part of an individual street clique—and any commitment to fighting its rival cliques— became much less important than being part of the car. The relationships between racial cars shaped much of parolees' regular routines and the spaces they had access to in the facility, so adjusting to prison life required learning the informal rules of prison politics. In this quote Jeremy, a twenty-eight-year-old Laotian parolee, explains the process and importance of learning how to be a part of the Asian car:

> The homie laced me up in prison. Us Asians, you know Asians funk
> [fight] with Asians out here, but when you go to prison that all dies. We
> have to stick to each other so we have to let us know. . . . Unless you
> were just like one of, [what] you call jaycats.[7] They the homies coming
> in where they just not all there, [but you] have to let them know. Cuz
> the drugs and all that stuff, I don't know what it was, [but it was] like he
> didn't know he was breaking the rules and he caused problems for us
> and we had to deal with it. That's how it goes too, that's what [causes]
> a riot to break off and stuff. When someone, I'm not gonna say in our
> car, like another car, like Blacks for instance, came in and disrespected
> somebody from a different race, and if the Blacks didn't deal with it
> then the other race would cause a riot and we would break off! Just
> break it off, boom. Just for not knowing.

Here Jeremy illustrates how in the process of learning about what he can and can't do, he also learned about his place in the dynamics of the carceral social order. As a street gang member in Fresno Jeremy grew up fighting with rival Cambodian gangs, but in order to survive in the prison he has to end these feuds and now support his former rivals. Additionally, he learns the importance of everyone in the car knowing and following the rules that divide physical space in the prison, and recognizes his role in informing new inmates about them. Learning these expectations is important because ignorance of them can inadvertently lead to a confrontation between racial groups that puts the whole car in danger. Understanding and following these tacit rules therefore becomes an important way for incarcerated men to claim and adopt the collective identity of the car. Doing so not only demonstrates that one is part of the group, but these rules or "politics" also become a lens through which the parolees understand how they can manage the carceral social order and negotiate their own racial affiliations. These sets of informal rules ultimately define the parolees' understandings of how the prison is structured, how it generates violence, and how they conceptualize their role in this environment.

The need for protective groups inside the punitive facility requires a coming together of otherwise fragmented gang cliques. For Black and Latina/o probation youth (as well as incarcerated Latino adults), this entailed street cliques from the same geographic regions grouping together to form larger collectives in the institution. But in addition to geographic ties, the need for protective groups also made race an important factor for group affiliation—especially true in the prison, where Blacks, Whites, and Asians prioritized racial identity over neighborhood or gang clique because they generally saw racial solidarity as necessary for survival. Research participants used the groups they were separated into for protection while they navigated the carceral institution, but doing so also required them to shift how they saw, described, and positioned themselves to fit the social order imposed by the institution. Part of this shift required developing an understanding of race and racial identity that fit in with how it was used by the institution: specifically, the probation youth and parolees learned to define race by how racial groups are institutionally separated in the facility.

## Reconceptualizing Race

There is a great deal of race-making work embedded in the prison sorting process that constructs specific racial identities (Goodman 2008; Robertson 2006). The division of inmates into rigid monoracial groups defines which identities are institutionally recognized, which people can meaningfully claim and use, and how one will be racialized by others. The socializing effect of this imposed structure is then to push people to identify with one of the few available categories (Goodman 2008), effectively collapsing the spectrum of racial and ethnic identities into a handful of broad categories that are institutionally useful. Individuals adapting to the carceral social order consequently then learn to understand their own racial identities in accordance with the racialized groups constructed and defined in the sorting process— even when this process conditions Asian inmates to refer to themselves as "Others," or designates Latinos from Northern and Southern California as distinct racial groups. This racial logic can resonate in criminalized communities outside of the penal facility as well, where the Norteño/Sureño split is oftentimes representative of the national, linguistic, generational, and cultural divides between Chicana/os and Mexicana/os (Mendoza-Denton 2008). For example, sixteen-year-old Emilio describes his Norteño affiliation and racial/ethnic identity as synonymous, explaining that "Chicanos and Norteños are the same thing. There's some Chicano Sureños out there, but they represent Mexico [and] Mexicans. They don't say Chicano, they say Mexico."

In the prison, the car and its specific rules of interracial interaction compelled some parolees to redefine how they understood their own racial identity and what this meant in terms of their relationships with racialized others. This kind of shift was especially noticeable for White men who may have never previously thought of themselves as racialized beings. For these parolees, Whiteness became defined by whom they got along with and whom they "had problems" with in the prison. James, a forty-seven-year-old White parolee, explains how his introduction to prison politics led him to discover his own racial identity (or "nationality"):

> I didn't know I was a Wood. I had to be taught that in county, the three months I was in county, and then three months I was in Delano. I had to be schooled on what I was. I didn't even know I had a nationality, a Wood, or a Peckerwood. I didn't know that. So I was schooled on that, but I found out that um, I had no problems with the Southsiders, and I had no problems with the Bulldogs. Now I had a lot problems with the Bloods and the Crips, but it wasn't with the Hispanic group, I never had any problems with them. They kinda gave respect, as long as you gave respect, they gave respect. Yeah, I learned that in the joint, that I was a Wood. But see I didn't know any of that. And I didn't know, and now I know the rules of conduct, and what we can do and can't do with them.

James describes cliquing up with other Whites in the prison as an experience in which he not only learned about how race was classified in the institution, but he also realized that he too has a racial identity.[8] But as he goes on to explain, part of learning this new identity included learning that he "had a lot of problems with the Bloods and the Crips," but not with Southsiders, Bulldogs, or other Latino inmates. James's newly discovered racial identity is defined by the rules that prison politics structure between racial groups, and by whom the White inmates do or don't get along with according to these rules. He learns to conceptualize his own racial identity in terms of his groups' relationships with other racialized groups of prisoners, and how he consequently can or cannot interact with them.

James's words illustrate how racial identity in the carceral facility comes to be defined by the boundaries between racial groups. The prison defined racial identity within a divisive social order that put racial groups into conflict with each other. Inmates therefore experienced and embodied race through unofficial but strict sets of rules that separated racialized groups and limited interaction between them. Such rules were most commonly about physical space (such as Jeremy's description of which spaces were permissible or forbidden), although some cars had very extensive sets of rules that regulated what they could and could not do with other racial groups.[9] Individual inmates were expected to know the rules for being with their race, as understanding and following these behavioral codes were fundamental to learning to identify with and be part of the car. Just as learning the "rules of conduct" was instrumental to the construction of James's identity as a Wood, the "jaycats" Jeremy describes as incapable of following the rules may not be recognized or accepted as part of the car because of the danger they may pose to the group.

Familiarity with and adherence to the rules of racial politics demonstrated who inmates positioned themselves with in the prison's carceral social order. At SJEA this position in the social order was performed not so much through observing an intricate set of rules,[10] but rather through one's presence with a specific group in their recognized space. Much like how belonging in a given car is demonstrated by knowing where in the prison one's group can and cannot congregate, performing this collective identity is similarly accomplished at the continuation school through the occupation of physical space.

Students' presence with one group or another on the blacktop were therefore seen as significant statements about the racial identities they were perceived to be claiming and performing, because the school's efforts to keep rival gangs separated effectively racially segregated the blacktop in much the same way as the prison. Not only were youth racially sorted into different affiliations based on how particular gangs were racially imagined and identified by staff, but the neighborhood-based identities that youth relied on for support in this context also re-created the residential segregation of Fresno's communities of color. Consequently, while the blacktop was divided by affiliations that were based on where in town students were from, these divides were heavily racialized as well. Here eighteen-year-old Angel, a Chicano student who is not in a gang but sits with the Bulldogs, describes how space at SJEA is racially divided and the effect this has on how students' racial identities are perceived and understood:

ANGEL: When a new Black person comes they go with the Black people. A new Mexican kid comes, they go on the other side. And if you see a new skater kid they go with the skater kids.
AUTHOR: Which is also where the White kids hang out right?
ANGEL: Mmm hmm. Or the kids that are Mexican but they act White.

Here we can see how both the institutional categorization of young people and students' need for protective groups teach them to conceptualize racial identity through a system of carceral affiliations. In the racially divided context of SJEA's blacktop (much like in the prison), one's race is not simply a matter of personal identity or family background, but rather something that students see as largely defined by which group one aligns themselves with. In this way, students' perceived racial identity may be tempered by gang affiliations or cultural identities, but is ultimately framed in terms of which racialized group they side with and support. For example, Angel describes the Mexican youth who sit with the skaters—and therefore associate more closely with the White students than with other Latinas/os—as racially different from his groups of friends, articulating a pattern at SJEA that was hard for Latina/o students to avoid: Mexican and Chicana/o youth coming in could choose between siding with gang-associated groups (by hanging with Bulldogs, Norteñas/os, or Sureñas/os) or being racial outsiders who were not recognized as Mexican. For students of color, being with their peers in this uncertain space meant being criminalized with them.

Alternatively, students who associated with other racial groups were not seen as legitimate members of their own race (i.e., the Mexican students Angel accuses of "acting White"), revealing how race comes to be conflated with the often gang-associated affiliations youth are divided into in the facility. The students at SJEA viewed being at a given table on the blacktop as something that made a powerful statement about who they are and whom they support within a social order in which affiliation is mutually exclusive. Consequently, identifying with a group that was racialized differently than oneself (i.e. a Chicano associating with the White students) jeopardized one's claim to their own racial identity. As youth appropriated the logic of the carceral social order that was institutionalized through continuous sorting and separation of students, they enforced it among each other by policing one another's presence at particular tables in terms of what they saw as appropriate for claiming one racialized identity or another. For example, one day while working with a small group of students on an assignment, two begin talking about a new boy at the school. Here Devin, a White student, and Amy, a Bulldog-affiliated Latina, complain about Chris because he sits with the White students but claims to be a Bulldog gang member:

DEVIN: The new Whiteboy, the one that was sitting across from me at lunch, says he's a Bulldog.
AMY: Why wasn't he sitting with us then?

D: I know! That's what I was saying! He was saying he from VEL.

A: What?? That's my hood! I don't know him!

D: He said that two of them put him on in JDF . . . he was all asking where the dogs are and where the scraps are and all that. I was just like "Man, you're fake!"

A: Why wasn't he sitting with us then if he's from my hood?!

D: I know! I mean why you gonna sit at the White table if you ain't a White person!

Devin and Amy both see Chris's presence at the White table as inappropriate if he is claiming to be part of a Latina/o street clique (VEL Bulldogs) and identifying himself as a Bulldog. Their complaints reveal not only the expected racial homogeneity of student groups, but more importantly their understanding of race in terms of the affiliations students are expected to choose between. Chris is White and self-identifies as such, but his claim to whiteness is dismissed when he reveals himself to be a Bulldog, and after announcing his affiliation Devin no longer recognizes him as a fellow "White person." In this context, students do not frame race in terms of identity or background, but as a category of affiliation that is made available to them and that is mutually exclusive from any others. In this sense, the students' understanding of being White mirrors the parolees' explanation of being White in the prison, particularly in that one cannot be White *and* be a Bulldog. One would have to be one or the other, but never both, and understanding this was essential to being identifiable as part of either group.

## Constructing Masculinity and "Bitches"

The routine enforcement of the carceral social order also socialized gendered identities that became important for navigating the punitive facility. The constant threat of violence made cultivating a masculine identity[11] that was based on physical power a crucial aspect of claiming an affiliation. However, embodying this physical masculinity further marginalized participants because while it was valued inside the institution, it was also stigmatized outside of it and validated one's "criminal" status. Masculinity is commonly socialized as a set of social practices that indicate dominance and control (Pascoe 2007), but physical power is often seen as inferior to rational power as a source of social dominance, and therefore often functions as a marginalized form of hegemonic masculinity (Connell 1995). Because the carceral social order necessitates fighting between affiliations, the masculinities that criminalized boys and men have available to them within punitive settings are associated with physical strength and violence. But conforming to this masculinity not only reinforced participants' criminalization as violent subjects who require punitive control, but also removed them from opportunities to access other forms of masculinity that are based on rational power and technical skills[12]—hegemonic masculinities that give people power on "the outs." Within punitive settings, this violence-based masculinity is cemented through a carceral social order that forces people to fight, even when they don't want to.

This form of masculinity was particularly visible in the conversations and interactions between students at SJEA. The centrality of rivalries to everyday life at SJEA directed how many of the boys came to understand masculinity. In this context, students defined masculinity in terms of one's ability to resist victimization, and performed masculine identities by "acting hard," demonstrating a readiness to fight and refusal to back down if provoked. However, the carceral social order directed when this identity was performed—namely, to defend one's peers and their physical space in the facility, and against youth with rival affiliations. Masculine identity at SJEA was designed to project one's commitment to an affiliated peer group. The carceral social order created the occasions for one's masculinity to be evaluated in response to confronting specific rivals, and ultimately defined what a boy was expected to do in order to be recognized as sufficiently masculine by his peers.

Boys who failed to confront rivals were marked as weak and subjected to social exclusion, which could leave one isolated and vulnerable. This understanding is articulated here by Nick, a sixteen-year-old Bulldog, shortly after he attacks a Sureño who sat at the Bulldog table. On this particularly hot day many students crowded around the Bulldogs' space to get under the shade, but Nick and his friends interpreted this boy's presence as an impending attack against them, despite the fact that he was simply eating his lunch. Because he was sitting next to him Nick felt pressured to act—first demanding he move, then punching him when he refused—and that ignoring this encroachment was not an option.

AUTHOR: So what do you think would have happened to you if you just walked away?

NICK: Oh I would've been the bitchest bitch here. They woulda been like "What? You gonna let him punk you? You're not down? You too scared to fight??" Especially against the littlest one, you know what I mean? Yeah, it woulda been all bad for me.

Nick understands not fighting as a decision that would have had worse consequences for him than being locked up again for assault. By not confronting this boundary violation by a rival, Nick risks being seen as fearful and unwilling or unable to defend himself or his peers against a perceived impending threat. Walking away from this altercation, and therefore failing to act hard, would have exposed him to being seen by his peers as a "bitch," a reputation that could potentially follow him to other facilities.

Avoiding this reputation is important for Nick because it could expose him to future challenges and assaults. The boys saw bitches as unmasculine subjects who were incapable of defending themselves and therefore easy targets for victimization. Acting hard was therefore an important means of resisting this label and avoiding being seen as a target by demonstrating that one could not be easily victimized, and that any attempt to do so would be met with violence. Sociologist Elijah Anderson similarly argues that young men in poor communities of color learn to develop tough "street" personas that indicate a capacity for violence in order to build reputations that protect them from assault (2000). He goes on to explain that these reputations become entwined with the masculine identities of young men because one's personal safety could be jeopardized if others do not respect one's masculinity, establishing physical strength and ruthlessness as valued masculine attributes (Anderson 2000).

Because the *bitch* label challenges this masculine performance, it functions in much the same way as the "specter of the fag"[13]—a disciplinary mechanism that crafts gender performances by teaching boys "that at any moment they could become fags if they were not sufficiently masculine" (Pascoe 2007, 60). In the carceral social order, boys risked becoming a bitch by failing to confront challenges to fight. This possibility disciplined boys' constructions of masculinity in a context that compelled them to prove that they weren't bitches by acting hard. Students policed one another's masculine performances by warning each other not to be a bitch and pushing them towards potentially violent clashes. Boys were regularly pressured not to "bitch out" of a fight anytime another student challenged them, and demonstrating that they wouldn't back down was often more important than actually fighting. Consequently, the displays performing this willingness— the unbroken eye contact, taking their sweatshirts off and stiffly putting their fists in front of themselves, taking tiny steps forward but never back, and yelling at each other to attack—generally characterized confrontations between boys far more than any physical attacks ever did.

But it is also important to recognize that in the context of the justice system facility, the term "bitch" marks one not only for social exclusion and isolation, but also as someone who would be vulnerable to sexual assault in the prison. As criminalized adolescents from high-incarceration neighborhoods, many students were regularly exposed to messages that they could be imprisoned one day, and understood the prison as a setting in which weak men were raped. This understanding is what made evading this label so important, and what structured how verbal challenges to one's masculinity were answered—either through fights, or if not facing an immediate physical threat, by discursively deflecting this label onto someone else.

Such is the case with Jackson and Garrison, two male friends reunited at SJEA after they roomed together at JDF, who now find themselves in the hallway after being thrown out of class for talking. When the security guard on duty askes how they know each other, Garrison points to Jackson and says "She my girl. [We] would bunk together in JDF, [I] would come in and just tell her to assume the position." Jackson howls in laughter and the two begin a back and forth over who controlled whom in the room, directing their statements to the guard and being sure to refer to the other as "she" each time. Even as they joke with each other, Garrison and Jackson perform and defend their masculinity each time it is questioned, displaying to their audience that they are dominant young men by identifying someone else as a subject of their sexual control. In this pattern the target is not only tagged as unmasculine, but is also feminized as a potential recipient of sexual violence. Revealed in this exchange is an understanding of one's relationship to violence as structured along a gender binary; just as masculinity is understood as the ability to resist victimization by inflicting violence, vulnerability to another's violence is constructed as feminine.

Consequently, any display of perceived femininity is quickly policed by other boys who frame the offense as an indication that one would be susceptible to sexual assault in the prison. For example, one afternoon in class a student fairly new to the school asks his neighbor to pass him a bottle of hand sanitizer sitting on a nearby desk. When he receives it he pulls down his socks and begins rubbing the sanitizer on his ankles, revealing fresh tattoos to the students sitting around him that read "love" and "hate" on opposite legs. As he starts rubbing the sanitizer over the tattoo of the word "love," the boy sitting next to him voices his disapproval: "You got 'love' tattooed on your ankle?? Better not go to ANY pen."

There is a moment of stunned silence from the surrounding students who hear this. They freeze with their mouths open in disbelief, but soon the shock dissipates into laughter. Another boy chimes in "They'll see him when he gets there and be like 'sup little girl!'" Everyone starts laughing even harder, except for the targeted boy, who keeps his head down and stays quiet while he continues to treat the aggravated skin around his new tattoos.

It is essential to remember that the institution has a central role in the construction of this masculinity, as well as the violence used to perform it. At SJEA this masculinity was not only learned from peers, but was also socialized by authority figures and directed by the social order institutionalized at the school. When Nick punches the boy who sits next to him at lunch, he doesn't attack any of the other non-Bulldog students who intrude on his group's space, or any of the Bulldogs he feuds with outside the school walls, but only lashes out at the student who is marked as his rival by the carceral social order. He attacks this boy because he is a Sureño, but in doing so he also actively defends the boundaries between groups that the school itself has imposed. In directing how this violence was used, the carceral social order at SJEA was effectively cemented through the boys' acts of conforming to the masculinity socialized in the punitive facility, i.e., doing what was necessary to not be a "bitch."

But law enforcement also participates in conditioning this aggressive masculinity, as officers regularly used violence, intimidation, and humiliation in attempts to control young boys in police stops. The "bitch" label was a common part of this experience, and these interactions with law enforcement similarly pressured the boys to defend their masculinity through acting hard. While reviewing a short story with my regular tutoring group, Ben describes what happened to his friend Richard, another SJEA student, the previous night, after someone else in our group asks what the word "accusation" means.

"It's like when someone blames you for something. That happened to the homie last night. Got arrested for tagging at like three in the morning."

"He did?" I ask.

Ben nods. "And the cop called him a bitch cuz they didn't see him writing. They just caught him with the cans, and he wouldn't tell her what he writes. It was a lady cop and I guess she was kinda fine, cuz while she was patting him down he was like 'Ooooh, ooooh' [simulating sexualized moaning]. So she was asking what he writes and what crew he's in, and was like 'Don't be a bitch, give it up!'"

In Ben's story we can see "bitch" invoked by law enforcement as a disciplinary mechanism when his friend won't identify himself as part of tagging crew—a group of young graffiti artists who are locally policed in much the same way as gangs. Here the term serves to establish the police as the dominant presence in this interaction and intimidate Richard into compliance by emasculating him, but it also reinforces claiming a criminalized identity as part of the expected criteria for masculine performance. Many of the boys described similar experiences in which police called them a bitch or a "wannabe"[14] if they refused to criminalize themselves as gang members, and felt this was used to try to goad them into self-validating. Richard resists this characterization by demonstrating his control of the situation, but because the officer is female he does this by sexualizing her rather than by performing a willingness to fight. More specifically, he undermines her authority by discursively reframing her as someone who is sexually pleasuring him. With this gesture he reclaims some sense of power by suggesting that he is the one benefiting from this interaction, and that he is in control because she is doing what he wants.

The masculinity that Nick and Ben describe relies on refusing to be passive when challenged and demonstrating this refusal by dominating a weaker counterpart. Asserting dominance in these situations becomes key to masculine performance and establishes a stark contrast between one who can act hard and one who remains passive. Students consequently come to see acting hard and being a bitch through a gendered binary in which the former becomes a masculine ideal and the stigmatized latter is read as feminine, in turn influencing how many of the boys learn to interact with girls and women. In addition to acting hard to prove that they could not be dominated, boys performed their masculinity by identifying girls and women as people who could be, often by talking about women and girls at the school as dismissible objects for sexual gratification. Some girls challenge this gender hierarchy that positions them as powerless by also acting hard to resist being treated as a bitch, but are often seen as behaving like boys when they do. One morning in class, David and Andrea talk about a fight she and another friend had with a third student some time ago, and he praises their aggression as masculine.

"I never seen girls fight like dogs before, you act like guys!"

"You gotta act like a guy, or they'll treat you like a bitch." Andrea then looks at me and reminds me of a discussion we had on this same point a few days ago in her interview. "Remember sir? We talked about that. You can be a dog, or you can be a bitch. I mean you'll have like a group of guys and like one girl, and they'll be like 'Oh this bitch, this and that,' and she'll just stand there! Like how's someone just not gonna do shit while someone calls them a bitch!?"

Andrea not only describes "acting like a guy" as synonymous with "being a dog," but she also explains that for girls to avoid being dismissed and disrespected they must adopt an aggressive persona and be ready to fight, behavior that she and her peers recognize as normatively masculine. In this sense the protective power of masculine performance—crafting a reputation as a tough fighter—is not restricted to the boys. In her study of how girls manage threats of personal violence in poor communities of color, sociologist Nikki Jones found that developing reputations as fighters gave girls the respect of their peers and helped them confidently occupy male-dominated spaces (2009). Andrea's reputation assures others that she is not a passive or submissive victim, but being a fighter also works to shield her from the treatment girls otherwise encounter in this space as "bitches." But while Andrea and her friends articulate acting hard in masculine terms, to say that she is simply modeling the behavior of the boys at SJEA misses that female students share the same concerns about reputation and survival (Jones 2009), and that acting hard functions to manage these concerns. Students felt that they could either be a "masculine" participant in the carceral social order by claiming an affiliation and being prepared to fight on its behalf, or be a "bitch" as someone who could expect to be abused. For Andrea and many of the other students at SJEA, the choice is easy.

CONCLUSIONS

For the participants in this research, the carceral facility was an institution that persistently worked to categorize them into one of the affiliations that it recognized. Parolees and probation youth had to negotiate being labeled by staff, but even more immediately they had to figure out how they were going to safely manage the rivalries that the sorting process spread throughout the facility's population. To protect themselves and maintain some agency in how they navigated the institution, individuals had to learn how to participate in and position themselves within the carceral social order. They primarily accomplished this by aligning themselves with collective identities that could help and protect them while they were in the institution. Most participants in fact made sense of the sorting process and the carceral social order as a need to "clique up" with other prisoners or youth like themselves in order to protect each other. Many therefore saw actively "choosing" or identifying with one affiliation as their best option, because the conflicts that structured everyday life in the facility were eventually going to force them onto one side or the other anyway. Understanding this perspective can help us recognize that young people adopt criminalized identities that they know will create risks for them because they are in situations in which this helps them find support in dangerous environments.

However, the collective identities that participants relied on while in the facility were also heavily shaped by the categories the facility used in the sorting process. Groups were very rigidly defined—and most importantly—mutually exclusive. Students and parolees therefore had to learn not only which group was appropriate for them but also how to be a recognized part of this group. This in turn shaped how they came to perceive their own racial and neighborhood identities, as well as broader racial and gang conflicts.

# 3. Negotiating and Resisting the Carceral Social Order

As was the case with many of the young women in San Joaquin Educational Academy (SJEA), Sara was first incarcerated following a dispute at her home. In this case, a fight with her mother led Sara to a domestic assault charge. Growing up, Sara's home life was often hectic due in large part to both her parents' and her siblings' gang activity. As a child she tried to sleep through regular late-night house parties that at times brought fistfights or drive-by shootings to her home. Sara's inability to avoid her family members' gang involvement also extended into the neighborhood, where more than once Sureña gang members assaulted her in the street because they recognized her as their rival's little sister. The risk that her own gang membership could bring more violence to herself and to her family shaped Sara's resolve to resist joining the neighborhood cliques that her relatives identified with. However, despite her steadfast refusal to gangbang, her experiences in the juvenile justice system ultimately compelled her to claim the same criminalized affiliations as her family.

While serving her sentence in juvenile hall for the domestic assault charge, a JCO (juvenile corrections officer) overhears Sara chastising one of her friends for socializing with a Sureña in the pod. Because of her family's history, Sureñas/os were a threat best avoided for Sara; they were always the people on the other side of fights that left her family members hurt, beaten, shot at, or stabbed. Sara scolds her friend as she explains that talking with the Sureña would make trouble with their mutual friends once they got back home, but Diana, the JCO, misunderstands this. She pulls Sara aside and accuses her of gangbanging in the pod, claiming Sara was "repping Sureños" and confronting the friend as a rival. Sara knows she isn't a gang member, but being labeled as a Sureña would mean being celled on their side of the pod, alongside girls from the same clique that would jump her when she was younger.

This possibility forces Sara's hand and she quickly counters Diana's assessment: "Hold on, Diana. If anything, if I'm gonna be gang banging, I'm gonna be backing up Bulldogs. If anything."

"OK," the JCO responds. "So you're a Bulldog then."

At her next court date, Sara sees the incident referenced in a file that designates her as a validated gang member.

Sara's experiences are reflective of many young people caught in the juvenile justice system. Similar to the parolees' narratives of the prison, adolescents in the Fresno Juvenile Detention Facility (JDF) and San Joaquin Educational Academy (SJEA) encountered facilities that interpreted their racial identities and neighborhood ties as criminalized affiliations, and frequently found themselves positioned within gang-associated groups by the institution itself. Within this context that presumed youth fall into one criminalized group or the other, students made the decisions they felt were best for them. In Sara's case, the JCO initially identifies her as a Sureña, a distinction she can only dispute by claiming an alternative affiliation instead. When forced to choose, Sara affiliates with those she thinks will give her the best chance to safely navigate the institution. Although the court now recognizes her as a gang member, Sara does not consider herself to be one or see "backing up Bulldogs" as gangbanging. Rather, it is a means for her to strategically position herself with youth she feels safe with while she is locked up.

In Sara's story we can see how people make sense of the carceral social order and maneuver themselves to make it through. Sara tries to stay away from any affiliations because of her family's history, but when staff threaten to position her anyway, this becomes difficult. From this moment her thought process is clear—in realizing when she must abandon her holdout, in deciding how she needs to identify herself, and what she understands the consequences of her selection to be. Her choice is informed by her family, her neighborhood, and the impending threat posed by the Sureña girls who already see her as a rival. Sara identifies herself as a Bulldog because within an institutional context that is built around gang rivalry, this identification is the only way she can stay away from girls who have attacked her before, even if it means facilitating her own criminalization. Outlining Sara's decision making complicates the carceral facility's socializing power by illustrating that the identities constructed by the sorting process are not necessarily fully embraced or passively accepted as assigned by the institution. Instead they are chosen strategically, at times reluctantly, and are constantly negotiated, resisted, and even rejected. When navigating the carceral social order, people use the roles that are at their disposal to do what is in their best interest.

In this chapter I focus on how those in the punitive institution negotiate, perform, and resist the identities that are constructed as part of the carceral social order. Through its ongoing processes of categorization and segregation, the carceral institution constructs situated roles (Goffman 1961) that individuals are expected to fill while they are in the facility—roles that are defined by the categories specified in the sorting process. These roles are ascribed, sometimes unilaterally (Walker 2016), by the institution, but it is important to note the extent to which individuals exercise agency in this matter. Individuals deliberate on which available role will best help them and how to communicate their position to others. People learn to not only claim but actively perform these situated roles in ways that will be recognized by their peers, particularly through the use of space and style. However, those who do not fit so seamlessly into one of these categories must then tailor these roles to fit them, or attempt to create a new alternative position. In examining how those immersed in the punitive institution make sense of the carceral social order, we can begin to understand the logic of choices and actions that may otherwise be interpreted as irrational criminality or as a commitment to a gangster lifestyle.

## FILLING THE ROLE

Inside the facility, the institutionalization of the carceral social order establishes it as a framework for making sense of one's experiences in the system, and for identifying sources of potential support or danger. Consequently, there is a constant effort on the part of those inside the facility to recognize how the people around them are positioned, as well as to ensure that their own position is clear to others. In this way the sorting process becomes an ongoing phenomenon, one the incarcerated and detained turn and impose on each other because they are taught that their safety depends on it. Individuals quickly become adept at racializing and categorizing each other—examining one another's appearance and use of space to place them into one of the carceral social order's recognized groups. At the same time, they learn to appropriately incorporate these same factors into their own scrutinized performances of the situated roles they aim to fill. In these efforts to interpret others' affiliations and to convey one's own, we can see how thoroughly the institution ingrains the carceral social order into the lenses of its charges. It becomes an internalized logic for assessing the marginalized body—both others' and one's own.

## Sorting Each Other

Learning to navigate and survive the punitive institution requires appropriating the logic of the carceral social order. Part of this appropriation entails recognizing affiliated identities as mutually exclusive and knowing where one fits within the rigid parameters of the groups available. But as much as safely navigating the institution calls for learning to position oneself into the carceral social order, it also requires knowing how to position others. The stakes are high for learning to do this correctly, as evaluating and categorizing the people around them enables prisoners and probation youth to identify and avoid potential safety threats in their social environment. However, the need for identification in this context means that individuals' own affiliations are in turn read by others. The dangers in how one could potentially be read pushes people to be clear about the roles they are occupying while in the institution.

Because of the strict and complex rules that dictate everyday interactions between racial groups, the parolees had to know whom they could interact with without creating conflict. To determine what they could share or do with other inmates, parolees learned to categorize them in the same way the institution does in the sorting process. Reading someone's race informed parolees which car they were likely in, and consequently what their politics were, which became particularly evident in interviews when parolees would try to categorize me while explaining how prison politics worked. These were telling instances, as parolees attempted to read my racial identity in order to place me in the divisive social order of the prison. In one such instance, while explaining the prison's racial politics James stops midanswer to ask me what race I am, and then describes how I would fit into the carceral social order as someone who does not obviously fit into one clear racial category:

JAMES: I don't know what nationality you are. You a, are you a . . .
AUTHOR: See that's the thing, I'm mixed.
    J: Oh really?
    A: I'm half White, I'm half Mexican.
    J: Oh so you're a *güero*.[1]
    A: *Güero?*
    J: *Güero*. Yeah, it's a White Mexican. *Güero*. They call 'em *güeros* in prison.
    A: Oh OK, *güero*.
    J: Yeah, yeah, *güero*, yeah. It's, I guess it means you're half White, half Mexican. Yeah. So, you can, and if you're a *güero*, that

means you particularly stay on the Mexican side. But you're, you're allowed in the Wood Pile side by, only by rep, talking to rep to let you in. You kinda get a leeway, a little leeway on things. But you're mainly [going to] go to [the] Hispanic side.

A: Were there a lot of *güeros* in the prison?

J: Yeah, not a lot, but there was a few. There was a few of 'em. But they lean more to the Hispanic side. The Wood Pile tolerated [them], but they're mainly Hispanic.

A: OK.

J: Yeah, you do kind of remind me of, yeah, *güero*. That's what I was kinda thinking, *güero*.

James asks me directly about my racial identity to confirm his own reading of my "nationality." He explains that as a mixed-race *güero*, I would have some agency in picking which car to go with, but that someone like me would generally side with the Latinos, needing special permission from a recognized leader[2] to be with the Whites. In this context James would be right to be cautious about determining my race—if I was with the Whites he would be free to trade or socialize with me as he pleased, but as a *güero* who most likely sided with Latinos, these same actions could get him into considerable trouble.

Noteworthy in James' compulsion to racially categorize me is not just that he mirrors the institution by sorting me himself, but that he finds a way to make my racial identity—one that exists between monoracial groups—fit the rigid template of the carceral social order. He explains that most likely I would affiliate with Latinos, but I could choose to be with the Whites, assuming the rep recognized my Whiteness. But essentially I would have to choose one or the other, and this choice was significant because at some point I would inevitably be read as part of one of these two groups. Controlling how my identity was interpreted by others by making it clear who I aligned myself with would be important for keeping safe, because ambiguity could be dangerous in a context where one is situated between rival groups. For example, Francisco explains that some of his unaffiliated peers socialized with Norteño or Sureño Latinos in the prison, thinking that this would be fine since they were not gang members. However, things ended violently once it was discovered that these friends were from Fresno:

I've talked to a lot of nonaffiliated people, and they tell me where they go, you know? They been to San Luis Obispo, you know, Donovan, places where—"Hey what happened to you?" "Hey man, just cuz I was from Fresno you know, I was there for a little bit, and guess they do a background check, and I was there for like maybe six months and then they just jumped on me one day." "For reals?" "Yeah." They don't play that shit you know? If you say the wrong thing to them, you know like "Oh I got cousins that are Bulldogs," you're known to them, you're affiliated, you know?

In this example, Northerners and Southerners interpret being from Fresno as being a Bulldog and resultantly attack Francisco's friend as a rival. Francisco explains that once the other inmates learn one is from Fresno through reputation, a "background check," or something said, this firmly positions one as a Bulldog. If this person is not already among similarly-categorized peers who can protect him, this identification can leave him vulnerable to assault.

Incidents like these, or more commonly stories of these incidents, reinforced the parolees' perceptions that the car was necessary for protection, strengthening their ties to it and identification with it. In the parolees' attempts to read and position others into the carceral social order we can see that incarcerated residents learn to replicate the prison's sorting logic, gauging racial identities to match them to recognized groups, then scanning the body for signs that may reveal one's hometown or gang loyalties. These attempts also hint at the stakes involved in terms of what is risked by getting these judgements wrong, as incorrectly reading another prisoner could expose one to harm. It becomes important then to hone one's ability to recognize where others fit in this social order. Where and with whom one is positioned within the institution's segregated environment serves as one of the clearest indicators.

## Space

Those confined to punitive institutions learn to see space as important in the same way that the facility tells them it is. Within these contexts segregated spaces become a manifestation of the prison's sorting template, and as one's racial category is significant there are also consequences attached to the spaces one occupies in the facility. Navigating the institution's carceral social order entails learning to properly use space within its confines, which becomes vital not only for ensuring that one's group ties are recognized but also for understanding one's relationship to others. As new students entered SJEA, they tended to gravitate toward existing friends or relatives in the school, making new friends through them. Because of the strict separation enforced by the staff, students became incorporated into—and gradually recognized as part of—one of the school's segregated groups in this process.

Consequently, others commonly assumed new students were gang members or supporters based on whom they sat with on the blacktop, and confronted them if they made the mistake of socializing with one's rivals. In Marissa's experiences coming to SJEA, we can see a clear example of how students' affiliations were interpreted through their presence in designated spaces, and how these interpretations worked to cement one into the carceral social order.

Before Marissa was sent to SJEA, her family had moved to Fresno from Los Angeles during the previous year. When she started attending the school, she sat with a small group of other Latinas/os who were also originally from Southern California. Consequently, she also sat with the handful of Sureña/o gang members who attended SJEA. Marissa didn't bang, but generated suspicion among the Bulldog students that she was a Sureña herself because she always sat with them. While working with Curtis in our tutoring group, one of these students, Andrea, describes her encounter with Marissa soon after she first begins attending SJEA:

A: I thought that new girl banged but I guess she doesn't.

C: You hit her up?

A: You have to! She could be the enemy and you have to know. She said something else to the homie, and I saw her sitting with the funk, so I was like what the fuck? So I sat next to her and I was like, "You bang?" and she's like, "Naw," and I'm like, "Back up?" and she's like, "Naw," and I said, "Nada nada?" and she's like, "Nada nada," and I'm like, "Alright."

The consistent potential for rivalries to become violent means Andrea needs to know whom threats may come from, and Marissa's presence among the Sureñas/os raises her suspicions that "she could be the enemy." Although Andrea seems satisfied that Marissa is not a threat after confronting her, her assertions that she is not a gang member ultimately did little to reassure the Bulldogs' mistrust. Within a few weeks at SJEA most of her fellow students associate her with the Sureñas/os, primarily because where she sits at lunch positions her in the social order of the school. This association subjects her to many students' contempt, particularly the Bulldog students who now consider her to be one of their rivals.

One afternoon, two boys I am tutoring begin talking about Marissa when she passes by our table on the way to the bathroom. As the teacher escorts Marissa and another girl to the bathroom, Johnny glares at her. After they pass by Michael asks Johnny, "Who is she?"

Johnny responds, "She's a fucking scrap!"[3]

"For real?? She is??"

"She always hangs out with them!! If she kicks it with them, associates with them, then she's one of them!"

Michael shrugs, then shakes his head conceding, "That's the code."

Johnny is convinced that Marissa is a Sureña because of her consistent presence around their space on the blacktop and the friendships she develops with the other students who hang out there. During her next several months at SJEA, regular clashes with the other Latinas at the school—almost all of whom associate with Bulldog or Norteña/o youth—cement her position in the carceral social order and the public perception of her as a Sureña. Throughout this time students confronted and challenged her as a "scrap" on a daily basis, and she routinely became involved in fistfights with other girls that resulted in suspensions and ultimately a probation violation that sent her back to JDF. Her implication into these rivalries reinforced her need for the protective support of other Sureña/o-associated youth, but also fed into the labeling that kept her entrenched in the juvenile justice system. Much like Sara, Marissa's conflict with one side reinforced the perception that she was affiliated with the other, and over time set her into a fixed position in the carceral social order.

For the young people at SJEA, occupying physical space was understood to say something about how students identified themselves. The growing collective conviction that Marissa was a Sureña was based on her consistent presence within the space recognized as theirs. This is because one's presence within a given space was an expected component of performing the situated and affiliated identities expected within the school. One's loyalties and position within the carceral social order are therefore read in large part by where one stands and whom one stands with.

Within the state prison, performing the situated roles constructed by the sorting process is tied to following the spatial segregation of the institution. After being sorted into a particular racial group, incoming prisoners then have to learn how to "program" with their group, in large part by learning about how to abide by a strict division of physical space. Jeremy, a twenty-eight-year-old Laotian parolee, explains that an essential aspect of being in the car is learning where one can go and cannot go:

> Whoever comes in, like if I came in new, the homies there would have to come hit me up, like "What's up? What's your name? We got your back. You can't walk through this driveway, you can't be in this space, this is theirs, you gotta eat at this table, you gotta shower over here." Know what I mean? Do this and that, pretty much program with them, with your people. At the same time watch each other's back. That's how it was. Then I had to do that to the new person that came in, to let them know.

Existing within the prevailing social order of the prison entails recognizing and respecting the spaces designated for each racial group, and as Jeremy learns coming in, being part of the Asian car therefore involves being in their space. Space within the institution then consequently comes to be understood as racialized and imbued with identity. As Jeremy describes, incarcerated men have to teach each other how to perform this aspect of group belonging, an item echoed by the many parolees who explained in their interviews that as you enter the prison, "someone will let you know." Being in a specific space is important for being (seen as) part of the car, but it is also crucial for avoiding unnecessary conflict with other inmates. A group's claim to space is something that is to be protected as a resource, as it provides some physical distance from other groups who may pose possible threats. Just as new prisoners must learn the specifics of these spatial boundaries in their particular institution, they also learn that failure to abide by these can inadvertently create problems that lead to fights between racial groups, or even jeopardize one's standing within their own car.

The spaces one occupied within juvenile justice facilities similarly communicated one's position within the carceral social order. As we see in Sara's story, the cells youth were assigned to in JDF were tied to their perceived affiliations. Being on one side or the other therefore strengthened this ascribed status, but could also potentially place young people in close proximity to dangerous enemies if this perception was incorrect. At SJEA this understanding of space was reflected in the tables that students used outside of the classroom. School officials steer students to one table or another, but students entering the school also have some agency in choosing where to go. Youth may have a sense of where they fit in based on family history with affiliations, recognizing old friends from their neighborhood or former schools, or simply going to the side that their enemy is not on. But because each facility's spatial boundaries need to be learned, some students have no idea where to go, even if they do have some sense of which affiliation they more or less fit into. For example, at SJEA Angel usually socialized with the Bulldog-affiliated students, but in his interview he explains that when he first came to the school, he sat on the opposite side of the blacktop:

AUTHOR: So if you didn't know anyone the first time you got here, when you went outside where'd you wind up going?

ANGEL: (laughing) I went to the Norteño side!

AU: Oh serious?

AN: Yea! Everyone was like, "What the fuck?" I didn't even know, I was just like, "What the fuck?" I guess cuz I had long hair too,

> like a ponytail, they were like, "Oh, this one's a norte." I was
> like, "What the fuck, I don't bang!"
>
> AU: So what happened after that, after you went to that side?
>
> AN: I was just sitting there and they came and hit me up, and I was
> like, "No," and I dunno. Later I just started goin' both sides,
> then after that I just stayed on one side.

Unsure of the specific meanings ascribed to tables at the school, Angel
gravitates to a space with other Latino/a students, but unknowingly associates himself with Norteña/os in the process. It is not until he is confronted
by other students that he begins to realize the resulting assumptions being
made about him. He gradually decides to change sides because he realizes
that space here is embedded with meaning, and although he is not a gang
member, his presence at this table is conveying a specific identity to others
in the school that he does not identify with. He is assumed to affiliate with
Norteña/os based on him being at that table.

Properly using and navigating space in the facility is an important part of
managing the carceral social order, but someone generally has to be taught
how to spatially perform their affiliation. A number of sources inform individuals about the specifics of a given institution's spatial boundaries—where
one can be and where one cannot. Much of this is shaped by the institution
itself as it directs newcomers where to go and whom to associate with. There
is also a good deal of peer instruction and socialization from individuals
already present in the facility; just as Jeremy was taught to recognize whose
space was whose inside the prison, at SJEA I would hear students like Ben
similarly explain to new students that "all the cool people are on this side,
and over there is all the busters."[4] Finally, individuals who have been
through the facility before may also advise their peers on where they are
"supposed" to be in the institution. For instance, Luis explains that when he
first came to SJEA he already knew where the Norteña/os congregated: "I
already knew where they kicked it at and everything, and they had told me
too before I came that we are always right there by the basketball courts.
That's our spot right there."

Community members in the punitive institution learn to recognize
where people fit in the carceral social order by the spaces they occupy in the
segregated facility. One's presence on one side or another is understood to
claim one of the affiliated identities recognized by the sorting process.
Residents therefore learn to convey their own ties through close proximity
to their peers and neighbors, and to see those in other corners of the yard
as potentially dangerous rivals or others.

## Style

By their design, carceral institutions generally limit and restrict individual appearance, perhaps most notoriously through requiring the familiar prison jumpsuits. These uniforms become part of the control that the total institution can impose over a person, functioning as an instrument of degradation that denies individuality and ascribes a powerless, criminal status upon all those held by the facility (Goffman 1961; Garfinkel 1956). However, despite the efforts of probation or correctional staff to control aesthetics, people find ways to work around them—because while particular looks and meanings can change as demographics and dynamics shift, style remains consistently important for performing the identities that the institution constructs in the carceral social order.

Participants' appearances in the prison and in JDF were both restricted to the clothes issued by the institution. While still restricted, personal style was more flexible at SJEA, and here my own identity as a young, straight, Latino man with roots in Fresno gave me extensive access to the boys' discussions and understandings of style and appearance.[5] This allowed me to see how the boys recognized and learned to embody the aesthetics they identified with. This was particularly evident as they evaluated my own appearance. For example, one day in fourth period I pull Juan, Edgar, and Mario out of class for tutoring. As we settle at our table I notice Juan looking at my hair. "You got a haircut huh?"

I respond that I did while rubbing the shortest hairs on the back of my head. Mario joins in: "Your girlfriend did it huh, or she made you get it?"

"Yeah, my girlfriend did it for me." She had cut it for me the way I usually have it done, trimming the sides and the back with hair clippers set with a #3 comb, and using scissors to cut the hair a few inches longer on top.

They quietly inspect my haircut for a few seconds more before Mario drags two fingers down each side of his face and asks "You gonna get your sideburns straightened?"

"Naw, I still gotta shave," I say, rubbing the stubble on my cheeks.

Mario goes on, "You should straighten it like this." He traces the hairline that runs down his thin sideburns with his fingers. "Then like this, and this." His fingers make a sharp turn, following the corners of his jawline around to the center of his chin, tracing the pencil-line of facial hair that runs from his sideburns to form a goatee. "That'd look tight. You'd look like a playa. Your girlfriend would be like 'Damn, I shoulda made him do that a long time ago!'"

Juan is still staring at my hair. "I would just bzzz, bzzz." He gives himself two swipes with imaginary clippers over the top of his own head, implying that I should have trimmed the hair on top of my head as short as I have it on the sides and back.

Edgar now stands up and leans over me, looking close and pointing to my hair. After a few seconds he leans back and taps the hairline in the middle of my forehead. "Naw, I would just cut this part to even this out and make it straight. Did you used to wear hats a lot?"

"Naw, not really."

"Oh cuz my uncle said that's where you get these, that when you wear hats a lot, when you get older it starts to go back here." Edgar taps the corners of his own forehead, referring to how far back my hairline goes on the corners of my forehead.

"Naw, I've always had these, even when I was your age. I can't really straighten it out cuz if I did I'd have a hella big forehead!"

Juan smirks "Show movies on it and shit!" Most of their recommendations advise me on how to change my appearance to more closely resemble theirs. All three boys have more or less the same hairstyle, as do most of the Mexican and Chicano boys here: they kept their hair very short (about a quarter inch long) with a precise, straight hairline across the front and a tapered fade on the sides and back. When I ask them how often they cut their hair, they all say every week.

This hairstyle was part of an aesthetic that most of the Eastside Latino boys adopted and commonly referred to as a "clean" look. The most common elements that rounded out this look in addition to the fade haircuts and precise facial hair were fake diamond stud earrings, Levi 501 jeans worn sagging with the bottom cuff rolled up, black Converse (Chucks) sneakers, and oversized, solid color T-shirts. Even these plain T-shirts—usually purchased at flea markets or discount warehouses—had to be the right kind of shirt: XXL or larger, cut extra tall to give them added length, generally black or white due to the dress code, and looking as clean and new as possible. Although the boys wore no logos on their shirts, the brands were still important and could be readily identified—AAA was acceptable, but the gold standard was Pro Club. Shortly after critiquing my haircut Juan asks the other boys if they think it is worth it to pay $60 for a dozen Pro Clubs, since he normally gets them for $7 each.

"That's what you usually wear?" I ask.

"Yup, see?" He pulls the top of his T-shirt up to show me the label under his collar.

"Why do you like Pro Clubs?"

"Cuz they're thick. Here, feel." He stretches the bottom of his shirt out towards me to feel how thick it is. "Plus the collar doesn't stick out like on yours," he says pointing to the old T-shirt I wore today. "It stays like this." Juan slaps the collar of his shirt under his throat. "It stays flat."

The "clean" style adopted by these boys was not necessarily unique to SJEA or set by its attempts to divide students, although in the context of the school's social order it could indicate where in Fresno a student came from. This was a common aesthetic in the boys' community, one they saw as representative of local Chicano masculinity. This was simply how many of the teen boys and young men in their neighborhood dressed, and many of the students at SJEA described learning to emulate this look as they came of age. Alex was a student who consistently came to school with this style, but here he explains how his current appearance contrasts with how he used to dress:

> ALEX: I used to have long hair back then. Really long hair. I would just flip it out [of] my eyes and all that, and it would be like to my shoulder. And then one day I was like "Naw, gotta cut it off." . . . You know the other Alex? The Alex with the curly hair? The White one? Yeah, I would dress like that, with big old baggy pants that would go underneath my shoe, and ripped up clothes and all that shit. Messed-up shoes. Cuz I used to have a lot of messed-up shoes, one side just tore up from the skating.
>
> AUTHOR: Why do you think you transitioned to the type of clothes you wear now?
>
> AL: I don't know, [I] just wanted to clean up. Girls don't really like fucked up clothes on a guy, so I was like "What am I doing?? I can't get girls like this!" So I just started [dressing] better.
>
> AU: Oh OK. Girls like the clean look a little better?
>
> AL: Yeah. There's other girls that skate but I wasn't really interested in them. I was more like the girly girl type. I liked the girly girls. Not the ones that are rockerish, wearing dark ass clothes all the time. I wasn't never into those girls.

In junior high Alex shifted from his "skater look" to a "clean" style that he now sees as a more respected image of masculinity. As a teenager he learned to see this as an idealized form of masculinity that is necessary for attracting conventionally feminine young women. But performing heteronormative masculinity is about winning the approval of other boys and men as much as it is about attracting women, and as much as Alex aspired to this masculinity, he was also pressured to conform to it: "They used to make fun of me cuz of my long hair and shit. That's why I would get into fights and all that shit. That's why I cut it. I didn't want to get into fights every day, every week. I didn't like the way people was talking shit about me so I kinda changed." Additionally, Alex's learned image has classed and raced connotations to it as well. His stylistic shift coincided with his transfer to a new school whose student body was predominantly Latina/o, working class, and criminalized. It was here that Alex "started hanging out with some of the Bulldog fools that I know now." Shifting his style was part of how Alex learned to incorporate himself into this group and express his belonging—in short, how he learned to grow into and perform the role of an Eastside Chicano that would be recognized at SJEA.

Just as this "clean" look was embedded with racial and geographic meaning, styles deviating from this were also seen as indicative of holding different raced and classed identities. Alex's previous skater style—tighter-fitting graphic T-shirts, old jeans with frayed leg cuffs worn on the waist, beat-up skate shoes, and long, shaggy hair—contrasted with the "clean" style adopted by most of the Chicano boys and was seen by these students as how middle-class White youth from Fresno's northern suburbs dressed. Recall how in the previous chapter Angel racializes the skaters at SJEA as Whites or "Mexicans who act White." In SJEA such stylistic differences intersected with how space was used to claim and recognize racialized identities. Within this punitive setting, the racial, class, and neighborhood identities that these styles embody or suggest work to position the wearer into the carceral social order. They become part of how affiliated identities are performed and interpreted, as they are presumed to indicate how one self-identifies and therefore whom . one aligns themselves with.

The role of style in performing an affiliated identity resultantly placed an imperative on students to socialize each other into the aesthetic expectations of being part of the group. Boys regulated each other's appearance through teasing each other for not appropriately embodying the stylized image of the identity they shared. One afternoon as everyone is lining up for class after lunch, Armando calls Daniel out for wearing a black polo shirt that looks like it's sized medium or perhaps large at most. He strolls up to Daniel while making his way to his own line, and in a voice loud enough for all to hear, shouts "Sanchez! What'd I tell you about wearing your little brother's shirts?!" A few days ago Armando had similarly teased Daniel about wearing another close-fitting polo. As he did then, Daniel laughs and shakes his head. Himself wearing black basketball shorts and an oversized white T-shirt, Armando grins and keeps at it as he walks past him. "Tomorrow I'm gonna bring you a shirt that fits right!" At eighteen, Armando is one of the oldest and most physically imposing boys at SJEA, a committed gang member, and occasionally rumored to be involved in shootings around town. He is an informal leader of sorts for the Eastside Latino boys, generally friendly and certainly influential. Soon after this teasing, Daniel too begins wearing the same oversized T-shirts, and a few days later even tries teasing Juan for his shirt being too small.

Juan defends himself against this accusation and flips it back at Daniel: "Fool you're wearing a small, this is an extra tall!"

"This isn't a small, it's an extra-large!" Daniel retorts.

Raul, standing by Juan, shrugs and offers a guiding rule. "If the sleeves are above the elbows . . ."

For the boys from Fresno's Mexican and Chicana/o neighborhoods, appropriating this style was part of performing the gender, racial, and class identities that comprised the affiliation they shared at SJEA. But in this context, this look also marked one as being from Northern or Central California. Conversely, boys from Southern California performed an alternative identity by incorporating an older, traditional cholo style into their appearance.[6] The small number of Sureño-identifying students at SJEA made themselves stand out stylistically by using an exaggerated embodiment of styles that originated from Chicano street culture in Los Angeles. These boys set themselves apart from the Eastsiders' clean aesthetic through adopting aspects of cholo style such as large-fitting Dickies or Ben Davis work pants worn high above the waist with a belt (rather than sagging), hair that was slicked back or shaved off completely, checkered button-up shirts, rosary necklaces, and dress shoes. This appearance not only referenced a recognizable image associated with Southern California, but also stood in sharp contrast to the dominant style utilized by most of the boys at SJEA.

This was particularly visible when Diego began attending the school. On the day Diego enrolls, both Black and Latina/o students immediately notice him because he dresses so differently from everyone else. While sitting in the back of the classroom that afternoon, I can overhear Jose and Lisa talking about him. Jose gestures towards Diego, who is standing outside the classroom door while he waits to meet with one of the counselors on campus.

"That fool's a Suuuuuureño." Jose, a Chicano, draws out the first syllable to exaggerate the Spanish pronunciation in a mocking accent.

Lisa responds without looking up or realizing the Diego is in the hallway. "There's one Sureño here who's a straight cholo-lookin' mothafucka."

"Yeah, that's the one I'm talkin' about!"

Lisa turns for a quick look and bursts out laughing. "He leanin' like cholo! Got the Dickies AND the cross! That nigga came ready for his first day! I would never . . ." She laughs too hard to finish her sentence before catching her breath. "Everyone here come in basketball sweats and 501s nigga!"

What was most interesting about how Diego and the other Sureños dressed for school was the extent to which they relied on an elaborate and fairly dated representation of cholo culture, one that—at least in my own experiences with gang-involved youth throughout Southern California—young people in and around Los Angeles do not really use anymore. But for these students, most of whom moved from Los Angeles as young children or had close family ties still living down south, this was how they imagined this identity. More importantly, it made them stand out, and despite the presumed dangers of making oneself such a visible target, there was a vital reason for this. Here Jaime explains why he made sure his outfit would be noticeable when he came to his school orientation: "When I came here for the orientation, I came in blue Dickies and a white shirt and my Cortez so everybody would *know* where I'm from. And when I was leaving school is when two Sureños here hit me up and told me so OK, now we know where [the] Sureños at. So I would know who's who" (emphasis in original quote). Anticipating that he would likely be in the minority as a Sureño within a probation school in Fresno, Jaime consciously creates a first impression that sends clear message about how he identifies. In doing so his appearance ensures that Norteña/o and Bulldog students will recognize who he is and therefore allow Jaime to quickly assess which youth will be hostile rivals.[7] But this approach also makes sure that any allies who might be there can quickly spot him and let him know where to go and whom he can be with.

The social order that students and parolees encountered within their divided punitive facilities dictated that it was important for them to be clear about whom they affiliated with, and that it was equally important to be able to interpret how others affiliated. Within this context, one's racialized appearance and how one used space inside the institution emerged as key aspects for both reading others' affiliations and for performing one's own. In the prison, one was officially categorized and housed into racial categories that prisoners themselves subsequently internalized and learned to assign to each other. A similar pattern unfolded in SJEA, but as I will elaborate in the second half of this book, the school also hosted a visible intersection of how affiliations born of the carceral social order blended with local identities from students' home communities. The distances between tables across the school's blacktop came to represent the city's geographic, racial, and class divides, and the stylized aesthetics students brought from these communities then marked where youth saw themselves falling along these schisms. But not everyone simply performs the identities that they are ascribed in the carceral social order. Many do not fit its rigid template, and must therefore negotiate where they see themselves fitting in or resist participating in it altogether.

## THE SPACES BETWEEN AFFILIATIONS

Not everyone fits cleanly into the rigid schema of the carceral social order, making it important to recognize that people do not uniformly match or accept its situated roles, but deliberate, question, challenge, and resist them. The mutually exclusive character of the categories constructed in the sorting process forces those with multiracial identities or who have connections to multiple affiliations to strategically decide how they will fit into the institution's social order. These individuals must then determine how to best position themselves into the carceral social order, either negotiating their inclusion into one of the recognized roles, or attempting to resist this system entirely. However, this latter option creates additional struggles for those who attempt it, in terms of an elevated risk of violence as well as the potential for additional punishments.

### Troubling the Racial Typology

The sorting process that structures the carceral social order is premised on the assumption that everyone must fit within a fairly simple set of racial categories. Of course in practice people's racial identities don't fall so cleanly into place. Mixed-race individuals do not fit into the rigid, monoracial categories recognized by the prison's sorting process, but are also not permitted to be in multiple groups, switch back and forth, or exist between racialized groups within this divided system. This essentially forces mixed-race prisoners to choose one aspect of their identity over the other while navigating this segregated system. At the same time, some factors may dissuade or prevent individuals from affiliating with their racial identity inside the institution, effectively choosing another race instead.

As seen earlier in this chapter when James attempts to categorize me into the prison's racial order, mixed-race prison inmates are generally expected to choose one race or another. James explained that someone like me would tend to go with one of the Latino groups rather than with the Whites. Perhaps this is because of the White supremacist groups present within the broader White car. But regardless of the reason, his caveat underscores that the dynamics, relationships, and context in the facility shape the decision one would make in terms of their "race." Consequently, some men go with inmates outside of their own racial identity when they are incarcerated because they see being with others from the same neighborhood or the same affiliation as more important than being with others of the same race. This was particularly true when someone was gang involved but their gang was predominantly made up of members of another race. However, this rupture of the racial typology was also frequently challenged by others in the institution. For example, despite being Filipino and Native American, Marcus was housed with the Bulldogs, an overwhelmingly Chicano group of jail inmates, because of his extensive history of involvement with a Bulldog street clique. But his presence was challenged almost immediately upon arrival:

AUTHOR: Coming up with F14 before they were Bulldogs, you said they didn't really trip on you being Filipino, or not being Mexican?

MARCUS: Well out here in the streets, no. But when I hit the county jail growing up, they used to trip. At first they start trippin'. They'll be like "The fuck you doing? What gang you from?" Cuz when I first start hitting the county jail and they put me in general population when I turned eighteen, the TRGs and Bulldogs didn't get along.

[The] first time I hit the general population, Bulldogs hit me up. "The fuck are you doing here homie? You TRG?" "Fuck no!" Know what I mean? [I'm] Amerasian. I'm Filipino [and] Apache Indian, but I be straight-up hundred-percent Bulldogs homie. Fuck what you gonna do. Know what I mean? I'll be real, I had it rough when I hit county at first, you know, cuz they didn't know who I was at first. Cuz I put a lot of work in, but then I was the type I always stayed in the shadow.

Once they recognized that I was gonna represent who I am, then people started coming in who knew me, and there was people [I knew] who was there already . . . when they came out and stuff, from sleeping and so forth, they're like "Oh, whassup! Whassup!" Cuz they call me Creeper. They're like "Whassup Creeper?" And then the ones who hit me up, they're like "Oh, you know this fool?" "Yup. What's up? What you guys . . ." My homie asked me, "They fucking with you?" I answered him "Ain't nothing I can't handle. I'll probably knock every one of 'em out!" (laughs) Know what I mean? And he's like "Oh, alright, you don't need to do that but, [told them] it's just the homie Creeper." And he started introducing all of them to me, and [then] they all knew who I was.

When Marcus first hits county he is sent to the Bulldog unit because of his gang involvement, but the other men in the unit see him as an outsider at first because he is Filipino. Magnifying this confrontation is that the timing of his arrival coincides with an emerging feud the Bulldogs are having with Asian gangsters from TRG. Yet despite the potential dangers, Marcus prioritizes being housed by his gang identity over his racial identity. When his identity is questioned because of his race, it is ultimately his neighborhood contacts that give him credibility, as it is the recognition of other men in the unit who know him from back home that verifies his claims about being a Bulldog and neutralizes a potential fight.

The prison's racializing project is not quite so explicit in the juvenile justice system, as youth are not officially categorized and housed by race. However, the extent to which the groups that youth are categorized into are themselves heavily racialized pushes young people to make similar decisions about which "racial" group they identify with. But as with Marcus's story above, racial identity is not the sole factor deciding one's racial group. In addition to one's racial self-perception, this decision is also informed by one's neighborhood, class status, family, and if applicable, any gang ties. When students fell outside of the parameters of monoracial categories, neighborhood identity—and the performed class statuses that were tied to these spaces—shaped both how youth were read and where they saw themselves fitting.

In the cases of JC and Ben, both are mixed-background Latino students who are uninvolved in gangs, but while Ben kicks it with the Bulldogs, JC hangs with the White students. Neither fits into the simplified racial categories that the carceral social order requires, but unlike JC, Ben grew up and lives on Fresno's heavily Chicana/o Eastside alongside most of the other students who are similarly categorized as Bulldog affiliates at SJEA. Ben doesn't gangbang, but what nonetheless ties him to this group of students is the everyday presence Bulldogs have had in his community from the time he was little:

BEN: Where I grew up, it was everywhere. Where I grew up, that's all there was.

AUTHOR: How old were you when you think you first started hearing Sureños, Norteños, and [Bulldogs]?

B: I was actually, I don't even know, but like elementary. Probably like yeah, cuz where I live that shit was everywhere, so elementary.

A: Were there are a lot of Norteños and Sureños in your neighborhood?

B: Nah. None at all.

A: It was mostly Bulldogs?

B: Yeah.

Ben describes Bulldogs as being so ubiquitous in his neighborhood that by the time he was in grade school he not only knew who they were but was even aware of their enemies who weren't there. As an identity that "was everywhere" where he grew up, it has touched many of the relationships Ben has with the people in his community; many of the people in his life either identify as Bulldogs themselves or have several friends and relatives who do. Ben also falls into this latter camp—he doesn't take on this identity himself, but many of his friends at school and at home do, as do his own father and uncle. For students like Ben this is simply a common characteristic of local and familial peer networks.

Yet as extensive and entrenched as this identity may be, it remains but one aspect of social life in the neighborhood, one that Ben avoids becoming too involved in by choosing to stay away from gangbanging. At SJEA, however, the school makes it a central one, as it institutionally organizes the Eastside students around their ties to the Bulldogs as a central identity. Here he is placed into a context in which that distance is a bit more precarious; rather than simply being someone who has a handful of friends and acquaintances who identify as Bulldogs, here he is grouped together daily with most of the gang members he knows while also in close proximity to their rivals from across town. While Ben maintains his reluctance to bang, he sees the Bulldogs as something that many of his close friends and relatives are a part of. Consequently, his loyalty to these relationships compels him to refuse to socialize with their rivals, or even see them as peers: "Nah, I don't talk to 'em though. Like if they were trying to talk to me or be cool with me, or be the coolest person ever, I won't talk to 'em just because if I kick it with like one group, why am I gonna kick it with their funk? That wouldn't make sense to me." The institutional context at SJEA rearticulates Ben's support for his friends and neighbors in ways that crystallize his affiliation with Bulldogs by compelling him to make a statement on where he stands.

Although Ben's mixed identity contradicts the mutually exclusive nature of the carceral social order's racial categories, his home community and peer networks tie him to the Bulldogs. JC on the other hand is also part Chicano, but differs on these factors and therefore doesn't sit with the Bulldogs or with any of the Latino students. Instead he sits with the Whites, despite the fact that he identifies as Mexican and Native American and is quick to correct anyone who assumes that he is White. JC is not White, but he does live in the predominantly White and relatively affluent terrain of Fresno's northern suburbs. Home community is again influential here, positioning JC with the White students not because he knows them from his neighborhood but because of the physical and cognitive distance his neighborhood places between him and the other students of color. Here JC describes the social order at work at SJEA and where he fits into it:

> JC: I'm always the guy that befriends everyone. Like I'm just [if] you're cool with me I'm cool with you. Not "I'm with this group, [and] I funk it with you" like fucking gangsters do. I'm not like that. You know Simon, or the white guy, Travis? He's like that man. He's a surfer, he's just like me. He surfs, he fuckin' loves that shit, man. He's just friendly, you know. Friendly is my word.
>
> AUTHOR: OK, so one of the things I noticed is the different groups in school, especially outside like in the lunch area. How would you describe that?
>
> JC: Alright well that big table where you see all of them, you know right under the tree? Right there on the sidewalk, those are the Bulldogs. In the middle, those are still kind of Bulldogs. Then on my side it's like the kids that are just, you know, fucking class clowns and shit and some of the White kids. If you [have] seen at my table there's a lot of White kids, so that's like a White table. And [on] the other side you got the Nortes, you know, what they call busters. Then you got [students] from Hoover [a Twamp neighborhood]. Hoova they like to call it cuz they're all Black (laughs). Yeah they're from Hoover High School, or no from the actual place in the ghetto, like a little town or some shit. I don't know, I'm not from there. But yeah, and then that's about it.

In laying out the different groups present on SJEA's blacktop, JC offers his perspective on his peer group as well as the others. He describes the White students at his table are primarily "class clowns," peers he found himself drawn to because they were friendly and shared common interests. Conversely, he does not see himself as part of the communities students of color come from, describing the Black and other Latina/o students as primarily gang involved or "from the ghetto." His perspective is informed by not only the physical and social distance between his home and the poor neighborhoods on Fresno's southern districts but also by the institutional organization of SJEA's students of color into criminalized groups. Consequently, JC sees sitting with the Whites as a convenient way to avoid the institutionalized conflicts between Latina/o students.

Despite being part Mexican, JC is essentially an outsider to the Latina/o communities in Fresno. This prevents him from developing the same ties that might otherwise connect him to Bulldog or Norteño affiliations. But just as his class capital draws him towards White peers and allows him to avoid the conflicts between other Chicana/o students, it also prevents this latter group from seeing him as one of their own. Living in North Fresno and developing some of the resulting tastes in popular culture (in music, for example) gave JC something in common with the Whites but also alienated him from Chicana/os. These students saw him as White because of how he spoke, dressed, and performed his class identity:

> JC: There's a lot of bullies here, there's a lot of assholes here. It's not even bullies, they're just assholes. Like they just say certain things. Like at [the former SJEA site], when I was first there they were like calling me "White kid" or whatever. You know I just got out of the hall or whatever. (pause) It doesn't bother me personally, it's just like come on, do you really want the attention that bad? OK well, there it is. Boom, there you go, [a] fight.
>
> AUTHOR: Why would they call you "White kid?"
>
> JC: The way I talk. The way I sound. Don't I sound, I bet you on this recorder I sound fuckin' White! (laughs) And they're like this kid's White! No, I'm actually 65 percent Indian and the rest is Mexican. . . . They wouldn't make fun of [my voice], but they'll just call me White. I'm like "Dude, I'm not White." And I'd say calmly, "I'm not White, dude." "Yeah, you are. You sound like a White kid. From Clovis! Hahaha!" They'd start laughing, cuz they said that [I'm] "from Clovis."

JC associates with the White students at school by his own choice, but also because he is somewhat rejected by Chicana/o students who tease him that he is from a wealthy neighboring suburb because of his identity performance. Unlike Ben, JC does not have other family members in the justice system and does not live in a criminalized neighborhood—factors that shape whom he sees as his peers as well as how other students read him. His perceived difference from other students of color allows him to opt out of the immediate conflicts between affiliations at SJEA, but to also avoid the persistent criminal status constructed by this labeling process.

Neither Ben nor JC expressed any question as to whom they saw themselves fitting with, but a number of Blaxican students discussed more conflicted decisions about how they identified and whom they ran with.[8] In these cases students were not choosing between communities with a great deal of physical or social distance, as Black and Brown neighborhoods often exist side by side, particularly in Fresno's Westside or sections of the North. However, they were contending with an institutional expectation that they identify with one racial group.

One afternoon I have a group of students out working on an assignment and they start talking about how the numbers of Black and White students have shifted over the recent months. Erika reminds the table that regardless of these changes, "There's still hella more Mexicans than anybody."

"Psch . . ." Ruben exhales dismissively without looking up from his paper.

Erika glances at him in humored surprise "Psch what??" She turns to the rest of the table laughing "He all smacks his lips cuz I say there's more Mexicans!"

Ruben explains, "It's cuz I don't know which way to go, with the Blacks or with the Mexicans."

Ruben is speaking to the presumed impossibility of being both Black and Mexican within SJEA's carceral social order, a context that constructs racialized peer groups as mutually exclusive affiliations. Consequently, performing one's racial identity here often carries with it an expectation to side with one such group, which can be challenging for multiracial students as groups come into conflict or racial jokes are thrown around in whichever group one settles into. After a few moments I ask Ruben to clarify: "Hey you said you don't know whether to hang with the Black kids or the Mexican kids, is that cuz you're mixed?"

Ruben answers again without looking up, "Yup."

Erika points her thumb at Ruben and elaborates, maintaining her sense of amused disbelief, "This fool sits at the scrap table!"

"It's cuz they're my niggas. When I was at Walker [another continuation school] Bulldogs was always trying to jump me, and those niggas always had my back."

Ruben describes feeling torn between identifying with other Blacks or with other Latinos, but associates with the Sureña/o students because in the past they backed him up when Bulldogs would challenge him. For young people like Ruben, decisions as to whom they ultimately sided with were largely informed by who supported them in this contested environment.

## Mixed Affiliations and Resisting the Carceral Social Order

The carceral social order is a blunt system, and because the groups that it constructs are so rigid and exclusive, many don't fit their narrow parameters, or disagree with the related ideologies or expectations for conflict. Whereas some simply try to decide where they best fit, others strategize and practice various levels of resistance against this social order within the institution. This could range from halfheartedly or indifferently affiliating to refusing to participate or be positioned in this system entirely. Not surprisingly, many of those compelled to resist this system were not only those hoping to avoid conflict but also those who did not fit the rigid template of identity categories recognized by the carceral social order.

Much like the multiracial students at SJEA, several of the Chicana/o youth similarly found themselves straddling identities that the carceral social order constructed as opposing forces. Many of these students had families with members that claimed conflicting affiliations, most commonly as families with both Bulldogs and Norteña/os. For these youth, positioning themselves into the school's social order was not always a clear choice, as they recognized siding with one group or another as potentially costly and dangerous for their families. Their decision could alienate parts of their family, splinter familial groups and networks, or expose their home to violence.

A subtle but important form of agency is found in the individualized degree to which one embraces or resists the rivalries that are imposed by virtue of being in one group or another. For Angel, his reluctance to get involved in any conflicts between affiliations is shaped by the fact that he has both Bulldogs and Sureños in his family. He frames his stance as a refusal to gangbang himself, although he does not try to remove himself from the carceral social order altogether. Angel still places himself along the divides between Latina/o students, mostly associating with Bulldogs because of his neighborhood and his friends. However, he never displays any particular animosity towards Norteña/os or Sureña/os in the same way many of his peers do. He isn't concerned with them as potential threats, and finds it annoying when people do get worked up about it. Angel isn't about to fight anyone over being a Norteño or Sureño, but like Ben he opts to consciously yet quietly avoid them: "Well I don't bang so it's just like, yeah, I'll be cool with them. I don't be lookin' at them, [but] like I don't try to chill with them, [or] hang out with them cuz I'm usually like around the Bulldogs." Angel doesn't see why he would have a problem with other groups if he doesn't bang, but he doesn't try to socialize with them either because of the people he usually does hang with. Angel identifies with Bulldogs and limits his peer networks and interactions accordingly, but is reluctant to fully buy into the rivalries that are presumed to come along with this identity.

Similarly, some Central Valley residents incarcerated in the prison spatially affiliate with one group while still mostly keeping the politics at arm's length—recognizing the spatial or social boundaries between cars in order to minimize confrontations, but staying away from the power struggles between groups by mostly keeping to oneself. In this way people resist the punitive institution's socializing power, superficially participating in the carceral social order as a formality without internalizing the accompanying identity. However, relying on this strategy may depend on doing one's time in lower custody levels where the racial politics are more relaxed, as this is where most of the residents who told me about this approach were housed. Alternatively, some of those held in more contested spaces resist by trying to exclude themselves entirely from the carceral social order—removing themselves by either claiming a religious identity that excluded them from the prison politics, or more commonly through going into protective custody (PC).

As we saw with Angel, a home with split affiliations gave some youth reason to resist the carceral social order by refraining from siding with one identity over the other. But while Angel negotiates this system by claiming an affiliation while downplaying the need for conflict, others refuse to acknowledge the divide at all, refusing to be labeled and engaging with anyone regardless of the rivalries involved. Like Angel, Rachel has a mixed-affiliation family; her dad's family has Norteña/os and her mom's family has several Bulldogs. She doesn't want to alienate herself from the members of her family, but also tries to avoid getting caught in the middle between the factions they claim:

> when [my cousins] were younger we'd all kick it. Just we grew up to that stage you know? And just everybody chose what they were gonna be. They're [banging] and it's just this side's telling me "Oh, go tell them this," this side's telling me "Go tell them that." "Oh, tell them when I see them this, and tell them when I see them that." You know what I mean? So it was kinda hard because I'm like "OK well, shut the fuck up." I don't bang so I'm not gonna go instigate something. I'm not like that so I'm not gonna start doing it now.

Again like Angel, Rachel's refusal to get between her relatives shapes her refusal to gangbang. But Rachel not only refuses to participate in these rivalries but also resists being affiliated or identified with either side at all, insisting on her freedom to associate and socialize with whomever she wants. Of course this carries with it its own set of difficulties.

Young people who resist this placement in the carceral social order must then regularly defend their individualistic stance. Rachel refuses to pick between Bulldogs and Norteña/os because of her family, and tries to ignore this divide while making friends on both sides; in her first stint at SJEA she mostly hung out with Norteña/os, but during her second time at the school she spent more time socializing with Bulldogs. However, when she greeted her Norteña/o friends as they returned to the facility during this latter term, it soon led to questions that prompted Rachel to insist on her own autonomy:

> [T]he second time I came back, it was like I'm kicking it with [Bulldogs], but when some of the people [who] had left before came back, I'd go and hug them "What's up? How you doing? What's good?" So they were like why the hell are you over there hugging him? Why are you doing that? Why are you doing this? And my words were always I don't bang, so (pause) it doesn't matter. Those are always my words. I don't bang, so it doesn't matter who I kick it with. I choose. I choose who I wanna kick it with. I'm not gonna stop kicking with this person to satisfy another.
>
> The first time I did it they did trip, then I let them know what's up. Even before they knew, like when they started kicking it with me [I explained], "Oh, you know, I don't bang," you know? I'm just me. And then when they see me do it, I remind you I don't bang, and I'm not gonna satisfy anybody. That was pretty much it. But now nobody trips here. Now, nobody trips. Now it's just I don't have problems with that no more. Just sometimes the new people do, like "What the fuck?" . . . Yeah, but pretty much because I've been here so many times, they know that I'm not [banging].

Rachel explains her need to take a firm stand on her position, and that over time people generally respected that she was not going to get caught up in the rivalries between affiliations. A handful of other students at SJEA also held similar positions, and the longer they had been at the school the more likely they were to be broadly recognized as someone who did not bang or represent a threat to anybody, allowing them to safely cross this divide. However, this is a precarious status; Rachel is still challenged by new students who expect to see this division upheld, and the reputation she has spent so much time building here may still not be recognized if she were sent to another facility. This expectation can be even more intense for boys, who at SJEA were more likely to be physically assaulted by others and scolded by staff for moving across group lines. For these students, handling the confrontations that result from this boundary crossing entails performing a similar—albeit more individualistic—"hard" identity as those who embrace these conflicts, one in which they demonstrate that they are willing and ready to fight anyone who challenges them.

## The Dangers of Resistance

Even those who stay out of the carceral social order learned to anticipate and manage violent confrontation, because resisting the expectation to side with an affiliation often led others to see one as a suspicious or untrustworthy "hood-hopper." This is a term describing someone who bounces from one gang to another, but the stigma of this term lies in being framed as someone whose support cannot be relied on and who may be spreading information or instigating conflicts with one's rivals. Alex explains: "[You] gotta pick a side. And once you pick a side, you gotta stay on that side. You can't be going back and forth, cuz they [will] think you're snitching or whatever. Think you're giving them information: 'Oh, that fool goes on this bus, catches this bus, he lives over here,' you know? 'He keeps his stuff in this bush' or whatever. You know, information. You can't do that."[9]

This perception shapes some of the violence one may encounter for trying to exist between affiliated groups, but this stance can also lead to deeper legal trouble. While growing up Rachel faced this accusation frequently because of her insistence on staying out of conflicts between affiliations, leading to many fights and arrests:

> At school, outside of school, they wanna call me a hood-hopper. So I don't know, at first when I was younger, when I was like sixteen, I would care a lot about what people said. I cared *a lot*. It's just that got me in trouble too: a lot of fighting, a lot . . . a lot. Just, I cared but now that I grew a little, it's just like [I'm] not, you know, [I'm] not. Cuz a definition of a hood-hopper is someone who bangs, someone who says they bang this but yet they don't and then the next day they wanna go bang something else and day after that there's something else. So I would tell myself you know [I'm] not like that so don't trip. My cousins, even people now, they started respecting me cuz "Oh, you know she isn't like that, she's not." Like [my] actions just spoke louder than my words.

Rachel explains that a hood-hopper is someone who switches gang allegiances, and that this does not apply to her because she is not promising any such allegiance, be it to a neighborhood gang or to a broader affiliated identity. She sees this is something that people eventually recognize, although not without considerable conflict up to this point; in her time at SJEA Rachel has been in many fights, leading to three probation violations (each resulting in an additional term in juvenile detention) and numerous school suspensions. The consequences that this stance has held for Rachel highlight the important point that punitive institutions rely on the carceral social order to manage the facility, to the extent that going against this system and conforming to authoritative expectations to eschew criminalized identities may actually lead to *more* punishment.

This potential for receiving additional punishment for not conforming to the carceral social order is particularly visible with Steven, a parolee we met in chapter 1 who was removed from general population when he tried to serve his time as an unaffiliated prisoner. Steven is a White guy who grew up with Chicana/os in one of the small farming towns of the Central Valley, and when he got to prison he was housed with the Northerners, both due to his stated preference and because by this point he had been validated as a Norteño gang member. But while he was imprisoned a rumor spread that Steven had snitched on a friend of his back home after a fight, when police had found him concussed and in a drunken stupor. He quickly had a falling out with the other Northerners and found himself as an outsider in the institution's social order. Steven hoped to move on and simply do the rest of his time on his own as an unaffiliated, uncategorized individual. But with no group affiliation the COs saw no choice but to transfer him to the Special Needs Yard, another term for PC. Steven countered, opting for solitary confinement instead. But like Rachel, the decisions he makes in attempting to exist outside of the carceral social order ultimately create greater punishments for him:

> I got myself in a lot of trouble to the point to where they wouldn't even put me with no one else. They kept me single celled, I caught SHU [Secure Housing Unit] time, and thank God I never had to hit a yard full of garbage [do time in PC], you know? I got so much SHU time, my SHU time will override my discharge time, so basically I should never have to hit one of those yards that I don't want to hit. So going back, whenever I go back to the system I got SHU time, so I go straight to the hole . . . they got [me] single-celled. Some people are like single-cell, walk-alone. You go to yard in a cage, know what I mean? They got group yards there, but they're only for certain individuals. The rest of 'em [use] what're called dog cages. They got 'em up to like, they'll have twenty. Any time you come out, you come out for shower, you get showers like three days a week, like you get ten minutes for each shower. Any time you come out you're handcuffed.

Everyone in general population is expected to go along with the carceral social order. Prison authorities generally send anybody who refuses to affiliate with one of the institution's racial groups into PC, making it the primary alternative for those who do not want to participate in this system. But this option also entails its own set of risks. Inmates in PC are commonly stigmatized as either police informants or sex offenders—this is why Steven is so disgusted by the thought of doing his time here, and it also potentially makes him a larger target for assault either inside or outside the prison. Because this alternative is so undesirable it effectively functions to enforce the carceral social order. One can either be part of a car, or accept this status as a presumed snitch, rapist, or child molester.

The prison relies on the carceral social order to manage the facility, and enforces this system by removing and isolating anyone who resists this system from general population. Typically staff would do this by placing someone in PC, but Steven resists this protocol by forcing the administration to place him in the SHU instead, the unit designated for the prison's most problematic and violent inmates. Here his resistance places him in much more restrictive custody, isolated by himself and shackled any time he leaves his cell. His confinement here—his escalated punishment—is a consequence of not only rejecting the carceral social order but also the institution's efforts to subsequently isolate him in PC. And while his placement in the SHU protected him from physical assault, it also exposed him to additional forms of violence, as his confinement began to take a toll on his mental health:

> So I mean as far as the harassments and the oppression goes, I've had a good share of that, you know? And at times I still, I'm working on my mind. I got a lot of garbage in my mind now, you know? Not so much garbage, but I got a lot of bullshit in there, you know, and I'm working on getting rid of it. The longer I stay out, it goes away. You know, it wears out. But once I go back, I'm in that same environment, around those same individuals who don't like me, and they pick up where they left off, you know?

The longer Steven remains isolated in the SHU, the more it erodes his mental health. The seclusion of long-term confinement in SHU units is well known to have damaging effects on one's mental well-being (Haney 2003). Additionally, the little social contact that Steven does have often comes in the form of taunts and harassment—from the Northerners who now reject him, the Southerners he was already enemies with, and even COs frustrated with him for not going along with a system that makes their jobs easier. Interestingly enough, the only people Steven feels still treat him like a person during this whole experience are the White inmates, giving him a different perspective on the racial car he would have been with had he followed the prevailing racial logic of the prison:

STEVEN: [People] used to tell me to stick with my own race and it'll be so much easier for me. You know in the long run, now that I'm outside of that prison circle and I can look and see for myself and, there's a little truth to that, you know? When you stick with your race, it's a whole lot easier. Even my first time going to prison, I had like the White dudes, they tried to kinda get at me, you know? Tell me like "You know what, when you get there, do this and do that, get with your people, you know?" woo woo, this and that, but I was hard headed, man. I was like fuck that, you know, I'm gonna stay with the people I grew up with.

AUTHOR: So the Whites would give you a hard time when you were locked up?

S: I mean not really. They wouldn't give me a hard time. Matter of fact, they were kinda cool, and even when everything went bad, I'm not gonna lie to you, everything went bad this time. Like growing up, when I was younger, I had this mentality where I didn't even like my own race, you know? The color of my skin, I didn't even like it, you know? But going to prison, when all that shit was going on, the White people, even the ones who were still like with the business, they're the ones who reached out to me. Hit me with soups, hit me with cleaner when nobody else would, you know? When it was all said and done and I was thrown out here on the side, it was my own race, like they really aren't my people because I'm not with their business, but just based on the color of my skin and who I am, they're the individuals who got at me in a respectful way.

A: So in retrospect, do you think it would have been easier for you if you had . . .

S: I can't even really say. I can't say easier, cuz if I would have went that route, I'd probably end up in the same shoes I'm in now, because I woulda been doing, it woulda been all fake, you know, because that's not what was in my heart, you know?

Steven's experiences in the SHU force him to rethink how he chose to affiliate in the prison, his punishment and harassment serving as institutional lessons reinforcing the carceral social order as a dominant framework. The removal of prisoners who grow tired of politics or decide that they don't want to claim an affiliation offers the institution a means for containing and controlling those who resist the prevailing system. This process helps maintain the carceral social order as the expected norm, and the added risks and stigmas experienced as part of this removal may discipline individuals like Steven for going against the status quo. But while this experience made Steven wonder about how his time would have been different if he had aligned himself with the other White inmates all along, he also knows that this role may not have worked for him either because it would not have been compatible with his own sense of self.

## CONCLUSIONS

The carceral social order organizes the punitive facility, but it also provides those held within its walls a framework for understanding their experiences and relationships in this environment. People in the institution learn which situated roles are recognized within this system, and draw from those at their disposal to help them navigate the facility. Rather than simply conforming to ascribed identities, people carefully gauge and consider which would be the most useful or feasible, and what the consequences of their decision may be. Whether or not one fits a given role, there is a certain degree of work involved in positioning oneself into the carceral social order. Those who adopt the facility's situated roles must effectively communicate this to others, adequately performing these roles through their use of space and managed appearance. People have to negotiate their participation in these roles, work to establish an alternative position in the institution's social order, or fight to stay out of it entirely. However, there are dangers in resisting the carceral social order; outsiders may be targeted for violence or subject to additional penalties from the institution, despite the fact they are rejecting the criminalized identities that are otherwise used to mark them as gang members. These risks reveal the extent and means through which the institution actively enforces the carceral social order by isolating and removing those who reject this system, and creating a context in which it is easier and safer for one to go along with this labeling process than to try to resist it.

PART II

# Coming Back Home

# 4. "The Home Team" at the Intersection of Prison and Neighborhood

Even after finishing the packet of worksheets they've been assigned for today, my tutoring students stay crowded around a round table in the small office that is tucked behind the classrooms at San Joaquin Educational Academy (SJEA); they prefer to wait out the period rather than go back to their classroom, chatting and doodling on their papers. Half-listening to the conversations around the table, Andrea's attention wanders to the whiteboard behind her, and while the others keep talking she grabs one of the nearby markers and starts writing. She lists five names in a column, each with the word "free" written in front of it, and as the other students begin to curiously watch her do this she explains, "These are all my main dogs who are down." She caps the marker and points to each name, starting at the top. "This one is never getting out, this one has a year left, this one just got locked up, and these two are still awaiting trial." She points to the last name on her list, elaborating that this person is her fifteen-year-old cousin.

Andrea knows several people who are ensnared at various levels of the justice system, and in this respect she is representative of many of the students here.[1] Most of the young people here know someone who is or has been in prison, some counting as many as twelve or fifteen people when they stop to think about it. Others have uncles or cousins who are in county jail, or siblings and childhood friends in state custody in Department of Juvenile Justice facilities. And almost everyone counts several more friends who are still waiting to get out of Fresno's Juvenile Detention Facility (JDF). These relationships bind the students here to the justice system beyond their own probation cases, oftentimes to penal and punitive institutions that they themselves have never been to. They are personally affected by what happens in these spaces even if they are not there, and learn to understand incarceration as something that consistently happens to members of their families and communities. As these ties are concentrated in marginalized communities with high imprisonment rates, they establish a connection between neighborhood and prison, one in which the identities that structure incarcerated life become influential outside the institution.

The carceral social order is socialized within punitive facilities at the state and local levels—institutional spaces in which staff members use the affiliations that comprise this system to manage overcrowded facilities. But as incarceration becomes an increasingly prominent feature of American social life, these affiliations inevitably leak out into the residential spaces from which the imprisoned are taken. Within the links that emerge between prison and community, the carceral social order comes to contextualize how what happens in one space affects the other. In this chapter I discuss how the carceral affiliations that inmates use to navigate the prison tie these individuals to their home communities, how they connect neighborhood youth to their incarcerated loved ones, and how they keep parolees returning to the community tethered to the penal facilities they are trying to leave behind.

## THE HOME TEAM

Henry is a big dude, and has a booming laugh that matches his size. As I ask him more about what has led him to the prisoner reentry center I am interviewing him in today, he squints his eyes at me every few minutes and asks his own questions to probe how well I know this area and what exactly I am doing these interviews for. But more than anything his laugh comes out as he leans back, crosses his thick arms over his white T-shirt, and remembers a younger version of himself. Henry grew up in Sanger, a "county town" about fifteen minutes outside of Fresno that is 80 percent Latina/o with a 30 percent youth poverty rate. Here he lived in a tight-knit neighborhood called the Chankla where he remembers everyone knowing everyone. But to those outside the neighborhood, the Chankla's close network of young people was seen as a criminal gang.

By the time he turns eleven or twelve Henry starts spending more of his time with the other boys from the neighborhood, and this starts to get him into trouble. At thirteen Henry is arrested for stealing a pair of gloves from Save Mart and is sent to juvenile hall for the first time. After his subsequent placement on juvenile probation he comes under closer scrutiny from local law enforcement and juvenile justice personnel, and eventually the court decides to remove him from his father's and grandparents' home. Over time he is sent to a number of local group homes before finally being placed in one hours away from home. Henry hates it here and badly misses home: "I wanted to be at [my] house, you know? I didn't wanna be in no dumb, no damn group home." Within two weeks he steals a car belonging to one of the staff members and escapes. He drives over 150 miles back to his home in Sanger, but police find him just two days later at his family's house. This is the incident that lands him in YA.

At sixteen Henry is sent to the Preston School of Industry in Ione, a century-old reform school converted into one of the largest youth prisons in the California Youth Authority (YA) system.[2] Originally built as a foreboding Neo-Romanesque castle in the Sierra foothills, Preston developed a reputation as a cruel place for young people almost immediately after its opening. In this way it has always been reflective of a broader YA system in which high rates of violence, sexual assault, and suicide attempts have been chronic systematic problems. As facilities intended for the state's most serious juvenile offenders, youth are only sent to YA when they have criminal sentences longer than one year. However, years of tough-on-crime campaigning gradually made youth sentencing increasingly more severe in California, compiling over 10,000 young people into YA facilities like Preston by the time Henry is here in the mid-1990s (Krisberg et al. 2010). This buildup led to facilities that were dangerously overcrowded; not only were teenagers' medical and educational needs largely unmet, but they were also exposed to "levels of ward-on-ward assaults [that] are unprecedented in juvenile corrections across the nation" (Krisberg 2003). When external reviewers examined youth violence in six YA facilities over a twelve-month period, they discovered over 4,000 reported cases of assault and battery—more than ten a day—and nearly 1,000 cases of sexual harassment and assault.[3] For Henry, Preston is violent, intimidating, and chaotic: "If you're not a survivor, you're not gonna survive. If you got it in you then you'll survive, but [you're] still gonna learn a lotta hard lessons, a lot in there. A lot of fighting, a lot of shit-talking, everything . . . the devil runs wild in there."

Henry spends the next two years of his life here, and it changes him. He explains: "You adapt to it if you're a survivor. You know, and surviving is what I do and, I adapted to it and um, did what I did, got back home." Part of how Henry adapts to survive this dangerous setting is learning to stay with other youth from his hometown or from Fresno County. In a context in which youth are coming in from all over the state and facing such pervasive threats of predatory violence, shared home communities offer peer networks that boys can use to mitigate this vulnerability and look out for each other:

You know, we'll see someone coming in from Fresno, and they're from Fresno but they're not really a gang member or nothing like that. Well, we'll be like, "If you wanna stick with the home team, you know, come on over here then. Kick back with us." And nine times out of ten it's gonna go that way, cuz everybody sticks together with their home town. You got a lot of big cities out there, like LA, and this and that, you know what I'm saying? They like, since they're larger numbers they like to do a lot of dumb stuff so, that's why people gotta stick together in there.

It is in YA that Henry first experiences the "Fresno car," a collective of incarcerated peers from his home county that he would learn to rely on both here and in the other state penal institutions he would enter throughout his life. But while Henry is here this group also shifts in a significant way—mirroring events in the state prison system a few years prior, the Fresno car separated itself from the other incarcerated Latinos from Northern California. Henry was not connected to the prison politics that generated this move in any way, but he embraced this change nonetheless—not so much out of spite for other Northerners, although this developed over time soon after the split. Instead, it was important for him to go along with it because, regardless of who else the car was affiliated with, it connected him to home and to others from his home. The car connected him to his neighborhood even when he was locked up, and let him associate with others from his home in a way that could maintain some form of community belonging. But most importantly, Henry needed to maintain his ties to the "home team" because it helped keep him safe in an unpredictable environment.

This change for the car made Henry new enemies, got him into fights, and consequently got him into more trouble. But in this context it was a group he needed, and that remained essential throughout most of his adult life as he struggled to stay out of correctional institutions. As Henry got older and went on to state prison for a weapons charge at age twenty-one, the Fresno car remained an important source of protection for him, but also continued to connect him to home while incarcerated: "Fresno's not really too much of a, too much large in numbers, you know? So we're small on numbers but we stick together. And that's basically the home team coming back, you know, without getting stabbed or without getting jumped or anything like that, you know what I'm saying? . . . A lotta people see it as a gang, and then some, you know, to me we're not a gang. We're just one big family man, where we just gotta come back home. Stick together and come back home. That's it."

Henry describes the Fresno car—more commonly known as Bulldogs—as staying with the people one might know or who may live by them while one is locked up, contesting the common assumption of a gang or criminal organization one joins in prison. Prisoners adapt to the penal institution by developing important group identities that are shaped by race, home community, and peer networks. For incarcerated Chicanos like Henry, hometowns became something that they were labeled with, something they carried with them as they navigated multiple facilities, and something that connected them to the affiliations they used to protect themselves. These affiliations become valued identities for the imprisoned, but they also begin to shape one's time inside, as prisoners are segregated and assaulted based on where they from, how they are racialized, and how they are resultantly sorted into the carceral social order. Consequently, these identities also inevitably shape this time for inmates' families outside the prison as well.

Similar to how the romantic partners of prison inmates have to learn to structure their lives around the surveillance and discipline of the prison (Comfort 2008), they must also become quasi-inmates in regards to learning to position oneself into the prison's carceral social order. Prisoners' families have to know how their incarcerated members are labeled, and are affected by what happens to them because of these labels. For example, on Internet forums dedicated to prisoners and their families,[4] users oftentimes share information (that many have difficulty getting from the facilities themselves) about how to arrange a visit. But planning a visit in California requires some knowledge of how an imprisoned loved one is categorized in the sorting process. Among the information shared by forum users trying to visit family members in Wasco State Prison are the restrictions listed on the institutional approval form, one of which is a sentence explaining that appointments are necessary to see some inmates:

> Appointments are necessary ONLY for:
>   All SOUTHERNER Hispanics in Facility "A," Buildings 3, 4, 5, & 6. SOUTHERNER Hispanics and FRESNO Bulldogs in Facility "C" and "D" AND FOR ALL NORTHERNER Hispanic and Administration Segregation Inmates in Facility "D" Building #6.

To know if they need an appointment to see their loved ones, Latino prisoners' partners and relatives need to know where in Wasco their partner is being held, but also if they are Southerners, Northerners, or Bulldogs. This distinction was understandably confusing for many forum users who did not understand if these institutional labels applied to their own partners, and had to help each other make sense of the sorting procedures that marked their partners as gang involved. For example one post asks: "my bf is hispanic and from fresno ca and is in facility C. he is not in a gang or anything. will i have to make an apt just because hes mexican? how do i know if hes labled as a southern or northern hispanic????"

We can see here how the prison's carceral social order begins to leak into residential spaces. Inmates' families are indirectly categorized into carceral affiliations, as what happens to inmates because of how they are categorized also impacts their families; maintaining contact with inmates made understanding their position in the carceral social order important for families outside of the institution, but it also exposed these families to the violence that stemmed from these divides. This indirect categorization can then in turn structure a similar attachment to a carceral affiliation among those outside of the prison. Before neighborhood youth ever encounter this social order in juvenile justice facilities or in the criminal labeling practiced in their community, they overwhelmingly first learn about it from older peers and relatives who have been to prison. The emergence of the Fresno Bulldogs provides an interesting case study of this fallout. First, the violence between a handful of gang members in prison leads to the separation of all Fresno-area inmates. The institutionalization of a distinct carceral identity soon follows, which then seeps into other institutions and eventually back to the neighborhood. Here community members similarly learn where they and their families fit in this system, and why these affiliations are important. The high rates of local imprisonment allow for the same identities, stories, and understandings of carceral affiliations to be passed down into the spaces most affected by the prison.

## Legend of the Bulldogs

When Henry was first sent to YA in 1991, Sanger's criminalized Latina/o youth primarily affiliated with Norteña/os. By the first time he was paroled in 1993, everyone had forsaken any Northerner identities and were now claiming, "backing up," or "running with" Fresno Bulldogs. Henry noticed this shift as he returned to his neighborhood, but he also saw it happen in YA as wards from Fresno County and Northern California who had previously socialized together began distancing themselves from each other and, before long, clashing with one another:

> [T]hey knew what was happening, and we knew what was happening too, so you know automatically the grudges already began, you know? And then everything was happening in prison, and so, but there were like people, people would get letters from prison and stuff like that. And so everyone was caught up on what was going on and stuff, with the politics and stuff like that so. Yeah, so little by little it just, you know, it started phasing out. We started, you know, started running over here,

so. And it was, after that it was just more fighting goin' on. Yeah, a whole lot more fighting.

As Henry's peers in YA learned of the Norteño/Bulldog split that was unfolding in the prison through correspondence with inmates, they collectively began to shed their own Norteño affiliations. The divisions and violence stemming from the prison's evolving social order were consequently reproduced among a younger generation within YA facilities.

Prior to the mid- to late 1980s, Fresno-area Latinos were sorted with the Northerners when they were sent to prison. But around this time a group of Fresneros decided to break away and form their own group within the prison's racialized social order, a move that had ripple effects across the state's prison system, other justice system institutions, and even back home. The accounts of those who remember this shift are all pretty vague, but it's a fairly consistent story. The common narrative is that the prison gang La Nuestra Familia (NF) would regularly issue orders to all Northerners on what they could or couldn't do in the prison while also demanding extortion payments from inmates. As part of this extensive control the inmates from Fresno were commonly used as NF's enforcers and ordered to attack its rivals. However, the story goes that eventually the Fresno car decided to break away from the control of this prison gang that was exploiting them. Here thirty-four-year-old parolee Martín offers an example of how this story is typically framed:

> They were trying to have us do everything they had to do. They tried to make us their torpedoes. And [that] wasn't happening, so all of us got together, no shot-callers. We didn't have no shot-callers. All of us just came together from [the] Fresno car and said "Know what? Fuck that. They're having us do all their work, we're gonna hit them and show 'em that we're not gonna do it. We represent but we are not gonna be their little torpedoes all the time. We're not gonna be their little . . . " in other words we just said we ain't gonna be their bitches. Know what I mean?

Following this split was an escalation of violence between Fresno-area Latinos and the Northerners. Prison staff responded by isolating the Fresno inmates on protective custody yards to prevent further clashes before sorting them separately from Norteños and Southsiders into their own housing assignments. Within these segregated units prisoners began developing a new identity as Fresno Bulldogs, appropriating the name and mascot of Fresno State University's football team (the most popular sports program in the region) and incorporating symbols like paw prints and barking to signal belonging. The prisons in Avenal and Pleasant Valley into which many Fresno Latinos were subsequently concentrated became known as "Bulldog pens," and before long, Latina/o street cliques in Fresno began switching over from Norteña/os to identifying as Bulldogs, re-creating penal conflicts in local neighborhoods.

It may be impossible to ever confirm a precise history of what exactly initiated the divide between Bulldogs and Norteños. But what is interesting about the collective memory this older generation of parolees have of this transition is that it matches the learned histories contemporary youth tell each other about why they identify as Bulldogs. While the details remains murky, this tale of standing up to the Norteños and refusing to do their dirty work anymore is the mythology that was passed down to future generations. Local parolees' understanding of their own collective identity *becomes* the story of what happened, the narrative that is retold and that becomes the local truth that is known by neighborhood youth. Latina/o youth in Fresno still repeat the narrative with pride, and this story of defiantly rebelling against the Northerners' hierarchy has become an important part of the culture that is learned as part of affiliating with Bulldogs. On SJEA's campus, high school students who identify as Bulldogs regularly recite this ideology through proud proclamations that they "don't take orders," "have no shot-callers," and recognize that "Every Fresnero's Equal" (EFE, the Spanish pronunciation of the letter F).

## TWO ENDS OF THE CONTINUUM

In young people's repeating the stories and appropriating the identities produced in the prison, we can see how families and communities outside of the prison are affected by the sorting and politics institutionalized inside the prison. But it also tells us something about why carceral affiliations are appropriated locally, and how young people in the neighborhood understand them in the context of mass incarceration. High community imprisonment, and more importantly the concentration of imprisonment among community residents, establishes a continuum between prison and neighborhood—both institutionally in terms of consistent surveillance, punishment, and criminalization (Wacquant 2001), but also experientially in terms of how residents encounter and adapt to these. The relationships that span these spaces, the frequent circular migrations between them, and the common (even anticipated) trajectory that sends residents to prison all facilitate the passing down of carceral identities into the community. In this section I focus on two ends of this continuum—residents coming back from prison, and those being set up to soon go to prison. Both before and after the prison residents describe the roles and functions of carceral affiliations, as well as why and how they see themselves using them.

## Imagining the Prison

The familiarity criminalized youth have with the carceral social order—and even more dramatically, their anticipation of what imprisonment would be like—speaks volumes about the prison's role in their communities. The number of people local youth see sent to prison compels them to imagine what the prison is like for their loved ones, and wonder what the everyday lives of their relatives and neighbors might be like in this environment. But because of how frequently young residents see this happen, and because of their own experiences with criminalization, for many this imagination inevitably turns to what the prison would be like for themselves. This impression is largely informed by the narratives of previously imprisoned family and community members, which teach local adolescents about how people manage the experience of incarceration.

Young residents of criminalized communities are impacted by what happens to their relatives and neighbors as they navigate the criminal justice system. Consequently, their understandings of prison life are significantly shaped by how their incarcerated loved ones experience the implications of racial sorting and the carceral social order. For example, sixteen-year-old Emilio learns about how racial politics work in county jail through the experiences of his stepfather:

> My stepdad was in LA. He was in county for two months, and he told me when he got out [that] he thought he was gonna die in there because some Mexicans told him that they were going to beat him up, that they were going to kill him cuz he [had] told this Black guy to do his hair. The Black guy was like, "Oh, for sure," [and] he was doing his hair. But the only thing, the only reason they didn't beat him up was because he didn't know about it. He didn't know nothing, he didn't know how it runs, so they told him how it runs. Mexicans stay with Mexicans, Black people stay with Black people, White with White. That's how they roll in there.

In retelling his experiences with incarceration, Emilio's stepfather conveys the importance of being familiar with the institution's racial politics by describing how he unknowingly violated the informal restrictions that limit interactions between Black and Latino prisoners; after naïvely requesting a haircut from a Black inmate, the other Mexicans confront and threaten him, only letting his indiscretion slide when he convinces them that he didn't realize he was breaking any rules. But as his stepfather learns this lesson, so too does Emilio. Through the experiences of their incarcerated loved ones, local youth learn that race plays a definitive role in shaping penal peer networks and interactions, and that failing to abide by this social order can be dangerous, as residents are held accountable to the rules of segregation.

Yet while White, Black, and Asian students at SJEA all seemed vaguely aware that inmates were segregated by race in the prison, the Latina/o students were acutely literate in the more complicated divisions between Norteña/os, Sureña/os, and Bulldogs. Most young people first learn about these affiliations through family members and neighborhood friends involved in rivalries between them. This was particularly the case when loved ones were hurt or killed in these feuds, leading many youth who were indifferent about joining gangs to recognize anyone affiliated with their friends' or relatives' assailants as personal enemies. In these instances, youth learn to understand the dangers of the prison in terms of the presence of these rivals in the facility, and to see carceral affiliations as communal means to manage these hazards that are passed down from older generations. As these youth get older, their familiarity with the carceral social order is refined though their own experiences navigating juvenile institutions that reproduce the same social order as the prison.

Many young people growing up in criminalized neighborhoods like Eastside Fresno are therefore remarkably aware of the need to use geographic ties to clique up in carceral settings. Mirroring the parolees' recollections of their childhoods, most of the students at SJEA remembered being familiar with prison-based affiliations long before they were ever arrested or incarcerated, often learning about Norteña/os, Sureña/os, and Bulldogs from older friends and relatives who had been to prison. In this excerpt from his interview transcript, Ramon, a fifteen-year-old tagger who does not gangbang, talks about two of his older brothers who have been to prison:

AUTHOR: Did either of them bang before they got locked up?

RAMON: No, they just want to back up Bulldogs.

    A: Just want to back up Bulldogs?

    R: Yeah, when they went in there they were Bulldogs, but on the outs I don't think they really like [gangbang] . . . my brother Gabriel more like wears Bulldog stuff, like Bulldog hats and red shirts and stuff. Yeah.

    A: Oh, but they don't identify with like a clique or nothing like that?"

    R: No.

    A: You were saying earlier that there are some taggers that would back up Bulldogs if they got locked up. Have you ever thought about what you would do if you got locked up?

    R: Yeah. I would be a Bulldog.

Although his brothers were never in a gang before they went to prison, they supported the Bulldogs while they were incarcerated. Through his brothers, Ramon learns that surviving in the carceral system requires cliquing up with other Fresno Chicanos and adopting the appropriate affiliation, regardless of whether he bangs on the outs or not. His brothers' experiences taught Ramon not only about how these affiliations are necessary in the prison but also about the Fresno car's feuds, and steered him away from ever potentially identifying with their rivals:

AUTHOR: You said you would probably be a Bulldog if you got locked up, why do you think you would?

RAMON: Because I don't think I would fit in [as] a Norteño or a Sureño. Plus that's how my dad is, and my brother is, and my sister. Like my family would probably be like, my family wouldn't like, see me as it, my brothers would try to fight me and stuff. They would be talking hella shit to me if I was something [else], like a different person.

Ramon already recognizes the racial separatism enforced in prison and frames being locked up as having to side with one of the Latino groups— Norteños, Sureños, or Bulldogs. Ramon knows that in the prison he would have to pick a side, and in this situation he feels he should be a Bulldog like the rest of his family. Ramon frames this affiliation as part of an identity developed through familial ties, and can't see himself affiliating with any other group because of the problems this would lead to with his relatives.

Ramon knows for certain where he would fit within the prison's social order because it is where his family fit. We can see here a clear example of how familial ties spread this carceral identity to the outs, creating both an appeal to appropriate it but also a pressure to conform to it. Affiliations consequently become something molded at both ends of the prison/neighborhood continuum—there are consequences at home for how residents identify inside, but there are also forces on the outs informing how it takes shape inside.

In addition to learning to recognize these affiliations as part of their identity, many youth also come to see this cliquing up as important in the context of the dangers other groups in the prison represent. Students with relatives who had been involved in carceral rivalries understood that as Chicanos from Fresno they could expect to be targeted by other groups in the prison, making it essential to stay together and have a strong group identity while incarcerated. Here fifteen-year-old Manny, a Bulldog gang member, describes how he understands the prison as a violent place in which predatory inmates from Northern and Southern California will rob and potentially rape anyone not ready to fight them back:

AUTHOR: Have you heard anything about like what it's like for folks from Fresno when they get locked up? Like, what they can expect?

MANNY: Yeah.

A: Like what?

M: Probably getting stabbed or killed.

A: Yeah?

M: Yeah cause there's a lot of scraps and busters up there, or in the pen you know? Just gotta fucking not be a bitch. You gotta do what you gotta do. Like if there's a lot of homies in the pen you should just, you know but they're just a lot outnumbered. But fuck it, you gotta do what you gotta do. Can't be a bitch. Gotta take care of business and shit.

A: Have you heard anything either about the prison or maybe just about the juvie, about how to protect yourself when you going through that?

M: Naw, not really. Just when you go in there, you can't look like a punk. If anybody tells you anything, you better hit him.

A: What do punks look like?

M: They let people take their trays, their clothes. Depends what you got, their stamps, their snacks. Whatever they have, it gets taken. They get their asses taken too. If you don't [hit him, you'll] fucking get raped and shit if you fuck around. That's why you can't be a punk.

A: So that's why you gotta hit someone for saying shit?

M: Pretty much. If you don't do that, they're just gonna take advantage of you. It doesn't matter if you're little, you gotta do what you gotta do. Cause there's a lotta bigger fools and shit that'll try to take advantage of you and shit.

A: Do you feel like most of that would come from Norteños or Sureños, or do you think other folks from Fresno would try to punk each other?

M: Depends. If you're in the hall or you're in probably like in the pen or something, like if it's a dog from Fresno I don't think they fuck with [you] you know, cuz they wouldn't fuck around with each other. But if there's scraps and busters from Fresno, yeah they'll fucking try to fight you and shit.

In this excerpt we can see Manny's understanding of how things work in the prison. He describes the prison as particularly dangerous for Latinos from Fresno and argues that one needs to violently confront any signs of disrespect before they lead to more serious victimization. Manny mentions demonstrating a potential for violence as critical for protecting oneself (Anderson 2000), but most importantly, he recognizes cliquing up as an important means of avoiding or minimizing the risk of assault or rape while in the prison. He also understands that this danger is shaped by geographic ties and rivalries; he has learned to see Bulldogs as a safe group of peers that won't victimize each other, but Norteños and Sureños as inmates who will try to fight him, rob him, and make him a punk unless he is willing to fight them back. Through what he has heard from incarcerated friends and relatives, Manny has learned to anticipate violence in the prison as a certainty—to the extent that one can expect to be stabbed—because it is a place where Fresneros are overwhelmed by enemies.

Manny's description of the prison gives us a clear picture of how criminalized youth of color understand the affiliations of the carceral social order as a means for managing a carceral status. Youth like Manny learn to see Bulldogs as allies who can help them stay safe and who can collectively stand up to rivals so as to protect themselves from being targeted for robbery or assault in the carceral institution. In a system that punishes men from all over the state, the bonds of mutual protection that characterize neighborhood identities (Harding 2010) are simply extrapolated to include individuals from a broader area. Manny's understanding of this system informs his worldview of where he fits in and what he can expect.

The knowledge of the carceral social order that youth gain from their currently or previously incarcerated loved ones shapes how they imagine the prison, their place in it, and how they would need to articulate their ties in order to survive the correctional facility. When youth like Ramon and Manny encounter punitive institutions themselves in the juvenile hall or the continuation school, their race and home communities serve as proxies for gang membership and affiliation in much the same way as they do for inmates in the prison. Through these experiences youth learn to identify with the appropriate sides inside the institution. The divisiveness imposed on them in these spaces mirrors the tales they have heard of the prison and strengthens the role criminalized affiliations have in their lives, which manifests a polarizing social organization that positions young people into rivalries that they cannot easily avoid.

Youths' experiences in juvenile institutions gave them some experience seeing the carceral social order in action, but the experiences they heard from incarcerated adults told a more complex story of life in the prison. Young people learned to understand carceral affiliations as based on family ties and the danger posed by other groups, but that they are also dependent on the racial organizing accomplished by the institution. So even if one's relatives, peers, or rivals steer them towards one affiliation, the institution may have final say in how one affiliates and may shape others' perceptions of where one fits. Criminalized youth understood that they would be expected to stay with their race in the prison, which could complicate things for some of them. For example, Frankie is a seventeen-year-old Chicano who bangs Northside Lao Bloods, a predominantly Asian street gang, and usually hangs out with the Asian students at SJEA. Frankie also has a very intricate understanding of how people were racially segregated in the adult system. During our interview, despite being too young to have ever been there himself, he described to me how prisoners are racially sorted in the Fresno County Jail, even explaining which racial groups went to each floor. At one point I ask him if he had ever considered how he would fit into this structure as an adult:

AUTHOR: Hopefully you wouldn't have to choose this, but if you got locked up as an adult and you went to county, would you go in with the Asians or would you go in with the Mexicans?

FRANKIE: See I be thinking about that too, cuz like how I hear [it is] in prison, you got to roll with your race. And probably that's what I'll do. But I won't kick it with my enemies. Cuz like I'm saying, it's not just all Asians. It's [got] Mexicans too, like we got Mexican homies that bang LB, we got Black homies that bang LB, we got Whiteboy homies that bang LB too. Like I know Bulldogs, Black Bulldogs that bang Bulldogs, I know Whiteboys that bang Bulldogs, I know Asians that bang Bulldogs, and stuff like that. So I don't know, [but] I'll probably have to stick in my race.

A: Do you think you would stay with Bulldogs then or maybe with the *paisas*?

F: Yeah I'd probably just kick it with just the *paisas*, not Norteños or Sureños cuz then they'll be like "Oh, you kick it with them, woo woo." I'll probably just ride by myself. But sometimes I'll be thinking too, like "Ah, I gotta ride with my niggas, with my Asian niggas." But then when I look at it, they probably ain't gonna trust me like that, cuz you know I'm a different race. That's mostly what it is.

A: That makes it hard.

F: Yeah it's kinda hard too. I be thinking it too, like damn, hopefully it don't get to that point.

A: But you've thought about that before?

F: Yeah.

A: Yeah, that's pretty crazy. I've wondered about that too, like what do guys like that do if they have to choose?

F: Yeah. Like I got a homie too, he's Black [but] he be like "Nah, I'ma keep it 100, [if] I go to the pen I'ma ride with my niggas! I'ma stay with my niggas, I'ma stay with my Asian niggas! I'ma go with the Asians, I'm a LB, I'ma go with the Asians!" But sometimes, how they really look at it, the staff ain't gonna put you with the Asians cuz they ain't gonna trust you. Something might go wrong, they might kill you or something. Cuz that's mostly how it is. In prison, they gonna put you with your race. That's how it is. It's mostly about race. Cuz I mean Blacks too, they don't get along but it's their race, know what I mean? [Enemies] are probably gonna talk, but when it goes down into a big ole race fight that's when you gotta back up your race.

Here Frankie demonstrates a very sophisticated understanding of how the carceral social order structures life in adult punitive facilities. He recognizes that the potential for racial violence forces people to "roll with [their] race," which can complicate one's ability to stay with their peers if they have a different racial background. He also sees this segregation as something enforced by the institution ("the staff ain't gonna put you with the Asians"). So even though Frankie would ideally prefer to stay with other Lao Bloods, he already knows that the racial politics inside would probably not allow this and that it would be easier for him to stay with other Latinos. Additionally, because he is also aware of the carceral rivalries between Latinos, he says he would choose to stay with the "*paisas*"[5] rather than the Chicano Norteños or Sureños in order to avoid the violence between these latter groups.

The carceral social order's reach into the community—accomplished here through both those Frankie directly knows, and more indirectly through the knowledge base concentrated incarceration establishes in his community—shapes how young people imagine the prison and one's experience there. Frankie is already well aware of the functioning social formations of the prison, and perhaps most telling is the extent to which he has already considered and mapped out what his options would be if he was sent there. The fact that he has been concerned about this as a problem he may potentially face says something drastic about his perceived likelihood of incarceration. Understanding how the racial politics of the carceral social order work in the prison allows neighborhood youth to know what to expect in carceral institutions and to be prepared for the process of prison sorting. So while Frankie may want to stay with the Asian inmates going into the prison, his familiarity with the carceral social order makes him more aware of the difficulties and resistance he can expect to encounter if he did so.

## Lingering Affiliations among Returning Parolees

The relationships that local residents have with the incarcerated help establish prison-based affiliations as identities that bridge residential and penal spaces and inform neighborhood youth about the experience of imprisonment. But on the other side of incarceration, many parolees are also compelled to cling to affiliations or struggle to shed them after being released. Residents who are released from prison return to communities that have few opportunities for stable employment or housing to offer. Former inmates are also even further marginalized from the rare opportunities that do exist because of their felon status (Pager 2007) and the restrictions placed on them by parole (Petersilia 2003). Parolees with little support for their reentry to the community may then rely on affiliations for help. Additionally, the uncertainty about staying out of custody and the persistent ascription of affiliations as criminal labels also work to maintain affiliations, and resultantly leave returning residents exceptionally vulnerable to being sent back to prison.

One of the most basic needs that goes largely unmet for parolees is housing. A fundamental requirement that residents need to provide when reporting to parole is an address a parole officer can visit. Most stay with parents or spouses/partners, but there are many more returning residents who don't have family they can stay with—some parolees' families have moved away or no longer live in the county, have no room for them, or the parolee may not legally be able to stay there. Many of these individuals stay in halfway houses or inpatient treatment centers for a few months, but eventually they still need to find their own residences. However, because parolees are isolated from already scarce job opportunities, for most their ability to afford their own apartment has not improved since their release. Additionally, they may be ineligible for public housing and can be legally discriminated against by private landlords based on their felon status. For parolees like Carla, their inability to find housing becomes a problem that threatens to send them back to prison. Rather than allowing her to share an apartment with another woman (falsely) identified as having a criminal record, Carla was told that she had to stay in one of Fresno's homeless shelters. However, because local shelters have no beds to offer, what this translates to in reality is a choice between staying in Tent City—a loose collection of encampments that surround the city's homeless shelters on downtown Fresno's southern fringe[6]—or being reincarcerated for violating her parole:

CARLA: OK, here's my situation. My release date is Monday, and I live in this halfway house right now and you're not allowed to be released unless you have an approved address where you're paroling to. So probation went and checked out my address, OK, well three weeks ago I didn't have an address. I didn't know where I was gonna go. So, I was gonna file papers so that I can extend my time at the halfway house so I can find a job and get a place on my own. OK, well so I filled those papers out three weeks ago. OK, well those papers still haven't, they have to go out to the central region, get signed and approved, and come back for them to allow me to stay longer after Monday. OK, well those papers are out supposedly doing their thing. In the meantime I found an address. Probation went to the address, approved the address, did a background check on the girl who I'm moving in with, my roommate, and they're saying she has a warrant out of Kern County for fraud. So they're not gonna let me move there, but we know for a fact that it's not her that has that warrant because this girl works for the IRS. She's approved to visit men in prison. You can't go visit anybody in prison if you have any criminal [warrant]. She's been approved to foster children. So they're trying to work that out with her. But today's Friday. I'm supposed to be out on Monday. So, when Monday comes, I have to leave that halfway house because my roll-over papers haven't come back to extend my time, and since my address hasn't been approved they're gonna kick me out and force me to go to Tent City, which is where they put tents all on the side of the road. And that's where they're saying that I *have* to parole to because I don't have an approved address.

AUTHOR: I didn't know they could parole people to Tent City.

C: That's where they're saying, they're *forcing* me to check into the homeless shelter, Tent City. And so that's what we were talking about. It's not cool, it's not fair, it's a setup for failure. What am I gonna do? We're trying to figure out other options, but if my probation officer is telling me that I have to go to Tent City, if

I'm not there I violate. And I'm not gonna go there, I'm not
gonna go pitch up a tent on the side of [the road]. I'm not, I'm
not gonna do it. I'm not, you know? So I was telling them in
there, so what, should I go out today and get drunk and go back
to the program and do my breathalyzer and blow numbers, so
that they'll take away thirty days of my good time so that I *have*
to stay here thirty more days? You know? So they're forcing me
to be homeless, or they're gonna force me to do something I
don't wanna do to get in trouble so that I have somewhere to
stay. But I'm trying not to go that route. I'm not gonna go that
route, I'm just gonna leave it with God and see what happens.

A: Damn, that's crazy!

C: That's the system. That's the system.

As a condition of her parole, Carla needs an address where she can be
contacted and visited or she will be locked up again, and if she cannot find
one she has to stay at one of the city's homeless shelters. However, these
shelters are chronically overcrowded, meaning that "staying there" would
actually mean living in one of the neighboring encampments. As someone
in recovery from substance abuse, Carla sees staying in the encampment as
a setup for relapse—she can either stay somewhere where drug use is ram-
pant and she is likely to use again, or she can get drunk on her last day in
the halfway house in order to violate her parole, delay her release, and keep
a warm bed.

Local resources for parolees in Fresno are sparse and in constant flux
because they are dependent on unsecure and inconsistent grant-based
funding that must continually be sought out and renewed.[7] This vulnerability leaves many parolees conscious of the constant looming possibility of
being sent back to prison or jail, and therefore of the need to retain affiliations that they relied on while incarcerated. For example, when I met one
resident named David to interview him about his experiences with incarceration, he spent several minutes closely inspecting his consent form
because he was concerned that it might have some language in it claiming
that he was renouncing his ties to the Bulldogs. When I asked him about
this, David explained that he has been through county jail forty-seven
times in his life, and therefore he was naturally wary of the possibility of
returning yet again. If he ever went back having "dropped out" from his
Bulldogs affiliation, it would be all bad for him because it would indicate to
others that he had incriminated somebody else.[8] Consequently, even
though he was no longer in custody, it remained important to keep his
claim to this identity intact:

DAVID: I'm still active but I'm just gonna change my ways and just walk away from everything. Cuz there's somebody else out there that can do it. I'm good. You know, somebody else can do that, live that lifestyle. I don't need to live that lifestyle anymore.

AUTHOR: You mentioned that you still wanted to be, that you were still active. Why is that important for you, to still have that?

D: Because that can, that could seriously involve situations in my life. As far as like me, I'm saying just harmful situations . . . Fresno County Jail already knows who I am. I've been to jail almost forty-seven times since I was eighteen. Forty-seven times when I was [going] in there, they would always ask me "You still wanna go status as a Bulldog?" You know what I mean, so yeah, all the time. But if I was to drop out and say something went down, they'd send me to a protection unit, you know what I mean? And if I go to prison it'll be all bad.

A: You would get hurt if that was the case?

D: Yeah, yeah. So therefore I decided to just, it's better for me to just step up and change my life and get out of the certain area where I live and stuff, hanging out with certain people. And check myself into this program and get help, you know what I mean? For my meth addiction but also for my alcohol and learn to better myself and get closer to God.

David explains that it would be dangerous for him to drop his Bulldog affiliation, but this should not be taken as an indication that he doesn't want to change his life. Rather, the precarious nature of his freedom forces him to hold on to this identity even while trying to redirect his life. But also noteworthy in David's explanation is that he sees getting out of his neighborhood (and therefore out of this carceral continuum) as necessary for staying sober and out of the justice system. His perception of addiction and arrest as inevitable within this residential space reveals how closely crime is commonly associated with his neighborhood, which says something important about the relationship his community has with the penal system; the criminal status attached to (and in some cases even internalized by) those living here makes an imprisonable status part of community life. David's neighborhood is not simply a place where more crime happens, but within a neoliberal state that relies on mass incarceration to sustain itself (Waquant 2009; Gilmore 2007)[9] it is one of the poor communities designated for imprisonment. Staying out of trouble for David is not just a matter of staying out of jail or prison, but of leaving the neighborhood that sends one into these facilities and escaping the continuum entirely.

The lack of resources available for reentering parolees pushed many parolees to turn to the same bonds they relied on while incarcerated. In Fresno many of the parolees felt that their prison-based peer networks helped them get resituated, particularly because there were so few forms of support available for prisoner reentry. James, a forty-seven-year-old White parolee, stayed in contact with some of the people he met while incarcerated, and they periodically asked him if he needed anything to help him get "back on his feet." Through his contacts in the Wood Pile (the White car) James was put in touch with someone who could give him some work boots when he really needed them, and learned about a lawyer in Fresno that would help him should he get in trouble again: "They told me when I got out, 'James, you get in trouble again, you go down and see this guy in Fresno, downtown Fresno. He's a Red & White (Hell's Angel). You tell him you're part of the Wood Pile.' See now these are things that I, not that I need to know, [but] I don't want any more public defenders! I definitely don't want a public defender. So if I ever get in trouble again, I'll call this guy here in Fresno."

It was difficult for parolees to shed their affiliations once they were released from custody, as this was one of the few resources they had access to when they returned to the neighborhood. This assistance could reinforce one's ties to an affiliation, but now that he was out of the prison James was actually trying to wean himself off of this assistance because he saw it as something that might get him caught up again or expose him to further criminalization. But this distancing was something easier for James than for parolees of color, as the experiences of criminalized Latina/os give their affiliations meaning outside the prison in ways that do not exist for Whites. The important difference is that Latina/os' carceral affiliations are ascribed as gang labels; even if residents wish to distance themselves from affiliations, they may still be recognized by rivals and jumped, or seen as gang associated by police. And as we can see with David, constructing these identities as gang ties also makes residents more reluctant to renounce them, because if they do then they are marked as police informants. Finally, it is essential for us to consider how concentrated incarceration also makes affiliations hard for community members to avoid. The presence of so many parolees in one space means that there are many people in one's neighborhood a parolee can get in trouble for merely being around, as released inmates can violate their parole by having contact with other parolees or with anyone validated as a gang member or associate. Many of the people parolees know in their neighborhoods or even in their families have also been marked by or involved in the criminal justice system, so when parolees come back home they are often already surrounded by other parolees and/ or recognized "gang members."

Although parolees' peer networks were one of their only resources on the outs, these networks were also criminalized and used to legitimize reincarcerating them. Relying on one's carceral affiliation could strengthen one's identification with it outside of the prison, but also increases one's chances of being arrested and sent back. Instead, parolees were expected to divorce themselves from their peer networks. But this expectation was unrealistic for poor people who as ex-cons were now even further removed from the connections or financial stability needed to reintegrate back into their communities. Some parolees were therefore forced to choose between violating parole for accepting help from their peers, or violating parole for failing to satisfy their conditions without it. These violations keep people trapped in the corrections system far longer than the extent of their original criminal sentence, and parolees with one or two felony convictions may be in and out of prison on parole violations for ten, fifteen, or even twenty years.[10]

## RACE, CLASS, NEIGHBORHOOD, AND THE STATE OF BEING IMPRISONABLE

The prison's socializing power extends into the neighborhood through a coupling of secondary prisonization with the reproduction of the carceral social order in juvenile facilities. Here, local youth learn the same identities, narratives, and social order institutionalized in the prison through the experiences of their loved ones and their own experiences with juvenile probation. At the same time, a lack of structural support and the ubiquity of antigang policing prolong returning parolees' reliance on criminalized peer networks after their release, making it difficult to leave their affiliations to prison cars behind. Within the resulting continuum established between prison and community (Wacquant 2001), residents are persistently subject to surveillance and punishment, and affiliations subsequently offer residents a means of managing punitive contexts that increasingly span both settings.

However, it is crucial to recognize that this extended socialization also marks residents as *imprisonable*, ascribing this status by framing particular intersections of race, class, and neighborhood as pathological communities that require social control. The association of specific communities with prison-based affiliations reinforces a perception of poor Black and Latina/o neighborhoods as the appropriate targets of imprisonment by defining local problems as the result of gang youth, violence, or deviant families. As Bulldog or Norteño affiliations become visible in residential spaces, it becomes easier to characterize the troubles in residents' lives as the result of their ties to criminal peers or identities, and not the political disenfranchisement, residential segregation, educational inequality, overpolicing, labor exploitation, poverty, and unemployment that shape life in the neighborhood. This framing serves as an ideological justification for how the state distributes its resources within a post-Keynesian political economy, one in which the prison and a delegitimized welfare state are necessary to buttress neoliberal capitalism (Gilmore 2007). Simply put, this spillover of carceral affiliation works to rationalize the mass imprisonment of poor communities of color by identifying community members as criminal, gang-involved threats who need to be contained.

This imprisonable status comes to contextualize how young people interpret their own experiences as members of criminalized communities. Many SJEA students associate their race and class positions with the social problems they experience in their neighborhoods and home lives, incarceration among them. For example, like many of the other girls here, Daniela has repeatedly been arrested and incarcerated after trying to intervene in domestic disputes between her parents. One day while working in small-group tutoring with me and Cameron, another student, she tells us about her most recent incident at home: following an argument between her mom and stepdad, her mom became hysterical and announced that she was going to throw herself out of their apartment window. When she started to climb out the window Daniela pulled her back in, only for her mom to then turn on her and accuse Daniela of hurting her. After telling her story, Daniela vents her frustrations: "She doesn't know how to be a mother." She sighs while shaking her head, staring down at the table. "Sometimes I wish I wasn't Mexican."

I'm stunned for a moment by how sad this sounds, then simply ask "Why?"

"Cuz Mexican moms are crazy!"

Cameron nods and responds with a seriousness uncharacteristic of his typically playful demeanor: "I used to think the same thing about being Black. But it is what it is, you just gotta make it work. No sense in being mad over that, cuz you can't change it."

Daniela and Cameron associate "being Mexican" and "being Black" with suffering through chaotic and painful home lives. And while their respective racial backgrounds have not caused the domestic instability they have experienced, the rigid residential segregation in Fresno has so limited their viewpoint that the only people they likely ever see dealing with these problems are Black or Mexican. Additionally, in Daniela's case "being Mexican" has also meant that these incidents have resulted in her incarceration, which is more likely for poor women and girls of color (Flores 2016). This isolation and criminalization not only characterize problems like domestic violence as products of Black and Latina/o deviance, but also reinforce a pathological view of these communities that legitimizes their carceral status. Even Daniela and Cameron internalize the assumption that their communities' residents are not incarcerated because they are the victims of structural racism, but because their racial backgrounds predispose them to being "crazy."

Some students saw the intersections of race, class, and geography that they occupied as tied to eventual incarceration. While most youth did not see incarceration as inevitable, they understood the prison as a real possibility that they had to be ready for, because they had seen it affect so many people around them. In this sense incarceration was understood as part of the consequence of being from their family and their neighborhood. Fifteen-year-old Manny, for example, explains that "everyone gets locked up at least once in a while," a perspective shaped by his experiences growing up in Fresno's Eastside. In his interview Manny explains that he identifies as a Bulldog gang member, a collective identity born in the prison conflicts of the 1980s. But unlike popular understandings of gang initiation in which one is violently jumped in, Manny, like many of the interview participants in this research, explains that he was "born into" being a Bulldog because it has always been so prevalent in his family and in his community. Here he describes this identity as something that he never really wanted, but rather as something he has had to accept because of who he is and where he is from:

> [With] a lot of people, I don't know, if they *could* choose, I think would rather just be like normal people you know? But it just depends on how you grow up and shit. Like if I could choose, I'd be somewhere else. I wouldn't even be in Fresno. I'd just be like a normal person. Wear normal clothes and everything you know. It's just a different way you grow up you know? A lot of people don't want it, it's just what happens. Just the way you get taught and shit. So like, I don't know, that's pretty much it.

Manny describes being a Bulldog as something he never really chose to do, or that anyone *can* choose to do, and feels that if given a choice most would opt for a different kind of life. Additionally, he frames being a Bulldog as inescapably tied to where one grows up and what one learns from their surrounding community, prompting his desire to "be somewhere else." A few minutes later I ask him more about how he imagines being somewhere else, and Manny describes an idyllic life free from the traumas he associates with his own community:

AUTHOR: You said if you could choose, you'd be like a normal person, like wear normal clothes and stuff like that?

MANNY: I'd be like those people who don't have any problems, you know? They don't have to worry about getting stabbed or shot or shit like that. They just go home and just have normal parents and shit. Normal house and shit like that. But it doesn't matter though, you just used to what you got.

Manny's wish to be somewhere else is not just a desire to occupy a new place, but to embody the improved social position that comes with it: he dreams of being a "normal person" experiencing a middle-class adolescence free from violence. He recognizes the privilege of other communities whose residents "don't have any problems" like those present in Eastside Fresno. But instead of enjoying a carefree life in a neighborhood where young people are safe and get to wear "normal clothes," Manny understands that he lives in a criminalized Mexican community that turns people into Bulldogs. This is how Manny experiences the carceral subjectivity of his community—he estimates he has seen ten to fifteen of his uncles, homies, and "just people from the neighborhood" sent to prison in his young life (along with approximately twenty of his teenaged peers sent to juvenile hall), which has sadly made his Bulldog affiliation an important learned resource.

In describing the fallout of state disinvestment in marginalized communities, Avery Gordon explains that "[w]hen the State abandons you, it never lets you out of its sight" (2007: 143). As state support for education, housing, employment, and public welfare have been withdrawn, the residents of communities most affected by these changes have increasingly become the subjects of intensified policing and the targets of mass incarceration. The affiliations institutionalized in the prison emerge as survival strategies for migrating between these two poles. Both returning parolees and young people coming of age in a system that criminalizes them learn to manage the raced and classed carceral subjectivity of their neighborhoods through affiliations. But these affiliations are also in their very origins a state-constructed criminal status, and as such perform the same work in the community of marking individuals as criminal that they do in the prison. Consistent with inside the prison, affiliations are regarded by law enforcement as ties to criminal gangs, and consequently used as criminal evidence facilitating the incarceration (and reincarceration) of neighborhood residents, perpetuating mass incarceration.

# 5. Carceral Violence Inside and On the Outs

When I get to fourth period to try to pull Ben out with the rest of my usual group, his teacher won't let me because she says he's about to be suspended. Standing in front of her desk smirking, he turns to me and says "It's cuz I said 'fuck.'"

She hands him a slip that he has to take to the main office. "You can talk to the person who cooks you dinner like that, but you won't speak to me like that."

On the way out of the room Ben shouts back, "I cook my own dinner!" I sign out a few of my other regular students and take them to one of the cafeteria tables. Once outside the classroom Anthony starts snickering and tells me that Ben said "Fuck you" to the teacher and "told her to suck his dick." Anthony laughs and shakes his head, "Stupid." Juan is sitting with his arms crossed, clearly less amused. I ask him what happened, and he just shrugs. But Anthony elaborates, explaining that someone in class hit Ben up right before this happened because he thought Ben had crossed out a tag he had painted: "He said he didn't do it, 'Then why'd I see your name there?' 'I don't know.' 'Well if that shit happens again you're gonna have to catch that fade.'" This challenge to fight from a boy much bigger and stronger than Ben contextualizes his outburst—one that seemingly comes out of nowhere and that he knows is guaranteed to get him kicked out of class. He certainly does not like his teacher, but his main objective here is to simply get out of the room and away from an impending threat to his safety.

When I come back the next week Ben's suspension is over, but he is absent from school again. When I pull the other boys out they start talking in urgent, concerned voices. As soon as we settle at a table Edgar sheepishly asks Juan, "Was his face all messed up?"

"Naw, it was just kinda red but it wasn't too bad."

"That's fucked up though. He shoulda hit him back."

"He was sitting down, he couldn't really."

"I even told my aunt, 'They're trying to jump my boy, let's go get him!' But we went to the bus stop and there wasn't no one there."

I ask, "Who got jumped?" and Juan points to end of table where Ben usually sits.

"Ben. Someone got him on the bus after school. He wanted to fight him but Ben wasn't gonna, so he just jumped him. Just snaked (sucker-punched) him. He was just sitting on the bus and couldn't even get his hands up or anything. It was kinda messed up."

"Why'd he snake him?"

"Cuz he was trying to fight him after school but it was a big scene and all the POs were there."

"But why'd he want to fight him in the first place?"

"Cuz someone's been crossing his name out and writing [Ben's] name next to it, to make it look like he did it. But you can tell it's not his."

Ramon agrees, "That shit doesn't even look right, it's all sloppy like . . ." He writes the name out quickly to try to make it look sloppy. "Even that's better."

I turn back to Juan. "So they set him up?"

Juan nods soberly. "That's what they did."

We start reading the text for the assignment they have today, but after a few minutes Edgar leans over to Juan and quietly asks, "I'm trying to think, who would write [Ben's] name in like that? That fool would cross out WFN [West Fresno Norteños] huh? Would he put his name [next to the crossed out tag]?"

"Naw he'd just put ESF [East Side Fresno]."

The boys never figure out what exactly led up to Ben's attack. When he returns to campus the next day with a black eye, the school's staff do not learn what caused his visible injuries either, and consequently do little to respond to the assault. His assailant, a White boy who mostly hangs with the Twamp students from the Westside, is never reprimanded for the attack and goes on to threaten other students at San Joaquin Educational Academy (SJEA) as well. It is certainly conceivable that Ben refused to answer if asked who attacked him, but it is also hard to not think that a lack of concern or sympathy also plays a part; many members of the staff see Ben as a pain in the ass, and taggers more generally as a public nuisance, such that when one security guard notices Ben's injury he tells me, "Hopefully it was a business owner." With the staff unresponsive to his victimization,

Ben opts to simply walk the three miles home each day rather than take the bus again. The institution cannot or will not keep him safe, narrowing Ben's options to avoiding threats however he can and relying on his friends' support when he can't.

Many of the people who navigate SJEA, Fresno's Juvenile Detention Facility (JDF), or state prison facilities are at some point confronted by others in the institution for being positioned with one group or another, and oftentimes these can result in physical assaults. In these instances, the carceral social order's influence in shaping people's experiences with violence is clear, but in the buildup and fallout of Ben getting jumped, we can see a more complicated relationship, one that weaves itself into personal feuds. Because it determines both one's peers and one's rivals, this system can shape who becomes involved in an individual's disputes. This prevailing social order informs how people make meaning of the threats they navigate in unpredictable spaces, as well as the decisions they make about engaging or avoiding the fight. Ben's friends are invested in what happens to him, and presume that Norteña/os are somehow responsible when he is attacked for something he didn't do. The boys have repeatedly backed one another up when they've anticipated such an attack, but when the threat first emerges in class, Ben acts out so as to evade the threat while still maintaining a defiant masculine performance, ultimately adding to the list of infractions that lead to his next court date.

In this chapter I explore how the carceral social order structures Central Valley residents' exposure to violence, both inside the punitive facility and back home in the neighborhood. Inside the institution it discourages individual fights between racial cars or neighborhood gang rivals. However, it also structures when violence is expected, and teaches and pressures institutionalized residents to use violence to enforce this system and its boundaries. Back in the neighborhood, the conflicts that the penal sorting process structures between racialized groups spill over into the city, and inmates' personal disputes are reproduced and extended back into their home communities. But it also becomes a framework for understanding the threats of physical violence that young people encounter or anticipate in their neighborhoods, and for learning how to manage these threats. Finally, I conclude this chapter by considering how the carceral social order also brings structural and legal violence into the community in the forms of marginalization and legitimized police violence.

## THE RULES OF INSTITUTIONAL VIOLENCE

Sorting practices rationalized as preventing penal violence instead structure its use. The identities and relationships constructed by this process and the subsequent segregation comprise the carceral social order, and this resulting system in turn socializes corresponding expectations concerning violence in the institution. These norms simultaneously restrict some forms of violence in order to defer to group management and stability, while at the same time relying on violence to ensure that group boundaries are recognized and implemented. These expectations ultimately function to bolster the carceral social order as a dominant logic among the institutional population by reinforcing the primacy of the identities created in the sorting process. Fears that individuals will be isolated from the groups they see as their only protection teach them to use violence to force the institution to maintain this system. But this ultimately enforces the divisions that the institution itself establishes and enacts, while confirming administrative perceptions that racialized violence is inevitable and that this type of social control is necessary to control the incarcerated.

## Restricting Violence

One of the interesting contradictions of the carceral social order is that its implementation within the facility institutionalizes racial conflict, distrust of other groups, and the expectation to participate in specific forms of violence, while at the same time regularly discouraging individuals from fighting with other prisoners across racial lines. In state men's facilities, prisoners who have a problem with someone else in another racial group are discouraged from simply fighting it out individually because this will create a brawl that the rest of the car is then obligated to jump into. Instead, inmates are taught to go through informal leadership channels (aka the "rep" for their racial group) so that disputes can be diplomatically addressed without exposing the rest of the car to unnecessary violence.

Ignoring this protocol could lead to discipline from the car, or worse could cause a "wreck" for the car—a larger conflict that draws the whole car into a fight or riot. Avoiding this kind of conflict was a common goal for all of the cars, and consequently each of them followed similar guidelines about starting fights with those outside the car—all of the parolees described being conscious that they could not go into another car's space or disrespect someone from another race, because this could start a race riot. Some of the parolees described learning about these rules when they unknowingly broke one of them, and someone had to explain to them what they did wrong. For example, when James, a White parolee, was first incarcerated in county jail, he got into an argument with a Latino inmate. He began yelling at him through his cell door until another White inmate pulled him aside and corrected him, explaining the rules of the racial order that he was now a part of: "I got mad at a race, a Hispanic race. And the Wood Pile, my rep in there, said 'Hey, you can't do that man, you can't yell at people like that, you know? Even yelling at someone behind the door, you can't do that.' He said, 'You're a Peckerwood, you just can't go yell at another race like that and go off on them. You have to ask me first, and I'll tell you what's going on.' So yeah, I learned, I learned quite a bit in the three months I was there." James was not supposed to yell at this other prisoner because starting a fight with this person could create a larger conflict that could pull both races into fighting each other, causing a wreck for the car.

Informal rules restricting people from fighting with someone in another car then function to control instances of interracial violence in the institution,[1] something sociologist Michael Walker also found in his ethnography of a Southern California county jail system (2016). Consequently, the violence that prisoners do encounter is actually more likely to come from inside the car rather than from those they are taught to fear outside of it. Here Eli, a forty-four-year-old Black parolee from Fresno's Westside, describes fearing the violence he saw when he came to prison, and feeling that dangers he had to protect himself from would come from the other inmates in his own car:

> ELI: [I was] thinking "Man, cat gonna probably try to rape me. I gotta make a shank, I gotta get ready." You know, and I had me one. You know when I first got in there, I had to have one cuz I didn't know what was gonna happen.
>
> AUTHOR: Were you more worried about getting attacked from other races or from other Blacks?
>
> E: Other Blacks.
>
> A: Other Blacks?
>
> E: Yeah. Other races, it wasn't going down. They can't, they wouldn't be able to do it, you know? It would have to [be] your own race that'll do it. They wouldn't cross races and try to do nothing, it'll be a riot up in there.

Eli is far more concerned with facing assault from someone within his own racial group than from another car. Indeed, despite the racial animosity institutionalized within the prison's segregated environment, one is more likely to be attacked by a member of their own race than by someone from another (Trulson and Marquart 2002). Within the car some inmates may bully others, personal disputes may come to blows, and violence may be used by leaders as a means of discipline or to ensure control of the group.

Neighborhood gangs, however, are expected to suspend their conflicts while imprisoned for the sake of ensuring the stability of the car. The division of institutional populations into affiliations within juvenile justice facilities similarly restricted or controlled violence between rival gangs within the same affiliated groups. While in the punitive institution, neighborhood gangs are expected to suspend their rivalries and defer to unifying their shared affiliation. At SJEA, students were in school during the day and returned home each afternoon, creating an interesting pattern in which members of rival gangs would be cool with each other during the day (so long as they were both Bulldogs, for example), then fight each other to satisfy their obligations to local beefs after school was dismissed.

Mario finds himself caught in this shifting conflict status one afternoon, then has the added misfortune of me asking him about it the next morning. He is unusually quiet when he comes out of class, and the black eye stands out to me right away. "What'd you get in a fight about?" I ask, pointing to my own eye to reference his injury.

Mario look down. "Oh, I dunno," he says unconvincingly.

He's trying to avoid talking about it, but I can't stop myself from chuckling at his response. "What, you don't remember?"

Ben watches with a sly smile, shifting his narrowed eyes over to me. "It's complicated, to the eye of the untrained nigga." He kind of sounds like he's in a bad kung-fu movie, although his point is that it might be hard to understand for someone unused to the expectations surrounding fighting here.

Mario sighs. "I dunno, it was just funk I guess." He pauses for a moment, then his frustration pushes him to vent. "That fool's not with it though, cuz he said we had funk but I know other fools from there that say they don't funk with us no more. But just the fact he called me out . . ." He trails off with a shrug, implying that even if he didn't agree with the fight, he had to go through with it if nothing else because someone challenged him. He goes on to explain that his fight was with a classmate from another Bulldog set, who Mario argues was falsely informed that their cliques were feuding.

I ask him more questions. "Did you run into him somewhere?"

"Naw, I already knew him from before."

"How did it start?"

"Well he came here and I was like, 'What's up, you still tag?,' and he's like, 'Naw, I got put on Calaveras,[2] where you from?' and I was like, 'Alright cool, I'm from Belmont.' and he's like, 'Ohh, I think you might be funk,' and I'm like, 'I don't think so. That was from a long time ago, I don't think we funk it anymore. I know a lot of folks from Calaveras, in fact I just met one the other day.' and he was just like, 'Well, lemme ask the older homie what's up.' and I was just like, 'Alright then.' Then I was gone for like two weeks on suspensions and stuff, and when I came back he came up to me and was like, 'Yeah, I checked, you are funk.' so I was just like (Mario shrugs his shoulders again), 'Alright, catch it after school, I guess.'"

Mario and this other boy already knew each other from the Eastside as friendly acquaintances, only to find out that they had joined rival gangs. However, this occasion was the only time they fought over it, as if it was a formality that they had to get out of the way so they could say that they addressed it. It never came up as an issue between them again, and they both kept hanging out with each other every day at school just fine. Waiting until after school to fight helps them avoid getting into trouble, but the fact that they do this while still amicably socializing with each other during the school day also accomplishes something else: it maintains a stable affiliated group within the institution. It demonstrates how so long as one is in the facility—on campus and during school hours—the affiliation is prioritized and neighborhood gang feuds are put on hold. They may be tended to once back in the neighborhood, but while inside, this type of violence is suspended within the carceral social order.

## Demanding Violence

Much of the violence that does take place inside is predicated on fear. This fear is established as one enters the institution and is told by staff that other racial groups represent dangers to them and that they need to stick with their own. But it also comes long before that, in the lessons one receives from previously incarcerated peers and relatives. The anticipation of facing physical or sexual assault prepares those entering the institution to then strike first, actually using the violence they fear to protect themselves against those they learn to recognize as enemies.

The process of socializing this expectation of violence extends across facilities, both in the institutional replication of sorting practices as well as in the lessons by which inmates teach each other how to do their time. As Vincent recalls his experiences facing incarceration for the first time, he remembers imagining a violent world full of dangerous rivals in which he would immediately need to fight back a slew of attacks. But this expectation is largely contextualized by what he has heard from older brothers, who have been through both the California Youth Authority (YA) and state prison:

VINCENT:  [In YA] you have to go to the receiving center first for like two
          months. You're basically in booking for months. I don't know

why, but you gotta be there for a couple months. That's where it gets popping in there.

AUTHOR: Like, fights go off in there?

V: Yeah, because it's usually everybody's first time going up there and they don't know nothing. They're just like, fuck, they just gotta start taking flight on anybody. My homies tell me it gets hella crazy in there. Like, for a Bulldog to go, they said it's hard. Like, you're just like fuck, you get rushed every single day. You can't go a day without getting rushed. Like, you go to lockdown for fighting. And you come back and you will fight again. Right when you go on mainline, someone goes, "What's up, where you're from?" "Fresno." "You a Bulldog?" Pow. What the fuck? That shit's all bad. That's straight up YA. Fuck, it's horrible there. Basically it's worse than prison.

A: So why do people go off in booking or in reception?

V: Oh, cuz they don't know nothing yet. Most of them don't know yet. They don't know how it's gonna be or nothing, so if somebody's tripping, they'll start fighting, you know cuz they have to. They gotta show that they're hard. They gotta show that they're with the business, they can't fucking be looked down on. They gotta show that they're up there. So when they go to regular pod, they'll just be like, "Yeah, that fool got down. They got hands." And a lot of people that don't bang and fight, they got *manos*, or hands, they'll recruit them most of the time.

A: Oh yeah. There's a lot of recruitment in YA?

V: Mmmhmm, a lot of recruiting, Mostly Norteños. Most of the time, you go to YA and you don't bang, you're gonna be a Norteño. Cuz they're the majority there.

Through his brothers' experiences Vincent learns that when entering the carceral facility, one needs to fight almost right away. Consistent with Anderson's "code of the streets" (2000), Vincent sees "taking flight" on anyone who challenges him as essential for developing a reputation that will keep him safe over the course of his confinement, and for gaining the respect and support of other youth in the pod. Ultimately, what he hears of his brothers' experiences in the prison shapes how he approaches his own incarceration at JDF:

P: Did you think you would have any problems going in [to JDF]?

VINCENT: I thought like, right when you walk in, the way my brothers told me about prison? I thought it was like juvenile hall. So when I

walked in, [I thought] I had to like, fight everybody and
anybody, but it wasn't really like that when I got in. . . . Ever
since I remember too, I remember some people telling me too,
yeah, locked up, you gotta fight anybody that says one word or
something like that. I'm just like, damn, so when I got in
juvenile hall, I was like, somebody says one little thing wrong, I
could just start fighting them cause if they're gonna start hitting
me first, I'm not gonna let that happen.

The violence that Vincent anticipates in JDF is informed by what he has
learned about carceral facilities—that as someone from Fresno he will be
challenged and assaulted immediately and regularly, so he needs to be
ready to hit anyone he suspects may be a source of such attacks. He illustrates how early lessons that span across institutions and generations teach
criminalized youth that it is crucial to stay within the parameters of the
carceral social order—that affiliations are important because rival groups
are always waiting to attack. But these lessons essentially repeat what correctional staff tell incoming prison inmates,[3] and are very much based in
how people learn to make sense of a dangerous place in which they are told
they are segregated for their own protection. Vincent fully expects to be
attacked by Norteños and Sureños in reception precisely because he is from
Fresno, and describes how even many of the boys who aren't gang members
will likely become affiliated with these enemies in short time. Organizing
the institution around the sorting process fundamentally frames prisoners
from other regions or racial groups as irreconcilable enemies (Robertson
2006), precipitating the expectation of those coming in to face violence and
to need to use it themselves. As one's time in the facility grows, the constant and ongoing fear of violence oftentimes prompts one to use violence
to ensure separation from their rivals, consequently maintaining the prevailing social order.

The policing of physical space at the school institutionalized the presumed threat that rival groups represented to students' personal safety, and
thus structured violence between students. Fights on campus were rare and
most students avoided fighting altogether, but when they did happen they
were often over the spatial boundaries that the school itself established. In
these cases, students fought to enforce these boundaries because they feared
their safety was at risk if a rival group imposed on their designated space.
They understood that if students associated with a rival group infringed on
their space, it was because they were planning to assault them. Assuming
this, if students wished to protect themselves and their friends, then they

had to enforce these boundaries to keep dangerous rivals away, and strike first if and when such enemies did cross into their space.

At SJEA, the ongoing struggles over access to shade during the summer months highlighted this logic concerning spatial boundaries. After moving the tables away from the trees back in April, the school's probation staff keeps the students at their tables in the sun for the next several months, shooing them away anytime they try to linger in the shade. However, as summer wears on it simply becomes too hot for everyone to stay outside for any length of time, and the staff decide to keep students inside during lunch and break times in a large, similarly divided multipurpose room. By August the staff begins to feel that keeping the students indoors all day makes them more restless in class and move them back outside, this time clustering the tables under two shaded canopies built of white mesh fabric and PVC piping. These seem to settle the problem for the next several weeks, until one of the canopies is destroyed in a wind storm. After this happens most of the students gradually begin to crowd under the one remaining canopy during lunch, and over the next several days the boundaries between groups begin to blur and some of the Bulldogs grow increasingly tense as rival Sureños begin to sit at their tables.

Later in the week, just as I am coming outside to observe the students' lunch break I hear one of the officers yelling "Code 3!!"[4] and see security guards quickly swarm one of the center tables. Several students back away from the source of the commotion and reveal the two security guards kneeling on the ground with their backs to each other, each pinning a boy to the ground while handcuffing him. They lift the students to their feet and bring them inside—first a short Sureño boy relatively new to the school and then Greg, a young Bulldog student I had seen around but just recently gotten to know. After a couple minutes I follow them inside and find Greg sitting outside the principal's office with his hands still cuffed behind his back. While Greg waits for the probation officers to process the other student's statement for an incident report, a school counselor scolds him for fighting and begs him to explain why he would act so irrationally about where another student sat. Still upset, Greg tries to explain but quickly gives up when she doesn't understand:

GREG: I mean he sat right next to me! He knows he's not supposed to be there! He should have known better.
COUNSELOR: All this over a seat! Would you have done that if I sat next to you, or if he (pointing at me) sat next to you?
G: No, but he's a Sureño!

> c: How are you gonna explain that to your parents, or to the judge?
>
> g: When you're enemies, and he sits right next to you, (agitated, stops to try to think of the words to explain, but can't) he knows!
>
> c: [The] judge isn't gonna give a shit about that! You're gonna tell him you fought just cuz he sat down??
>
> g: It wasn't cuz he sat, it was cuz of what he said when he sat down. That shit just pissed me off.
>
> c: What'd he say?
>
> g: Just talking shit.
>
> c: So what'd he say?? Enlighten me!
>
> g: Just talking shit.

Greg tries to explain to the counselor (and later to myriad other school and probation officials) why he started the fight, but they simply cannot understand why he would get himself into so much trouble over a Sureño sitting next to him. The irony in this is that many of the authority figures who are so puzzled by Greg's actions are some of the same institutional figures who invest so much energy into structuring the very division that he took upon himself to enforce. SJEA institutionalizes a social order in which such proximity is unacceptable because of the potential for violence, but disapproves when students react to this same perceived risk. After the counselor leaves I keep talking with Greg, and he explains how the fight was not simply about a rival trespassing into the Bulldogs' space or even saying anything disrespectful, but about the threat of impending violence implied in these actions:

> AUTHOR: So what was he saying when he sat down?
>
> GREG: Just talkin' shit. Like, it was basically he move or I move. (Greg looks over shoulder to see if any of the staff members are still around before continuing in a lowered voice.[5]) He called me a mutt. And like, if I'm a Bulldog and he's a scrap, and he comes over and sits right next to me, he's trying to start shit. I'll tell you what happened. You know how there used to be two shade areas and now there's just one and it's over on the Bulldog side? Well now those fools are thinking that they can come over and make all these guys all tense. So I was just sitting down on the end where I usually sit, I had just gotten my chips, and this fool came and sat right next to me and started talkin' shit. So I told him to move and he's like, "Fuck you, you move," and then [his

friend] came and sat there too, so I'm thinking all his friends are gonna come sit over here. Like, they're just gonna act like it's theirs. So I told him two more times and then I stood up kinda pissed off, like, damn this fool's not gonna move, and it's gonna look all bad on me, like, if I just walk away.

A: So it would've been worse for you if you didn't do anything?

G: Oh yeah. If I came back and they were like, "You're a lil bitch, you're a dropout," that'd be bad. Even as I was fighting him, all the Bulldogs were like (Greg starts nodding approvingly), "Alright." It's not good or bad, it's just how it is. I know it sounds stupid but that's just the way it is. I understand [I should be] keeping myself out of those situations, but he sat right there! There was nothing more I could do. It's not even like, "Oh, this is our side" or whatever. We just didn't want them getting too close to us, cuz if they're getting close then they could try to fight, you know? Like, when they first moved over there it was when there were only a few of us, so we thought, "Oh, they're getting a lil braver. They think there aren't that many of us, so they think they can like push us a lil bit." You understand what I'm talking about, right? Cuz everyone else here acts like they don't know what I mean, like, "Oh, you're just being stupid."

A: Yeah, yeah, I know what you mean.

G: And did you see? When [security] called their side to the bathroom, they were waiting for our side to go until the POs were like, "No you guys go too," cuz they knew something would've gone down in there. They all went when they called them but they were trying to wait for us! So then we started making sure there were like, two or three guys sitting at each table so they wouldn't try anything, cuz if there's just like one table between you, something bad's gonna happen. It should be like, I'm gonna sit on this end as far from you as I can get, and you sit way over there as far as you can sit away from me. I mean what people don't get is that it's been like that since before I got here, since before I was even born. It goes way back, you know.

A: Yeah, I noticed they started sitting over there last week, but yesterday they weren't over there and instead of all the Bulldogs being on the far two tables they were kinda spread out.

G: (Starts laughing) Yep! Yep! You know what I mean?! That's why we made sure we had like two or three guys at each table. That's why I was sitting [where I was], but then he sat right next to me and then [his friend] sat across [from us], so I thought all his friends were gonna come sit right there. I got up and went to get my stuff and then I saw [all the Bulldogs] there, and I was like, "Aww, shit." I sat back down and I was like, "Dog, you need to move," and he was all, "Fuck you, mutt, I ain't moving," so then I stood back up and went off on him. I mean, I really didn't want to do it, you know? But I mean, what're you gonna do when you have a whole table of your homies watching what's gonna happen next?

I argue that Greg does not see his actions as attempts to prove his toughness or defend turf to impress the gang, but as an effort to confront and stop the threat the Sureños' spatial encroachment represented to the safety of the rest of his group. Greg sees the Sureños' gradual movement closer to the Bulldogs' tables as evidence of plans to assault him and his peers in the bathroom or on the blacktop. As a self-identified gang member, he feels particularly accountable for protecting other Bulldogs and understands that failing to meet this obligation of mutual protection would lead his peers to shun him and potentially even turn on him. Greg describes the expectation to stop this intrusion as "not good or bad, it's just how it is," conveying the extent to which the carceral social order has become an engrained common sense understanding for him of how the world works.

This understanding also gives us some insight into why he sees this situation as one in which there was nothing he could have done individually to avoid fighting. Greg interestingly equates refusing to fight—and thus not confronting the intrusion of his groups' recognized space—with being seen as a "dropout," the same term the parolees used to describe inmates in protective custody who were stigmatized for betraying or abandoning their car, suggesting that the affiliated groups at the school have the same fundamental functions and expectations associated with them as the cars in the prison. Greg finds himself in a situation that the social order he is embedded in demands he respond to, even if he is trying to stay out of trouble. As is also often the case in the prison, Greg is punished for using violence to enforce the boundaries that the school itself establishes, and the institution in turn uses this violence to justify dividing youth into opposing camps.

Residents in the punitive institution may use violence to enforce the carceral social order themselves in large part because they have learned to see the subsequent segregation as necessary, and the designation of specific spaces in the facility for each racialized group as important. Here Steven, a twenty-nine-year-old parolee who ran with the Northerners, explains that institutional sorting functioned to send inmates into units that were designated for their car, but one had to be sure they were going to the right place: "Just being from the Central Valley or Northern California, if you're not a person from Fresno or any other spot, they label you, they throw that Northern label on you, you know? But once you get that label, they shoot you to D3. If they shoot you anywhere else, [or] you don't want to [be in] D3, then you do what you gotta do to go where you belong, you know?"

When parolees felt that they were not housed with the appropriate group, they had to correct this mistake by "doing what you gotta do to go where you belong," perpetuating group separation. In these cases, inmates often used violence to force staff to transfer them into the units that they are "supposed" to be in. This was because the parolees' physical safety was directly affected by their experiences navigating a segregated system and the labels it ascribed to them. Many of them had been assaulted by their institutionally determined rivals, and only felt safe when they were isolated with their sorted group. Consequently, many resorted to violence to ensure this separation. For example, when Francisco was in Chino, another reception facility, he was vastly outnumbered by the Southsiders housed in his unit. Having been stabbed by Southerners during a previous prison term, he felt unsafe in the unit the COs placed him in. So when they sent his unit out to the yard, Francisco used it as an opportunity to assault one of the Southerners who strayed from the group. Here Francisco explains the rationale of attacking someone when he's so outnumbered:

FRANCISCO: The trouble starts when they make a mistake. Like, say if I got out of prison [and] I come back from a violation. I already know that, you know, it's been war with these guys, and [COs] so happen to call my name out (to the yard). And there's Southern Hispanics out there (pause) um, I feel threatened. I don't wanna feel threatened. I don't wanna get, you know, cuz there's so many of them, I'm not trying to [fight] all of them right? Cuz that would just get me hurt. So that'll be my opening, you know?

AUTHOR: You fight one that you can . . .

F: Yup, to attack so I won't be hurt. You know I been a victim once, I'm not gonna be a victim again. They'll put me in ad seg, then place me in the proper, in the place where I'm comfortable in. Know what I mean? So when inmates find themselves in groups where they're not supposed to be

around, they're gonna attack. You know? And hey, it's only
thirty days, sometimes it's ninety days, you know three
months inside the hole or ad seg or whatever. That's nothing
compared to you getting stabbed.

Francisco uses violence as a strategy to protect himself by changing his
housing assignment. Believing that he would eventually be attacked by
several Sureños at once if he stayed in the unit, Francisco attacked one of
them as soon as he got a chance because he knew it would get him transferred to the "appropriate" unit where he would be housed with other
Fresno Latinos. In doing this he also reinforces the prison's divisive social
order—and thus the perceived need for institutional sorting—by contributing to intergroup violence. Trapped in the rivalries of the prison, parolees
like Francisco saw segregation as the only thing protecting them from these
racialized conflicts, meaning the only way they could protect themselves
from the violence of the carceral social order was to perpetuate it.

Finally, its implementation in the institution enables some to use the
carceral social order as a tool to manipulate others and leverage violence
against one's personal foes. When Christian, a sixteen-year-old tagger from
the Northside, first comes to SJEA he doesn't know anybody at the school
except for one boy who is a personal rival he had fought with before.
Taggers from his neighborhood usually hung out with the Bulldogs, but his
rival Darren is already stationed here. Consequently, Christian stays on his
own at an empty table. Darren sees this and uses it to his advantage in their
personal vendetta, telling the other boys around him that Christian is a
Norteño. Many of these students immediately confront Christian, which
went on to characterize his experience at the school for the next several
weeks:

> Right when I started I had problems with like, a lot of people, and then
> like, a lot of people seen that I was in a fight like every day that I was
> here for like three weeks straight. Just like random people just all hating
> on me cuz I was the new guy, you know . . . [All] because uh, there's
> one guy that didn't like me. This one guy who didn't like me, but um I
> don't know, he was just talking to everybody that I was a buster. Like, a
> buster's a Norteño. He was trying to tell everybody that I was a
> Norteño and that my brother's a Norteño, and I was like, what the fuck?
> You know I'm a tagger to be honest. I'm a Northside tagger, but that's
> that. And he knows that, but he just has problems with [me], like, it's
> just between me and him.

The steady stream of challenges gradually pushes Christian closer towards
the Norteña/o table, further from the Bulldogs. He doesn't bang, but he

begins to primarily hang out with these students while at school, and eventually they offer to help him if this trouble persists. When I take Christian and a few of these students out of class for tutoring, Christian tells them this same story. A few minutes later we begin to focus on the assignments, but to the side I overhear Auggie, a Norteño gang member, talking to Christian in a hushed tone.

"Those niggas givin' you problems?"

Christian shakes his head and sighs, "Some of those dogs are trippin' . . ."

Auggie nods. "Just lemme know if those niggas givin' you problems." The ability to wield the carceral social order as a weapon against personal rivals ultimately fortifies the respective positions of those involved in the system—those targeted are pushed closer into the affiliations that may protect them, and those manipulated feel their fears of rival groups fueled and ignited.

Individuals use violence to try to protect themselves from the threats generated by the carceral social order, which ultimately works to reinforce this same system. Additionally, these clashes and confrontations also reinforce the assumption that criminalized residents NEED to be segregated and kept apart in the institution because violence will inevitably result otherwise.

## NEIGHBORHOOD PRISON VIOLENCE

The violence that unfolds inside the punitive institution is not all that is structured by the carceral social order, as the rivalries constructed by the sorting process also spill over into prisoners' home communities. Here this system shapes residents' experiences with neighborhood violence—for those released from the prison, as paroled residents see the conflicts they dealt with inside follow them back home, as well as for local youth growing up in these spaces, as it shapes what threats they are exposed to and how they make sense of the dangers present in their community.

### "Things from Prison Are Coming Out to the Streets"

David grew up in Corcoran, a small cotton town in Kern County at the southern end of the Central Valley. For most of his young life he had a long history with drugs, using as a child and selling them by age fourteen. Less than two months after graduating high school he was locked up for selling weed, spending the next eighteen months in county jail before finally being sent to state prison. A second drug possession felony and a total of eighteen parole violations—all for dirty drug tests—would keep him cycling through the system for the next ten years. Inside he was sorted as a Norteño and positioned firmly into the prison's social order. But the prison changed David a good decade before he ever went inside.

As a boy David saw the prisons come to town, built almost literally in his backyard and bringing with them thousands of prisoners who would soon outnumber the town's population. The first opened in 1988, when David was five, the second in 1997 when he was fourteen. About halfway between these two points, something crept over the institution's walls and began spilling into his community and home life. By ten David began seeing himself as a Northerner, no doubt informed by his older brother's incarceration and the other young men in his neighborhood who already claimed this identity. In his final year of high school he became a Norteño gang member, but by this time being a Norteño in Corcoran was different than it was for his predecessors, as the divides that structure life inside the prison began to consistently appear throughout town:

> I'm from the Southside of Corcoran. I grew up looking out my back window and seeing the prison lights. I've heard the sirens every day at five o'clock. They have a shooting range, so you hear the pop, pop, pop, pop. And the street I grew up in, there was drive-bys there, shootings. But back when I was getting raised up, it was families. It wasn't really the gangs, you know what I mean? Just til recently, know what I mean, the gangs started. But we had nothing but Northerners in town, know what I mean? Now, just recently, we started getting Southsiders just cuz of the prison. Lot of lifers go there from LA, or down south. So we get families that move in. A whole family of Southsiders, know what I mean? So it's like, right now it's kinda getting a little hectic . . . cuz things from prison are coming out to the streets.

The carceral social order established a presence early in David's life, but beyond learning how to affiliate, he saw his community changed by its proximity to the prison. He saw his neighborhood become more violent, and once incarcerated himself, he witnessed a certain consistency as he cycled in and out, as the same feuds continued on regardless of whether he was at home or locked up inside. David saw violence with Sureña/os increasingly characterize life in Corcoran, and—fueled by the threat he saw in them moving in, the stories he heard from his older brother, and his own early experiences in the pen—he participated in it himself as this violence escalated and intensified:

> [W]e burned down houses, beat up whole families, just to get 'em out of there. But they would come gangbanging on us. Cuz that's where they

came from, you know what I mean, LA. They're Southerners. See a lot of Southerners [in LA], they fight amongst themselves. They don't know who we are. And they come down this way, and they run into us, like, "What the hell?" and then like, they'll [start problems]. But we don't take nothing from them, know what I mean? And, it's just a lot of things happen. Houses getting burned down, people's moms getting beat up cuz they're trying to get involved [and] stab us. But it's not [that] we *intended* to do it. Think about it, what're you gonna do if somebody's mom comes up to you with a knife? Are you gonna sock her in the head or you gonna get stabbed?

In David's story we see the conflicts that are structured by the carceral social order extended to inmates' families, dramatically affecting their home lives. The institutionalized violence between Norteño and Sureño inmates is reproduced as prisoners' families move to follow their incarcerated members and find themselves in conflict with locals related to an opposing group of inmates. Mirroring what would happen in the nearby correctional facility, young Northerners feel compelled to use violence to drive Southerners out of town because of the danger they are presumed to pose.

Interestingly, David also sees himself having a role in aligning neighborhood feuds with how conflicts are structured in the prison. Not only has he participated in clashes with Southerners as they moved into Corcoran in greater numbers, but he also feels some responsibility to foster cooperation across the previously warring Norteña/o neighborhoods. When I asked him if Norteña/o neighborhoods fought each other the way he said that Sureña/o neighborhoods did, he explained:

Yes. See we grew up that way in Corcoran—feuding. But once we got to prison, we understand what it's about now. Understand what I mean? Growing up, [we were] not knowing it cuz a lot of the older homies are gone. They know about it, [but they were] not there to guide us or help us, enlighten us on what it's really about. Instead, now there's some, a majority of us [who] have been to prison. We know. So we go out there and know what I mean, and [tell the youngsters] "That's not cool, that's not cool." So we're getting along now, compared to the way it used to be.

As an adolescent Norteño, David claims that he and his peers fought with other Norteña/o neighborhoods because—cut off from older, then-incarcerated Norteños—he and his peers didn't know what being a Northerner was "really about." But as someone who has now been to prison, David feels that he now has a better understanding of what being a Norteño means. Consequently, he feels that he and several other former prisoners now back in the neighborhood are obligated to extend this carceral identity construction by teaching local youth to prioritize this affiliation over their own neighborhood gang rivalries. But this unification is also accomplished in the face of a common Sureña/o enemy, reproducing the divides institutionalized inside.

The high rate of neighborhood residents subjected to incarceration, and the adoption of sorting practices by local institutions to categorize criminalized youth as gang involved, collaborate to connect the prison and the community under the same carceral affiliations. But one of the consequences this system creates in the prison is that it structures violence between racialized groups of inmates. In this bridging, much of this violence is then reproduced or extended back to the communities that prisoners disproportionately come from. In Corcoran, secondary prisonization (Comfort 2008) subjects the families of the incarcerated to the socialization processes that position their loved ones into the prison's racialized rivalries. But carceral identities are also socialized and learned locally, meaning that even when residents leave the prison they can still find themselves in environments in which the carceral social order remains constant, and the violence built around this system therefore also remains consistent.

Like the labels ascribed to them, formerly incarcerated residents may also see the more individualized conflicts they become involved with in the prison seep back into their communities. The personal disputes that residents get into inside—themselves still by and large structured by the carceral social order—can continue even after being released back into the neighborhood as these conflicts are picked up by locals who themselves relate to the carceral identities that are at stake. This is particularly the case when residents have a falling out with the car, or parole somewhere where another rival affiliation is prominent. Steven, whose falling out with the Northern car and attempts to go unaffiliated landed him in solitary confinement, continues to encounter violence as a result of his conflict with the car after returning home on parole:

> I finally got all the police reports, I got the medical facts, I got deposition from like the Department of Justice. Any deposition you can think of, I got it. And I submitted it to 'em, right there in uh, I was in Tehachapi and 4B was the security housing unit. I got to the yard where the northerners are at and I went to go submit it to 'em, but they weren't [receptive]. They moved on me. They didn't move on me with a weapon or nothing like that. They sent one dude at me. I mean [the COs] shot the little blockguns,[6] bust him in his snotbox. Nothing happened to me. I walked off with my own two feet, twitched my lip at 'em and went about my business. Ever since then I been doing my own thing. I come

home, I see some of the individuals in my town, like the dudes I grew up with. They don't really harass me, they don't give me a hard time. [But] the younger ones, the younger ones that are trying to make their names, I been jumped [by them] once or twice on occasion. Know what I mean, nothing major, no broken bones, nothing like that.

Steven is exiled from the northerners while in prison, and when he tries to argue his case to the members of the car, they attack him. When he gets back home, local Norteño youth attack Steven after he is released, re-creating the assaults directed at him on the yard in Tehachapi. The forces that collaborate to import the Northern car identity into the neighborhood—the geographic concentration of imprisonment and the local appropriation of penal sorting practices—strengthen local identification with this carceral affiliation, and for Steven perpetuate the violence he experiences for his crimes against this identity. Within this "carceral continuum," the Northerner identity constructed by the sorting process remains influential in shaping criminalized residents' relationships and worldviews, explaining why community members in both locales attack Steven for his presumed betrayal to the group. His is a conflict structured by the expectations of the carceral social order, and this system's connection to the neighborhood is what facilitates its continuation.

Individual conflicts like Steven's leak out from the prison, following those involved back into the neighborhood and continuing to haunt them after their sentence has ended. But these conflicts don't necessarily end with those originally or directly involved, either. The connections built between the neighborhood and the institution give them the power to carry on, impacting young people who have never been to prison yet still find themselves caught up in hostilities that originated inside. Earlier in this chapter we saw how rival gangs who identify with the same affiliation postpone their fights until they are no longer inside the punitive institution: when Mario and his classmate realize that they are from rival neighborhood gangs, they wait until after school to ritualistically address the conflict through a fistfight, only to return side-by-side to the same lunch table the next school day. But what is also interesting about Mario's clash is that the feud between these two neighborhoods originally stemmed from a personal conflict among some Bulldogs inside the prison, which he begins to explain after I notice his black eye and ask him what happened.

"It's a long story, started from like some prison shit. But that shit's hella old, that ain't even funk anymore. I dunno who told him we still funked, but they don't know nothing. They probly just some kids. I asked him how old was the homie that told him we still had funk, and he said seventeen, and I told him he ain't with it, that's just a little kid."

"Who was his homie?" asks Ben. Mario tells him and Ben widens his eyes and starts nodding. "That nigga's hella with it, he was in the same pod as me. He's hella with it."

Mario snaps back at him. "Well, he didn't know shit about this!"

I ask Mario to elaborate on how this all got started. "You said it started with some prison shit, what, from Wasco?"

"I dunno, most likely from Wasco. My older homie was in Wasco, he was just in reception. He was there for six months for a violation, and he was in D4, the dorms. And when he was in there, he said that they jumped the homie Speedy, and that it was the fools from Calaveras. So then we jumped them back, and then they didn't want it anymore. But now they funk with the people that we funk with."

Although he says that this feud is now over (even if his classmate doesn't seem to think so), Mario's explanation of this conflict reveals that rivalries between affiliations are not the only fights passed down from the institution into the community; prison-based personal squabbles and intragroup violence within the car, in this case from Wasco, can inform which similarly affiliated neighborhoods fight with each other on the outs. Part of identifying with the car means deprioritizing neighborhood gang identities, so gang members are generally expected to suppress their conflicts while inside together for the sake of presenting a united front. But here we see a personal fight within the car quickly rematerialize these identities as members rush to support their neighborhood friends. This fight then establishes "funk" between neighborhoods 100 miles away back in Fresno, as what happens inside affects what young people back home are exposed to.

## A Framework for Neighborhood Violence

The carceral social order shapes local young people's exposure to, and informs their understanding of, neighborhood violence. The system that young residents are organized into in juvenile justice facilities continues the residential segregation they already see in their neighborhoods, but within these neighborhoods it also comes to organize local gang violence. Local gang youth, seeing their older peers incarcerated and sorted, come to appropriate carceral affiliations as umbrella identities that inform their collective ties to the neighborhood and establish a set of rival neighborhood gangs. The carceral social order therefore has a very clear role in structuring violence for gang-involved youth, but it also becomes a significant force for young people uninvolved with gangs, as it shapes the social environments that young people have to navigate regardless of their level of gang involvement. This impact becomes particularly visible when we examine the experiences of young taggers in the community.

Like other taggers at SJEA and throughout Fresno, Anthony goes out at night with friends to practice painting, sign his alias, and find visible public spaces to display it to impress his friends and other taggers. But venturing out into the night to create these displays requires navigating community spaces that are claimed and defended by neighborhood gangs that organize themselves into opposing affiliations. Consequently, Anthony and his friends must be wary of how the carceral social order structures rivalries in local spaces, and be aware of how they may be read as subjects within this social order. Although he does not bang, Anthony explains that he generally gets along with the Bulldogs in his neighborhood, but also has to be cautious of them when he is out, as it can be dangerous to be seen as unaffiliated, or worse, as an enemy:

> [They] don't even fuck with us, they just alright. We walk through their hood and [they'll] be like, "Hey, you guys bang?" "No, we taggers." "Alright dog, woot woot woot woot. You guys kick it with busters?" "Fuck no!" "Kick it with scraps?" "Nope!" "Alright though. Alright keep on walking." But sometimes when they're all drunk and high, "Sup blood!" You don't even answer. "What the fuck?" You keep on walking and they gonna come after you, oh shit! I got chased hella times from Bulldogs. I'm cool with them but [when] they're drunk they're dumb as fuck. "What you bang, Bulldog?" "I don't bang!" "What! Don't bang!?" Son of a bitch, I got to run!
>
> I remember when I was walking last time, [we] came back from like, chilling hella places, tagging 'n shit, and we had a backpack. [My friend] had a blue belt and I had a red one. For some reason this fool is dressed in all blue and I was dressed all in red. I told that nigga, "You better not dress in all blue." I called him up before we went painting. "Nah, nah, it's all cool. I hate this color, I'm going to go get [these clothes] painted up." We came back with hella paint on it. The Bulldogs are like, "You walking through my hood, you fucking blue jay?" And that fool gave him a scary look and [my friend] was like, "Nah, nah, I don't bang, I don't bang!" Alright, kept on walking thinking he wasn't going to do nothing. We kept on pushing, [then hear] "Fucking scraps!" hella loud. We see like, four or five dudes running. I was like, "Ah fool! I told you not to wear blue!" I was like, "Fuck!" We had to take off running. We ran like four or five blocks. They didn't stop chasing us until the homie turned around, pulled out a can, and threw it straight at them, bink! Hit one fool. He was like, "Oh shit!" Got 'em and took off running. They just stopped and seen the can and that's I guess [when] they realized we were taggers

and shit. They knew some scraps wouldn't be holding fucking spray cans and shit.

Anthony explains that his safe passage hinges on his ability to convince local gang members that he is not gang involved by forcing them to recognize that he and his friend are taggers. In most cases this is not a problem, but when intoxicated the local homeboys may be stubborn, belligerent, or difficult to convince. Instances in which Anthony has crossed paths with Norteños or Sureños have led to similar experiences being chased, threatened, or jumped. Consequently, one of the prevailing risks of physical violence Anthony has to navigate in his community is the constant danger of gang members seeing him as a member or supporter of a rival affiliation.

The dangers that Anthony encounters are shaped by the rivalries that are constructed within the prison's carceral social order and exported into the community. Even when not confined in the punitive institution, he still has to navigate this system and be conscious of which affiliations are present, navigate the violence between opposing groups, and understand where he fits. Anthony does not bang and as a tagger is generally given a pass on neighborhood gang feuds, but he is not immune from the battles between affiliations. He has had guns pulled on him and seen friends hurt by both Norteños and Sureños, and has even been chased by the Bulldogs he is usually cool with if they don't know he's a tagger. But just as the carceral social order reproduces the prison's violence locally, it also functions as a framework for understanding this neighborhood violence. Even though Anthony has been threatened in fairly consistent ways by Bulldogs, Norteños, and Sureños, he describes these latter two groups as lingering threats to his safety while forming friendships and close relationships with several Bulldogs, viewing them instead as peers who will have his back when he is in danger.

We can see here the carceral social order emerging as a prevalent framework that shapes the threats youth navigate in the neighborhood, and what they have to look out for. Anthony and his friends learn to distance themselves from Norteños or Sureños, and to ensure that they cannot be mistaken for them in order to avoid being chased down the street. But at the time of this research there was also a rising level of violence among young taggers; some taggers formed crews of close friends that began bickering with other groups, in some cases escalating to stabbings or shootings. This situation in turn led police to equate tagging crews with street gangs—even though taggers and gang members didn't see it this way—and to surveil and punish young graffiti artists as dangerous public threats. Individual conflicts between taggers can also grow if one becomes upset with another if they feel their work is disrespected or "slashed" out, leading to fights and in the worst cases lethal violence. Many SJEA students knew friends who had been killed over these conflicts in the previous year or two, and one young tagger I got to know through both JDF and SJEA was killed during this research when he was stabbed at a party.

Many taggers commonly become Bulldog gang members as they get older, in part because the violence among taggers in Fresno has gotten so bad. In this context in which tagger violence is intensifying, claiming more explicit carceral affiliations via gangbanging then becomes attractive to some youth for the same reasons many prisoners appreciate these identities inside—it offers an element of structure and predictability in an otherwise dangerous and chaotic setting. Edgar began tagging as he started junior high, but by the time he reached the ninth grade he transitioned from being a tagger to identifying as a Bulldog gang member. A large part of his rationale for making this change is that he felt gangbanging would actually be safer for him in the neighborhood than being a tagger:

AUTHOR: So why did things start getting really violent with the taggers? I'm still trying to like, figure that out.

EDGAR: It's just because people slash each other and then nowadays nobody wants to fight, they just want to start shooting.

A: And so you got into it in sixth grade, so you had a good two or three years where things were kind of cool?

E: Yeah.

A: And then ninth grade, shit just started getting crazy?

E: Yeah.

A: Damn, so how did you feel when you started seeing . . .

E: If I'm gonna be a tagger and all of this is happening, might as well gangbang. Because gangbanging, I think tagging is worse compared to gangbanging.

A: Like, gangbanging is safer?

E: Yeah, I think so now because all the taggers are just shooting each other and gangbangers you just go after your funk. Like, after the scraps and all the Norteños.

As Edgar explains, violence structured by the carceral social order feels more predictable than the risks involved in tagging, where seemingly any random tagger who thinks he slashed them on a wall somewhere could be a threat. He now has a clear understanding of who his enemies are—mostly rival affiliations who generally live on the other side of town—and perhaps some sense of protection knowing that he is part of a group ready to fight with him against those threats. For Edgar, formally adopting a carceral affiliation through gangbanging offers him a means for making sense of, and having some influence in directing, the violence he may encounter in his neighborhood.

## A Final Thought on Violence

The connections between the prison and high-incarceration neighborhoods that the carceral social order establishes expose local youth to a final yet crucial form of violence. When Ben was a young boy, he heard a commotion coming from his family's living room that drew him out of his bedroom. When he opened his door and stepped out into the hallway, he was met by a handgun pointed at his face. Standing on the other side of the gun was a police officer, part of a contingent storming his home in search of his father, a validated Bulldog gang member. Ben estimates that he was perhaps seven or eight years old when this happened.

The threats and assaults that local youth experience in police stops—when they are pulled over in the street, their homes are searched, or their family members are arrested—represent an additional form of violence brought into the neighborhood by the exportation of carceral identity. The growing prevalence of Bulldog affiliations in Fresno's poor Latina/o communities established an identifiable image of nonwhite criminality that quickly became the subject of calls for law and order. Claiming them responsible for a majority of the city's violent crime, in 2006 the Fresno Police Department launched "Operation Bulldog," a zero tolerance policing initiative explicitly focused on "making life miserable" for residents identified as Bulldogs. Like similar campaigns that soon emerged in the city's poor Black neighborhoods on the Westside, these efforts sought to drive their targets into jail or out of town by prioritizing the cases of residents listed on gang databases; subjecting them to random and frequent searches of their homes, vehicles, person, and even cell phones; and pursuing criminal charges against them whenever possible, no matter how minor the offense.[7] But as has been seen with other forms of zero tolerance policing, these operations ultimately legitimize police harassment and violence against poor youth of color by designating neighborhoods with "high levels of gang activity" as the appropriate sites for aggressive policing, and the young people living in these communities as its targets.

For many of the young people at SJEA, the first time they ever had a firearm pointed at them or had their life threatened was by law enforcement. These students encountered police violence from an early age, regardless of their level of gang involvement or if they had even done anything illegal. Edgar had a similar experience at age fourteen as he was walking to school:

AUTHOR: Can you remember the first time you got pulled over?

EDGAR: It was like, 7:30 in the morning, I was walking to school and um, it was me and two of my homies. They used to go to my house every morning so we could all walk together. And then we were walking and then we got pulled over and then the cops pulled a gun out on us and told us to get on the ground. Cuz they were accusing us that we stole, like, PSPs. Because there was a group of three guys, all dressed in black, and all three of us were dressed in black. And they were all in front of Roosevelt, the three guys [were] in front of [the school] punking all the kids for their iPods and PSPs, and they thought it was us. So they pulled us over and that was the first time I ever got pulled over.

A: So damn, they just came out and pulled a gun?

E: Yeah, they came out cuz they thought, um, they said that one of the boys had a knife and he was punking everybody with a knife. And they thought we had weapons so they came out with the gun pointed at us. They had it like, this close to my face (Edgar holds his hand a few inches from his own face). And they made me get on the floor and then they threw me in handcuffs and they searched me. And then they just, the principal came and he was like, "No, those ain't the three."

A: How do you remember feeling like when the police . . .

E: I was scared. I got shocked. I was like, "What did I do?" and they are like, "You know what the fuck you did!" I was like, "I don't know what I did, what did I do??" They were like, "You know what the fuck you did!" They were all cussing and I was just in shock, like, "What the hell I didn't even do nothing! I just come from home right now!"

A: Did you ever feel like that kind of influenced the way you saw police?

E: Yeah. Like, I didn't, I don't like cops because of that.

Edgar is profiled on his way to school, threatened with a deadly weapon, and accused of something he didn't do until the principal convinces the officers that he is not the guilty party. The experience leaves him scared and confused, but more than anything, distrustful of police. Such intimidating and unwarranted encounters with law enforcement create an overpolicing/ underpolicing paradox in which criminalized youth are stopped and punished for minor offenses or simply looking suspicious, but these experiences discourage them from ever calling on police themselves when they need help or have been victimized (Rios 2011). Instead, youth learn they have to rely on themselves and their peers to manage the dangers they have to navigate daily. Not surprisingly, Edgar decides to become a gang member not long after this incident.

It's not terribly hard to imagine how Ben's or Edgar's encounters with the police could have ended with these boys being killed, shot down by armed men hunting for gang members and other criminal archetypes in Fresno's poor Chicana/o neighborhoods. In the years following the killing of Michael Brown—and the far too many similar instances since—the perceived danger ascribed to the bodies of young men of color is repeatedly cited in the explanation of police shootings, and their criminality is routinely suggested to defend whichever officer pulls the trigger. Fresno's communities of color certainly have histories of police violence that pre-date the carceral social order's affiliations appearing in the neighborhood. However, much of this violence has been legitimized and perpetuated in recent years by appealing to constructed fears of "gang youth" as dangerous subjects who require such aggressive social control. It is crucial that we recognize the harmful actions of local law enforcement carried out in the name of fighting criminalized affiliations as a form of physical, interpersonal violence that the carceral social order brings into the community. At the same time, we must also see this as an aspect of the structural or legal violence that comprises mass incarceration's collateral consequences—as part of the harm of the cumulative disadvantage piled into high-incarceration communities that is rationalized by framing residents as criminal.

# 6. The Carceral Social Order and the Structuring of Neighborhood Criminalization

At the onset of first starting this research project, Mrs. Arroyo—an administrator from a local nonprofit that helped place me in San Joaquin Educational Academy (SJEA)—drives me to the campus, introduces me to the counselor I would initially be shadowing, and arranges a quick tour of the building to help familiarize me with the site. Afterward she brings me back and drops me off at my car, but leaves me with a final word of caution. She tells me a story about how her organization's parenting classes got kicked out of a local community center on Belmont after one student from the class shot another in a drive-by. She warns me: "Never forget this is who they are, this is what they are capable of, this is what they will do if they're desperate enough. We learned the hard way. You think you know them, that they're just kids, and you forget that they're not. They're dangerous."

Her words always stood out to me. I had received similar warnings many times before, especially from worried family members who imagined gang members as vicious, even sadistic predators. But unlike my frightened relatives, Mrs. Arroyo actually works with gang-involved and gang-labeled youth every day. This regular contact might typically help one recognize the multiple dimensions that comprise who a young person is. In the time I spent at SJEA and the Fresno County Juvenile Detention Facility (JDF), I came to know students who were awkward and unsure of themselves, who tried to impress their friends, who got shy when talking about other students they had crushes on, who could be short-sighted and defiant when they felt misunderstood, who would call me "sir" and excitedly come up to shake my hand when they saw me in public, and who would daydream about what they wanted to do when they grew up. However, for Mrs. Arroyo, as with many others, these dimensions of adolescence—their insecure self-awareness, youthful enthusiasm, painful self-doubt, and hopeful aspiration—are overshadowed by the blanket recognition of these youth as dangerous criminals above all else. So important is this point that her closing advice to me as I prepare to begin working with these teenagers is that I remember that they are not really children at all, because on a fundamental level, "this [criminality] is who they are" as people.

The perception of gang youth as fundamentally violent and dangerous figures is rooted in the social construction of the gang member as a politicized image of racialized criminality designed to agitate the fears of White voters. Stemming from caricatures historically used to legitimize and elicit public support for the colonization of the American Southwest (Romero 2001), in the twentieth century gang members served as vital public threats that could be sensationalized to justify law enforcement spending, legal powers, and violence that primarily targeted poor communities of color (Davis 1990; Durán 2013). The extended socialization of carceral affiliations represents a key component of this ongoing construction—as the prison expands its ability to define criminality beyond its own gates, it uses the trope of the gang member to do so. Consequently, the delinquent status (Foucault 1977) ascribed to high-incarceration neighborhoods is produced by identifying these communities with carceral affiliations, and subsequently framing them as gang-infested spaces that require punitive social control. In a contemporary context that relies on mass incarceration to facilitate an increasingly polarized form of capitalism (Gilmore 2007), the carceral social order continues this pattern of defining poor youth of color as criminal social subjects who need to be incarcerated.

In this chapter I focus on how the carceral social order implemented in punitive institutions becomes an authoritative template for identifying high-incarceration communities, and the young people in these communities, as criminal. Sorting probation youth by their presumed affiliations inside the institution ultimately defines them as gang members, a constructed status that comes to officially define them. For the young people ascribed with these labels, many of the creative abilities they develop to communicate or express themselves are resultantly interpreted as forms of gang activity. But this template is also exported into local policing by establishing a logic of "polarized labeling" that follows the institutional sorting process—youth are identified with a racial category, then assumed to fall on one side or the other of the rivalries within that racial group. This logic establishes a parallel process within criminal labeling in the neighborhood that identifies local youth as the same types of gang affiliates as inside the punitive facility. The affiliations constructed and socialized by the prison and extended into targeted neighborhoods are then recognized as evidence of criminality both inside and outside the institution. This process ultimately serves to attach an imprisonable status to the residents of poor communities of color. To this end, structuring institutional life around the carceral social order socializes those who work with probation youth to ideologically identify them—and the families and communities they come from—as irresponsible social burdens that require punitive management and social control. Framing young people of color as fundamentally criminal then structures punishment as a default response to address the social and personal problems they experience, such as drug addiction, abusive households, or mental health struggles.

## THE CARCERAL SOCIAL ORDER AS TRANSFERABLE LABELING TEMPLATE

The appropriation of penal sorting practices in juvenile justice facilities establishes the carceral social order as an authoritative template for labeling poor youth of color as gang members at the local level. The presumption that youth fall into one of a handful of gang-associated groups institutes a logic that in turn interprets many of their activities, particularly the means by which young people express themselves, as criminal and gang-related. This logic does not remain contained in the punitive facility however, as it goes on to inform how local neighborhood police identify poor youth of color as particular types of gang members. Following the same conceptual process used to sort incoming prison inmates, officers racially categorize youth to determine the applicable affiliations, then interpret one's home community, peer networks, and personal style as gang related in order to slot youth into one affiliation or another.

### The Presumption of Gang Activity

Inside juvenile justice facilities, the positions that young people occupy (or are assigned to) in the carceral social order are constructed as ties to criminal street gangs, which creates the common perception among both staff members and institutional youth that all or nearly all of the young people in these spaces are gang involved. As more than one SJEA student responded when I first explained my research, "So, you're writing about the school? You know pretty much every kid here is a gangbanger." However, in contrast to this presumption that "everyone bangs," in reality most youth in JDF and SJEA are not gang involved. In spite of this, the sorting of youth into gang-associated clusters subsequently evokes gang-centric discourses to interpret youth behavior, style, and identity as criminal.

One product of this framing is the understanding of several forms of young peoples' creativity as criminally suspicious. For example, many students at SJEA practiced their skills writing calligraphy, elaborate cursive, or artistic lettering constantly. It became an appreciated and competitive art form for many while they were locked up, and the most talented were even able to make some income from developing their skills into tattooing. But as excited and invested as many students were in refining this ability, they were not offered or allowed any type of creative outlet to strengthen or channel their talents into productive endeavors. Instead, most of their creative work was heavily discouraged by the school and criminalized as tagging. Calling it tagging associated their doodles and penmanship with defacement of property,[1] even if it was done on their own worksheets and scrap paper. The mere act of writing in any creative way was prohibited, and would oftentimes get students into more trouble.

Despite the school's general disapproval of it, when I took them out I usually let students doodle or write on their scrap paper after they finished their work. I even let some of them practice their lettering on my folders or notebooks, encouraging them to try to show off their skills. One afternoon Juan pulls a folded piece of orange paper out of his pocket and asks me if I want to see it. "It's badass!" he promises. But his eyes quickly widen and he pulls his hand back. "Wait, a PO's [probation officer] right there. I'll show you later." A few minutes later he unfolds it and reveals a page covered in drawings that he and Ben have been tracing and shadowing in during class. Filling the lower half is an elaborate set of letters that look like erratic lightning bolts flowing out from the center. They watch me as I stare at it for a few moments, then they start laughing.

"He can't read it!" chuckles Ben.

Juan leans in and points to the left side of it. "Here's the P, A, this is the T. . . ."

I start laughing once I recognize my own name. "Oh, I see it! Thank you guys, this is awesome." I refold it to put it into my folder. "Do you get in trouble if you get caught with this?" I ask, thinking of how Juan waited for the PO to pass.

Both boys nod yes. Ben adds: "I got in trouble for tagging my own name! They told me that if it's not 'normal writing' then I'll get in trouble."

The creative writing and lettering styles that students developed were stigmatized and dismissed as vandalism, but they were also criminalized as vaguely "gang related" by many of the school personnel. These styles

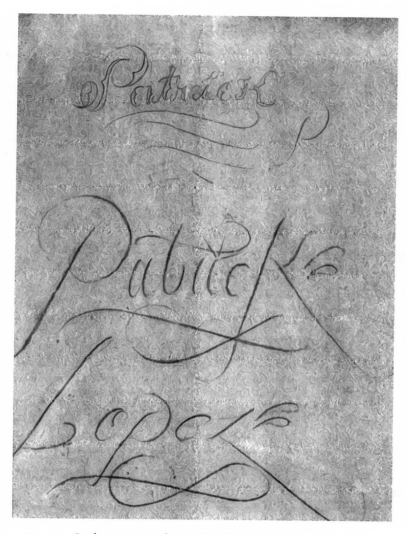

FIGURE 2. Students practice their stylized writing by customizing my work folder.

Patrick Lopez-Aguado

themselves were seen as somehow promoting gang involvement or identity, which became a rationale for punishing students who were caught drawing them. This perspective was also apparent in how staff members would make sense of this activity, arguing that it was appropriate to suppress it as criminal rather than allow youth opportunities to showcase it.

After observing the students' lunch period, I go to eat my own lunch in the break room, and I'm soon joined by the probation and administrative staff who have just been supervising the students outside. They start venting about their frustrations with some of the students, and one of the teaching assistants mentions writing a student up for "gang writing" on his worksheet. Flores, one of the POs, mentions that the same student had been drawing out a list of all the honor roll students on the bulletin board in the hallway.

"He was all excited because they got him to tag in the front of the school, on this board over here by the double doors." I had noticed the list in progress; over the past few days someone had been writing out students' names in round, bubbled letters in pencil and then filling them in with ink, but today it was gone and replaced with a simple typed list.

Alvarez, another PO, shrugs her shoulders in bewilderment at Flores' mentioning of the bulletin board. "Who allowed that anyway? Who said that was OK??"

Sharon, a classroom assistant, agrees, "I know, I don't know why they let them do it anyway."

The receptionist from the front desk then updates the table on the outcome of the troublesome list. "They took it down. [An administrator] took it down because it was unacceptable."

"Just cuz of the way it was written?" I ask, confused.

She simply repeats herself, this time closing her eyes and slowly shaking her head, "It was unacceptable."

Sharon tries to explain but is equally vague. "Yeah, well first of all you can't read it, and it's just the way it's written."

Alvarez elaborates, "It's the way it's written, plus they know how to do all the secret stuff in it."

"Yeah, it's like, we don't want you to tag but go ahead and tag on our school," Flores chuckles.

Many of the school's staff members are repelled by this style of writing because they don't understand it and even seem to see it as vaguely offensive. But the POs also see it as criminally suspicious and capable of communicating dangerous messages. The staff consequently agree that suppressing this style altogether is important for maintaining consistent discipline among students and discouraging them from being gang members. Their reaction to the honor roll list reveals that even something celebrating students' accomplishments is threatening and deemed unacceptable if it is written in this "tagging" or "gang writing" style.

The creative products that young people fashioned in JDF were similarly criminalized as gang activity and subsequently prohibited. Inside JDF, the

Fresno Youth Network (FYN) managed a recreation room that youth from each pod could come and use for an hour about twice a week. That spring we received a bunch of donated art supplies—mostly paper, markers, and colored pencils—and decided to make them available to the young people who came in. Almost everybody used them, stenciling out their names, writing inspirational mottos, and even inventing cartoonish caricatures. These drawings decorated the room's walls and windows until one afternoon, when we came in and found every picture taken down and piled onto a table under a note that read:

> Several of these drawings have gang related writing on them and are not allowed at the JDF. Please Do Not post drawings on the walls and/or windows in this room without permission from the Watch Commander.
> Thank you for your Cooperation!
> JDF Staff

Similar to the POs' suspicions of stylized lettering at SJEA, JDF's juvenile corrections officers (JCOs) become concerned that the drawings youth are making in our clubhouse are gang associated and possibly sending hidden messages to allies or enemies. After several weeks we are eventually able to get permission from a supervising officer to hang pictures in the windows again, but only after agreeing to regularly stress to the young artists that they cannot draw anything "gang related." We also have to start counting the markers and pens after each session, while the youth who come in are now patted down as they leave to make sure they are not taking any markers back to the pod. Despite these interventions, the works that the youth create are still routinely questioned and denounced by personnel on the site who insist that the drawings are forms of gang activity.

A few weeks later, while most of the youth in the facility are eating dinner in the cafeteria, one of JDF's mental health workers walks by the clubhouse and stops to look at the drawings we have hanging in the window. Most of them are cartoon portraits created by Alberto—one of the most artistically talented teenagers to frequent the clubhouse—who draws a new one almost every week. Tom, who works with me in the clubhouse, spots the mental health worker and opens the door to the outside quad to talk. He mentions that the drawings caught his eye as he was walking past, adding "They're real clever about putting hidden messages in their drawings."

"You see anything here to be concerned about?" Tom asks him.

"Yeah, a few things. Step out here and let me show you." We go outside and he starts pointing out the details in the drawings that he sees as related to Alberto's gang identity. "One of his things is that all of his pictures have a strong theme of blue. [And] the blue ice dripping from the face in [this] one, they'll tell you he's chillin,' but what that really is is the drugs." He goes on to say that the fact that all of his characters have "droopy" eyes—as Alberto drew eyelids on his characters as opposed to having their eyes opened wide—means that they are under the influence; he even points out a tooth with a hole in it and explains that this is a "tweaker tooth" meant for putting a blunt up to and smoking through it. Finally, he claims that there are also several hidden numbers in the faces. Pointing to various crossed pen strokes and scribbles, he says that they are supposed to be the number 13 (representing Sureña/os), although they don't seem to be in any real order. "On this one he has a 1 under one eye and a 3 under the other," he claims, but I don't see it. He continues, "And [in] this one he has what are called the Locs (sunglasses), but if you look closely you can see the 'x3,' which is his set, southsiders."

In analyzing the drawings, the mental health worker tellingly slips from talking about the artist Alberto specifically to referring to probation youth more broadly, describing them as drug users and gang members who lie to conceal their true deviance. The messages about drug use and gang representation presumed to be hidden in the cartoon drawings particularly highlight this perception. Drawing faces with eyes wide open can make a character look overly excited, surprised, or frightened, so drawing eyelids half-closed is commonly used to convey a wider range of emotions such as boredom, annoyance, mischief, a clever smile, or even a fairly expressionless resting face.[2] However, Alberto's character is assumed to simply be high. Also blended into this interpretation of drug-using cartoons is the perception of shading and small details (such as hairs or dimples) drawn onto characters' faces as covert gang symbols. As he points these supposed symbols out, I find the accusations to be a bit of a stretch, and more importantly claims that likely would not have been made at all if the artist were unknown or not in the hall. When she hears about this assessment, Valerie, the clubhouse manager, makes this very point, rolling her eyes and arguing: "Well yeah, that's how they're gonna see it in here, because that's their mindset. But if you were to show it to anyone on the outs, they wouldn't see any of that. They would just see cartoon characters!"

For the young people detained in Fresno's juvenile justice system, many forms of creative expression were regarded with this kind of suspicion, to the extent that many felt that seemingly all aspects of their lives were perceived as some form of gang activity. A few days after the pictures are initially taken down, I have the boys from one of the pods in a focus group and explain what happened. They are hardly surprised. After explaining that the facility staff alleged that the drawings were promoting gangs, I ask them, "Do they ever think stuff is gang related that isn't?"

Hector, the oldest and most outspoken of the group, is quick to answer. "They think everything is gang related! Like, if we do this"—Hector bumps fists with the boy next to him—"they'll tell us 'Hey, stop that! [That's] gang related!' Like, even if we just shake hands, like a straight handshake, they'll say it's gang related. If we sign to each other they'll think it's gang stuff. Like, not real sign language but ghetto sign language." He starts twitching his fingers, making them quickly resemble each letter of the alphabet.

"When'd you learn how to do that?" I ask him.

Hector laughs, "Man, my second time I was locked up, everyone was talking to each other through their windows. Like, someone was trying to say something to me, and then at rec they were like, 'Why didn't you say nothing back??' I was like, 'I don't know what all this is!'" He starts moving his fingers again, this time randomly to re-create the senseless spasms they originally resembled to him. "I don't know how some of these guys do it so fast though. [Like] this guy." He points towards Daniel, who starts grinning shyly. Valerie, the FYN clubhouse manager, asks him to say, "I love the Fresno Youth Network." He signs the message fast, much quicker than Hector did, before leaning back with a quiet smile and a shrug while we all cheer.

Many of these expressive forms that young people practiced inside—the cursive writing, their drawings, the improvised sign language—were developed in response to being locked up. Having little opportunity to do much else, youth find ways to communicate, pass the time, and express themselves with the few resources at their disposal. However, the institutional preoccupation with identifying probation youth as gang members then interprets many of their activities as promoting or advancing criminal groups. The alphabet system that youth develop to communicate with each other when they are locked in their rooms is consequently included in the range of activities institutionally presumed to be gang affiliated. Messages that have nothing to do with gangs could be interpreted as such by JCOs, and become evidence of "gang activity" in one's probation file that leads to additional punishments. This remained the case as students transferred to SJEA and used some of the same hand motions, even if they were just messing around.

In Mr. Castro's sixth-period class it's approaching the end of the day. Colton and another boy are talking loudly, mostly because Colton's laugh is pretty loud, to the point that other students notice and look at him with their own confused amusement. Mr. Castro asks the class to be quiet before singling him out. "Colton! Stop!" Colton stares at him for a few seconds in surprise and asks what he did. Mr. Castro answers him, clearly annoyed, "You're being loud and disruptive, [and have] been fooling around since you came in!"

A few minutes later the school's Resource Specialist Program (RSP) teacher comes in, and Colton wants her to take him out. Mrs. Tanaka specializes in working with students with learning disabilities, and she usually takes Colton around this time for one-on-one assistance. But today she can't; she has to take the girls out for a weekly young women's program the school is initiating. Colton complains to his friend about not going out, at one point putting his arms up in the air and hanging his forearms down like a marionette, and yelling out "R! S! P!" while he forms the letters with his fingers as he yells them out.

Mr. Castro rolls his eyes and pulls out his radio. "That's it. Castro to security." Colton already realizes what's happening but is confused as to why. He raises his palms up in a confused shrug. Castro continues his radio call, "I have one student who needs to go out."

"What'd I do??" Colton asks incredulously.

Mr. Castro responds with seriousness, done with it for today. "If you're gonna flash gang signs, then you're going out."

Colton cannot believe that he is being accused of throwing gang signs and simply laughs, "What???"

Castro hangs his forearms from his shoulders and twitches his fingers around to impersonate Colton. "I don't know what *this* is!" he says, referencing Colton's unfamiliar letter signing.

Colton doesn't bother to wait for security to come to the room. He gets up and starts to leave on his own. "I'm just trying to do my work, but if you're gonna act like an asshole about it. . . ." he counters as he walks out the door.

Across the room, a student I hadn't met yet makes eye contact with me after noticing my notetaking. "Sir, you're just writing all this down, huh?" he asks. I chuckle and nod. He continues with a stern face, "Write it up and get the school shut down."

Gang identities certainly have an influential presence inside juvenile justice facilities, because they are important to many of the young people who are cycled through these institutions. But it is inaccurate to view all youth coming into the facility as gang involved, or to characterize everything young people do here as gang inspired or driven. In relying on a systematic organizing principle that categorizes young people as one type of gang associate or another, the institutionalization of the carceral social order creates a lens through which probation youth's actions are interpreted. This lens becomes a crucial contribution in shaping a broader dominant logic that then makes meaning of the actions and behaviors of poor youth of color, both in the institution and in their home communities.

## The Carceral Social Order in Neighborhood Policing

The logic that governs how criminalized youth are categorized as potential gang members—and that subsequently interprets their behavior as gang related—also leaks out of the punitive institution to inform how police label youth in the neighborhood. In Fresno's poor communities of color, officers utilize what I term "polarized labeling" in stops to identify youth as particular types of criminal threats. Using a process that mirrors penal sorting practices, officers racially categorize the young people they encounter, then assume them to be on one side or the other of rivalries within the selected racial category. In these stops, officers commonly validate youth as gang members or associates by tying them to these broad affiliations rather than to specific neighborhood gangs, illustrating how the classifications constructed by the sorting process ultimately become proxies for criminal gangs. These experiences often represent students' first encounters with the carceral social order, formally marking them with labels that later inform how they are categorized in juvenile hall.

When identifying materials or actions that may be promoting gang identities, Fresno's gang unit police officers rely on a conceptual framework that is consistent with the logic of the punitive facility. A few days after all the drawings are taken down from the clubhouse walls and windows in JDF, Tom asks a couple of police officers from the city's gang unit he met during a ride-along to come in and check the pictures out themselves. He introduces me to Clayton, a tall Black man with a shaved head, and his partner Ricardo, a shorter Latino man with angry eyebrows and sunglasses pulled up over his black hair.

They walk into the clubhouse and immediately start inspecting the pictures that are spread out over the table. After a few moments they say that they don't see anything gang specific, but note that "the style is like tagging, [like] when they write on walls or in their books." Still curious if this means that some of them may be gang related, Tom asks about identifying which youth may be gang members, recalling: "From what I remember from riding along, you guys took a lot of pictures of tattoos, and there are a lot of tattoos here. A *lot*."

Ricardo asks him, "You guys have cameras?"

"No, we're not allowed to bring anything in." Tom replies.

Ricardo frowns and looks over to Clayton. "That might be the way to go, get 'em while they're young. Ch-chk, ch-chk, ch-chk." He holds an imaginary camera and snaps his forefinger down as if he were taking pictures. "Get them while they're putting in work, getting their marks. You know how it is."

Instead they start advising us on what to look for in terms of identifying gang-involved teens who may be coming into the clubhouse, telling us to be mindful of nicknames, numbers, and students who have tattoos, hang out together, or even draw similar style pictures. Clayton adds verbal cues to these means of identifying gang youth, explaining "Bulldogs say 'fool' a lot, and Norteños—and I've heard some Bulldogs say it too—will say like, 'Whatup nigga,' like we would," waving his hand between himself and Tom, another Black man.

Ricardo pulls out another drawing. It's one Jayvon, one of the boys who comes in regularly, wrote his name out on with "Feelin' Good" written under it. Half of the letters are colored in with red. Ricardo starts to explain "Sometimes with Hispanics, they'll color in an N like this for Norteños, to represent their colors."

"So would that one be suspect?" Tom asks.

Ricardo clenches one side of his mouth, considering it. "Mmm Jayvon? He's Black? Maybe if it was like, Juan or something like that and it was filled in like this, that might be something to look out for."

Clayton nods in agreement. "Yeah, sometimes you can tell from the name."

These gang unit officers, who primarily work in Fresno's poor neighborhoods of color, use the carceral social order as a template to determine one's potential gang affiliations; it informs the tips they provide us and shapes their assessments of which of the teens' pictures may be considered gang related. As trained gang specialists working in the field, they identify which material may be gang related by first racially categorizing the individuals involved. Racial identity, here assessed through one's name and language, serves as a key factor for them in tying teenagers to the proper criminalized affiliations, and therefore interpreting their actions as gang related or not. Ricardo explains that the red lettering in the drawing could be considered indicative of Norteña/o gang ties if the artist were Latina/o, but because he is Black it is not. The process that these gang unit police have learned to use to recognize young gang members in the community mirrors the carceral institution's sorting process, in which incoming inmates are racially sorted, then slotted into particular affiliations depending on that racial classification—Latina/o youth are identified as Norteña/os, Sureña/os, or Bulldogs, and consistent with Fresno County's jail and juvenile justice systems, Black youth as regarded as members of either Twamp or the Squad. The punitive institution's sorting process and its resulting carceral social order have established a standard template for criminalizing poor youth of color, and for understanding "gangs" and affiliations as rigidly racialized constructs.

The carceral identities socialized in the prison are passed on to neighborhood youth through the relationships local youth have with imprisoned loved ones, and the appropriation of penal sorting practices by local juvenile facilities that categorize young residents into the same groups. In this process, the prison's influence as a socializing force is extended into high-incarceration communities. But a vital aspect of this socialization is the construction of these identities as criminal. Consequently, what also accompanies these identities as they spill over into the community is the institutional procedure of categorizing residents as the appropriate types of racialized criminal threats. Emulating the process institutionalized in California's prisons, local police are taught to use the carceral social order as a template for learning how to identify gang members and associates in their own cities—racially categorizing youth they encounter and interpreting local identities and peer networks as indicators of criminal affiliations.

This process is particularly visible with the criminalization of identity performances that are influenced by carceral affiliations. The extension of prison socialization into the neighborhood informs local styles, gender performances, and racial identities with the carceral affiliations institutionalized in the facility. For example, while prohibited from doing so during school by SJEA's dress code, many of the Latino boys would wear solid red T-shirts as part of the "clean" style they developed as a masculine aesthetic. However, these boys did not necessarily see this as identifying with a gang or promoting gang culture, but rather as part of claiming a racialized regional identity. Here Alex, who is not gang involved, explains that he sees this learned style as part of being from Fresno:

AUTHOR: Would you usually wear red or blue or something they wouldn't let you wear [at SJEA] if you were at home?

ALEX: Yeah, I would. Usually I got a lot of colors that are red like, if not solid red then bits of red on it.

AU: When you wear something like that, do police ever trip that you're affiliated or something?

AL: Yeah, they do. They always do. I tell them no, [but] they don't believe me. They had me pulled over and pick up my shirt and see if I got tattoos or anything.

AU: Oh really? How often does that happen?

AL: It happened twice already. One was by MAGEC.

AU: The gang task force?

AL: Yeah, "the gang cops." One was by them and one was by regular county police.

AU: Did that ever discourage you from [wearing] red?

AL: No, I still wear it.

AU: You feel like it's worth it to wear it even if . . .

AL: Might get in trouble? Yeah, it's still worth it. You know, it's Fresno. I was born in Fresno, you can't say nothing. That's the color for Fresno. Just like LA, the LA Dodgers, they're gonna wear blue. If I lived in LA, then I would wear blue.

AU: Yeah.

AL: It's just where you grow up, where you live. If you see that in Clovis, they're not gonna be like, "Oh, that's a gang member," cuz it's in Clovis. It's different.

Alex doesn't bang, but he has learned to see his style—an aesthetic regularly viewed as gang related—as very important. He learned to adopt his current style after he changed middle schools. When he couldn't use his aunt's address to go to the newer, middle-class school anymore, he transferred to the junior high near his home, one that was almost exclusively composed of working-class Chicana/os and that had a reputation for being "kinda gangsta, kinda hectic." Before this move he used to identify and dress as a skater, wearing tight, frayed jeans, faded graphic T-shirts, and worn-out skate shoes. But in his new school the other students teased him about it, to the point that he even got into fights over it. Eventually he learned to conform to his current "clean" look, learning to see this as not only how the other boys dressed but also as what girls were supposedly attracted to. But his new style was contextualized by the racial makeup of the school, as well as the extent to which the students here were criminalized. More so than his previous school, Bulldog affiliations informed the identities that many of the young boys learned to perform here, consequently shaping Alex's own individual style. Its location in a neighborhood impacted by mass imprisonment and the carceral social order made indicating regional identities an important learned performance for students. By the time Alex got to SJEA, this was even more prevalent.

Now, Alex sees wearing red as a valuable part of his own identity, even if it gets him unwanted attention from local police. He understands wearing red as how he expresses himself as someone from Fresno, and sees this use of color as something people in other towns do as well. But just as he notes that where one lives determines the styles or colors one may identify with, it also affects if this is regarded as gang related or not. For young people like Alex in Southeast Fresno, local law enforcement interprets this style as indicative of gang allegiances; they use this rationale to justify pulling over youth who dress like Alex, putting them onto gang databases, and charging them with violations once they are on probation. It is also interpreted as gang involvement when youth are sent through booking in JDF, shaping how they are sorted once they are actually in a punitive facility.

Teenagers who are arrested and sent to JDF are first processed through booking, and during this time JCOs attempt to determine whom they are affiliated with. Paperwork filed by an arresting officer, notes from previous police stops, or one's listing in the state's gang database can all inform this decision. In this process youth have their probation files updated with their suspected affiliations, and some are even officially validated as gang members. Here Angel describes his experience being processed through booking at JDF: "When you first go in booking, they ask you 'What are you? Are you affiliated? You're a tagger? What?' Most likely you'll probly tell 'em, or you'll be like, 'No.' [But] if they look at your profile and see what you are, they're gonna be like, 'Oh, he's a tagger. Oh, he's a Bulldog.' I think they got me labeled down as a Bulldog cuz I was wearing red when I went in."

While Angel was being processed through booking at JDF, he was labeled as a Bulldog based on what he was wearing when he got there and who he already knew in the facility. This categorization was then used to determine where he would be housed in JDF, associating him with similarly labeled youth and shaping the peer group he would navigate this and future institutions with. This experience also marks an important step in a long process of ascribing Angel with a criminal label that keeps cycling him through juvenile justice system institutions. Importantly, Angel also describes his "profile" as being influential in defining him during this process, indicating he was likely put into Fresno's gang database as a "gang associate" at some point before he was sent to juvenile hall. Indeed, later in his interview he explains why he suspects this label stems from a previous experience in which he was stopped and profiled by police at the Fresno Fair: "I think it's because I had a red and black San Francisco hat. Now I think the cops think San Francisco means 'scrap free,' cuz I went to the fair one time and they labeled us like, 'Oh, scrap free, so you're Bulldogs.' My friend was like, 'No.' He's like, 'You got a Bulldog hat on.' [My friend] was just like, 'Oh, that don't mean I'm a Bulldog, sir.' [The cop] was just like, 'Yeah, you are,' and then he was like, 'Scrap free, huh?' [and] pointed at my hat."

While most sports fans in Fresno follow teams that are based in the San Francisco Bay Area,[3] when Angel is stopped by police his cap is interpreted in terms of the slang used in carceral rivalries. His experience demonstrates how the carceral social order imposed inside punitive facilities shapes and informs the processes used to criminalize youth in the community, as the same framework used for identifying and categorizing youth inside the institution is used to mark them as suspected gang members in their own neighborhoods. Angel's race, association with other boys from the Eastside, and stylized appearance act as cues that prompt police to interpret the letters on his hat as representative of anti-Sureña/o slang. Using the carceral social order's logic of polarized labeling, this casts Angel as a Bulldog gang member.

The criminalizing framework of the carceral social order is used by police to categorize him into an affiliation and justify creating a gang file on him, one that JCOs then use to categorize and position him in the social order of the juvenile hall. Probation files outlining young people's suspected affiliations (often based on the mere suspicions of teachers, staff, or other authority figures) functioned as negative credentials (Rios 2011) that were consequential in shaping youths' experiences and reputations in new spaces. Youth felt these files were held against them, and that the reputations they carried from one institution to the next magnified punishments they received and cemented perceptions of them as criminal youth. These initial contacts that youth have with neighborhood police inform how they are later categorized, meaning that the sorting process begins long before one ever reaches the prison. The extension of this process then represents the ability of the prison to construct criminality beyond its own walls.

## CARCERAL STATUS IN NEOLIBERAL CALIFORNIA

The spillover of the carceral social order into high-incarceration neighborhoods extends the prison's ability to construct criminality by imposing a racialized template for categorizing youth as gang members into local policing. But what this ultimately accomplishes is that it establishes a status for affected communities, one that designates residents as the fitting targets of incarceration within a social order that increasingly relies on the prison to facilitate an otherwise unsustainable globalized state economy (Gilmore

2007). California's shift from the welfare to the carceral state depended on shaping public perception to view social welfare programs as wasteful, and establishing a status for program recipients as public threats unworthy of public support rather than people in need. This process was largely achieved by framing the poor as criminal (Wacquant 2009; Parenti 2000).

SJEA offers an interesting example of how the neoliberal state has shifted resources from public welfare to punishing poor families. In a deindustrialized California that has struggled to incorporate the working class into a polarized service economy (Gilmore 2007), working-class students expunged from public school districts are now essentially warehoused—much like prisoners—in classrooms in which the primary lesson is docility; students are often simply graded on their behavior rather than any work completed, given a passing grade for the day if they sit passively and fill out word search puzzles or coloring book pages, and a failing grade if they talk or cause any kind of disruption. Naturally, students hate this and frequently try to skip or leave early. But SJEA receives its funding based on the number of probation youth present in the facility each day, actually losing about $30 each time a student is absent. This arrangement has subsequently shaped how the county distributes its resources, as well as how it secures its own financing. When the Probation Department had a budget crisis that in turn jeopardized funding for the government agency that oversees SJEA, intervention workers contracted by the county to provide gang outreach and awareness classes at the site were instead reassigned to help the school raise its average daily attendance. This effort not only protected state funding by keeping youth in the institution, but also extracted money from students' families by docking parents' welfare benefits—or fining them if they were not welfare recipients—if their children missed too many days of school. This was of course in addition to the fines that these parents have already paid to the county for processing their child through booking, incarcerating them in JDF, and monitoring them on house arrest. In the wake of the dismantled welfare state, diminishing state support for poor families not only shapes local governments' economic dependence on incarceration, but also in many cases forces the poor to finance their own subjugation.

Recognizing poor residents of color as gang members has been particularly effective in criminalizing their communities and rationalizing state divestment from supporting these spaces. In exporting penal affiliations to inmates' home communities, the carceral social order plays a crucial role in establishing this status, for example by identifying poor Latina/o communities as Norteña/o or Sureña/o gang neighborhoods. This situates high-incarceration neighborhoods into a discourse of delinquency (Foucault 1977) that resonates with the public imaginary, one that makes the community's presumed criminality legible by framing it as "gang activity." The sorting process used by punitive institutions constructs and instills criminalized affiliations, but when appropriated by juvenile facilities it also socializes staff to see probation youth as social subjects defined by criminality and therefore bound for eventual imprisonment. Consequently, many of those responsible for helping criminalized youth instead learn to see and talk about them, their families, and their communities in terms of an imprisonable status that establishes criminal punishment as a default method for dealing with the myriad problems that poor youth of color encounter.

## Socializing Perceptions of Youth

Defining students as criminal through the carceral social order facilitates a more extensive and elaborate framing of poor youth of color, their families, and their communities as social subjects who need to be punitively managed. The ultimate accomplishment of extending the prison's socializing power into marginalized neighborhoods is the establishment of these communities' residents as the fitting targets of imprisonment. Penal systems construct popular understandings of criminality, and ascribe to those who pass through its facilities a status that is presumed to warrant incarceration (Foucault 1977), but this status also comes back home. As already discussed, this status is passed on through local youth who identify with incarcerated loved ones, and through juvenile facilities that label young residents in the same terms as the prison. But establishing this status also requires socializing a public recognition of these youth as the proper recipients of incarceration. This perception is in large part legitimized by those who are tasked with managing criminalized youth—and subsequently recognized as experts about them—who themselves learn to see, frame, and talk about these youth in terms that fit this imprisonable status. By constructing an environment in which students are defined by their presumed gang loyalties, the carceral social order does much of the groundwork necessary for facilitating and giving credence to this discourse.

The unfolding of this process becomes plainly visible in the candid discussions among staff members at SJEA. Learning to be part of the staff and socializing with the others commonly entails learning to talk about the young people here in ideological terms. Complaining about students is common backstage interaction across educational environments, but in this context this dialogue also functions to frame students as particular social subjects—specifically, as both social threats and economic burdens.

As soon as they wrap up their diatribes about the "gang writing" used to recognize the students on honor roll, some of the lunching staff members in SJEA's break room expand their complaints about students. Officer Alvarez is particularly agitated, simply grunting "Ugh, kids."

"Yours?" asks Celia, an office assistant.

Alvarez answers, "No, these kids. Little monsters."

"Oh, I know, some of these kids are a pain in the neck!" Celia agrees before focusing her complaints on the pregnant girls specifically. "And the girls, we've got a lot of pregnant ones here, like Jones. And she's just in the office, laughing like it's a party."

Alvarez explodes: "It is a party for her! She's gonna get a big fat welfare check, and can stay home and have everyone tell her she's such a good mother." She rolls her eyes and starts shaking her head as she imagines this.

Celia again confirms the PO's assessment, describing the expectant young mother's incompetence: "I know, she came in today with a Dr. Pepper and Pringles. Security is holding it for her until she gets out."

Alvarez grumbles back: "She can be feeding soda to her baby, and make sure the next one comes out good and healthy. My tax dollars at work."

Building off a previous conversation that characterized student creativity as criminally suspicious, Alvarez and Celia go on to discuss the pregnant girls at SJEA as irresponsible young women who waste public resources while serving as incompetent mothers to their children. In drawing on images of poor young women of color as deviant social strains undeserving of social support, they evoke a discourse historically deployed to rationalize dismantling the welfare state and shifting state priorities towards crime control. This change was largely accomplished by criminalizing the poor recipients of public support as sources of social disorder that needed to be controlled. Consequently, it is no coincidence that we see both constructs of welfare burden and criminal conflated here when SJEA staff members speak disparagingly about students.

Much of this discourse not only frames youth as criminal, but also scorns or mocks the presumed criminality of students' families and communities. For example, in the fall the school initiates an effort to involve students' fathers in their education and progress at school by inviting them to come in and share breakfast with them. Upon learning about the program, one of the classroom assistants complains to another staff member about having to contact students' fathers for the event at the school. Holding a list of students' home contact information, she laments "I gotta call all of these and be like, 'Would Michael's dad like to come to [SJEA's breakfast program]?'" She immediately answers her own question, "'No, Michael's dad is doing twenty-five to life,'" before erupting in laughter.

In complaining about the work that this program creates for her, the staff member jokes about the program being futile because she imagines that students' fathers will be absent and imprisoned. Framing students' families as criminal contributes to an implication that students are bound for imprisonment themselves. Camaraderie within the lunch room and among staff members during breaks like these is often based in participating in and contributing to this type of discourse. Not everyone talks like this, but it is certainly common.[4] In the context of institutions that manage youth on juvenile probation, this discourse helps establish a status that rationalizes the ongoing criminal labeling and punishment that these staff members participate in or are incorporated into. In her book *Crook County*, sociologist Nicole Gonzalez Van Cleve describes how racist workplace cultures are institutionalized in the positions of power responsible for processing the criminal cases of the city's poor people of color (2016). However, unlike the prosecutor's office in Chicago that Van Cleve examines, most of the school and probation staff in Fresno are themselves Latinas/os, matching the demographics of the young people channeled through the county's juvenile justice system. Consequently, criminal status as constructed through the carceral social order is instrumental here in establishing an ideological distance between workers and the youth they oversee. For many of these workers, socialization into their roles as the managers of criminalized youth entails learning to talk about not only students, but also members of their own communities, as criminal. One of the most common discursive methods that workers use to establish this status among students is highlighting the presumed differences in how they were raised and how the youth here are brought up.

This discourse commonly frames parents as modeling or passing this criminality onto students by being poor role models, describing students' imprisonable status as multigenerational. While I sit in one of the counselors' offices writing up fieldnotes, Mr. Dominguez and Officer Taylor—a school administrator and PO respectively—come by to ask the counselor about a student who wants extra time to get to school. Students are required to be in school before 8 A.M., but most do not have access to a car or a family member who can drop them off, so they have to take the bus (or oftentimes multiple buses) to get here. Depending on how far away they live, school officials sometimes give students extra time to arrive before being marked as tardy, as these journeys can take over an hour for some students. However, both Mr. Dominguez and Officer Taylor object to this particular request because they say that this student already lives relatively close.

Mr. Dominguez takes the student's request for more time in the morning as a reflection of the parents' inability to raise their son as a responsible member of society. "The parents are modeling laziness for these kids," he laments as he shakes his head. In complaining about the late student, Mr. Dominguez slips into generalizing about the parents of all the students. His critical portrayal allows both him and Officer Taylor to contrast these parents' presumed incompetence with memories of how their own parents taught them to get to school/work on time and to be responsible adults.

Officer Taylor agrees with Mr. Dominguez, but also makes a telling jump to what he sees as the proper social roles for these young people: "They should be learning trades here. Not everyone is cut out for algebra. Someone has to be the janitors."

Mr. Dominguez sighs resignedly, "The way they're going, these kids are going to be a strain on the system."

There is much to unpack in these comments. Both critique students' parents as irresponsible role models who pass their poor work ethic onto their children, evoking old culture-of-poverty arguments that essentially blame impoverished communities for their own marginalization. Officer Taylor shifts his comments from blaming parents as irresponsible to arguing that the school should be training its students for industrial labor in light of these parents' apparent failures. He frames blue collar work in terms of presumed abilities, identifying janitors and trades workers as students who were incapable of learning algebra. He describes the probation youth at SJEA as intellectually limited and therefore candidates best suited for industrial labor, as skilled trades workers if they're lucky, but Mr. Dominguez takes this a step further in painting them as likely strains on society based on "the way they're going." It is ambiguous if he is referring to them as impending socioeconomic burdens as unemployable laborers, as incarcerated prisoners, or as both.

Ruth Gilmore argues that, in addition to addressing surpluses in land, capital, and state capacity, mass imprisonment in California emerged as a state response designed to contain the workers made obsolete by the state's transition to a globalized service economy (2007). Facilitating this response was an ideology of individual meritocracy that overshadowed the state's failure to incorporate industrial labor into the new economy. In their comments, authority figures at SJEA follow this same pattern in discursively linking students' educational shortcomings to the laziness and irresponsibility of probation youth and their families, rather than the institutional failure of a system that (1) hasn't taught these students algebra, and (2) has instead funneled them and many more poor youth of color out of public schools and into the juvenile justice system. Similarly, they describe the lack of future job prospects they expect students to face as resulting from "the way they're going," not deindustrialization or the lack of work available for poor students abandoned or pushed out of public school systems. In the ideological discourse that accompanied the shift from the welfare to the carceral state, working-class Black and Latina/o communities that were shut out of the changing job market were commonly blamed for their own unemployment. Connecting joblessness to the presumed deviance of poor communities of color effectively rationalized the mass imprisonment these surplus workers were now exposed to. This pattern is reproduced here, as students' criminality is framed as related to poor learned work habits, identifying their families as the producers of ongoing social disorder that calls for being controlled.

The carceral social order produces and socializes criminalized identities that help ensure that students are surveilled, arrested, and punished in the future. But it also accomplishes the production of a logic that dictates we should view probation youth not as children, but as members of a burdensome and multigenerational criminal class. To an extent all workers vent, complain, and make jokes about their work or about those they encounter on the job. For those working with youth, this inevitably includes backstage discourses about these young people. But it is significant that here these jokes and complaints take on a neoliberal discourse that identifies students as social liabilities unworthy of support. Students' poverty, race, and ensnarement in juvenile detention and probation subjects them to being targeted by this discourse. However, the carceral social order magnifies this situation by defining students by affiliation and subsequently as criminal first and foremost, establishing the school as a punitive space rather than a nurturing one. These labels facilitate denigrating critiques of students' families, parents, sexuality, or other targets of moral judgment, which in turn reinforce perceptions of probation youth's deviant nature. But most importantly, these ideological constructions establish a social standing for students beyond the school itself, as staff members' perceptions of students' potential shape their willingness to either help students transfer back into public school districts, or to send them back to juvenile hall and keep them circulating in the justice system.

## Punishing Social Problems

A product of the criminal status attached to students, their families, and their communities, is that the criminal justice system becomes a default mechanism for managing many of the personal, family, or health problems that they experience. Students' problems with substance abuse, domestic violence, or mental or emotional health are often channeled through the juvenile justice system, which for many is the only source of treatment or counseling they receive. However, this means that as problems persist they risk subjecting youth to additional punishment, or authorities' scorn if they are legally forced to call for medical assistance.

When I'm first getting to know Anthony, I find him sitting in the front office one day late in the morning. He has just been suspended and is waiting for his parents to pick him up, but the front desk receptionist can't get a hold of his parents, and according to school policy cannot let him go without them.

Anthony can't understand why they are making him just wait in the front office if he has already been told to leave school. "Why can't you just give me my tokens and let me go? It's not like I'm gonna die if I go early."

The receptionist retorts, "Actually it happened before, a student was stabbed over here walking home from school." She points over her shoulder to indicate which street this stabbing took place on.

"Man I would rather die than stay here. Then I could see my homie, [and] my lil cousin. [She] was only nine years old when she died." I sit next to him and ask him what happened. "Leukemia. Doctor said she wouldn't last two weeks, and she wasn't even on life support then. That's when I stopped giving a fuck." Behind him I see the receptionist silently get up and leave the room. I stay with him and ask him about why he's being sent home. "They hate me here. This school is fucking gay. I can't wait to get off probation so I can get out of here."

"How much longer is that?"

"Til February." He counts on his fingers. "Damn, ten months! I would rather they just lock me up for the rest of my probation than do this shit. In there I wouldn't get no dirties, wouldn't have my PO in my face, wouldn't get sent out of class. . . . I'd just get in less trouble."

"But wouldn't you rather be home than locked up?"

"That's true. But I'd rather be locked up and be cool when I get out than be on probation." As Anthony starts to explain how being on probation makes him feel like he is unfairly judged as a bad person, an on-site nurse comes in with the receptionist and asks him if needs an involuntary psychiatric hold because of the comments that he made.

She explains, "You said you would rather die than come here." If a student makes any comments that can be regarded as suicidal or indicating self-harm, even if made in jest, staff legally have to report what they call a 5150. A 5150 immediately summons an ambulance (which the student's family must later pay for) and requires that the juvenile be placed on a medical hold until it can be determined that they are no longer a threat.

Anthony fires back, defending his statement: "Being here is like being dead! They take your soul! They take your things, they take everything!" He exclaims his protest with a hint of playfulness, belied by the smallest trace of a smile, as if he knows he is perhaps a bit dramatic but at the same time not altogether wrong. His comments are an objection against the school that he is not ready to abandon quite yet.

The nurse lets him finish before patiently asking him if he is considering hurting himself, emphasizing the importance that he be serious for a moment and not take this lightly. He stares up at her with an awkward grin while she explains this, perhaps cautious to let his guard down in front of her. After a moment he breaks his smile and shakes his head. He responds that he isn't, that he lost a good friend to suicide and would never do that.

Anthony's PO comes into the office and immediately gets into his face, scolding him for causing the 5150 scare and warning him that his mouth keeps getting him into trouble. "I can tell your dad what you said, I'll bet he'd like that!" she tells him, threatening to get Anthony in trouble with his father over the potential costs of calling an ambulance for his comments. Fresno's juvenile justice system already places great expense on students' parents, charging some of the poorest families in the county fees for going through booking and detention in JDF, placement on house arrest, and even for truancy at SJEA. Few can afford an extra thousand dollars to cover the ambulance on top of these costs. Anthony's off-the-cuff comment made in frustration from wanting to go home leads to a confrontation from a PO who sees him as a hassle, potentially creating more trouble for him both at home and on his record.

As much as Anthony puts up a front, he deals with a lot of pain and struggle. His parents work in the agricultural fields that surround the city, and from a young age have regularly brought him out with them to help pick crops for the farm owners. This background, combined with a history of hyperactivity and trouble focusing, has made it difficult for him to adjust and stay consistent in the classroom, jeopardizing his educational progress and leaving him behind his grade level. On top of this he has also experienced much loss as a teenager, experiencing the deaths of a young family member and a close friend. But he does not feel that his problems are necessarily recognized or taken seriously by the punitive officials in his life, such as his PO who instead tries to force him to take her seriously through intimidation and threats. For him SJEA is a place where he feels defined by his probation file, and a place that he feels makes things worse for him rather than helping him catch up with school, to the extent that he thinks he would actually get in less trouble if locked up. Anthony's experience reflects a broader pattern that distributes punishment as a default state response to poor youth of color. For young people with problematic home lives or mental/emotional health issues, the outbursts that may stem from these struggles often lead to more punishment rather than help.

The reliance on crime control to confront social problems brings many of the poor youth of color victimized by these problems into the system as criminals to be managed. Sociologist Jerry Flores argues that this is particularly true for Black and Latina girls who—when struggling with abusive home lives—are often criminalized as juvenile delinquents rather than recognized as domestic violence victims who need help (2016). His findings are consistent with the experiences of young women in Fresno's juvenile justice system. For example, when I ask Marla about incidents that led to her going to JDF, she answers:

> Well, just cuz of my family. I guess cuz my mom and her boyfriend would always get drunk and everything. They would act like dumbasses. So . . . (pause) they would start hitting each other and I would always get in between. He would hit my mom and I would go and I would beat his ass. With like a bat or something. I would like, mess him up and he would call the cops. I wasn't tripping. You know, cuz I went in for a good cause. The three last times I went in there [were] for that.

Marla's growing criminal history is not the result of gangbanging or a drug problem. Instead, she is repeatedly arrested and incarcerated because she insists on intervening when her mother is being beaten. This same bind was sadly true for many of the girls who came through SJEA, as several of them were placed on probation for charges that stemmed from domestic disputes with parents or step-parents within a violent home. In the course of navigating juvenile institutions because of this probation, many girls were then subsequently marked as gang affiliated through the labeling processes institutionalized here. This marking was similarly the case with Marla, who instead of receiving support as a victim of domestic abuse, was criminalized, incarcerated, and ultimately validated by her probation officer as a Norteña associate because her cousins were already documented as gang members.

Not unlike prisons, a great number of youth passed through juvenile justice institutions have problems with substance abuse, domestic violence, or mental illness. The prison building boom and sizeable public investment in crime control has largely come at the expense of financing social welfare for the nation's most vulnerable families (Gilmore 2007). In many places county jails and prisons have consequently become some of the largest providers of mental health care (Torrey et al. 2010). For the poor young people in Fresno, the only treatment that many are able to access is that provided through the justice system. For example, young residents who need rehabilitation for substance abuse problems but cannot afford a private facility may have to go through juvenile hall to get it via a six-month stay in JDF's designated addiction treatment unit. Similarly, a number of youth I encountered in JDF reported being diagnosed with mental illness, but most of the treatment they received for these issues was accessed through the juvenile justice system.

These young people generally had little access to treatment before their arrests, meaning that the juvenile justice system became a significant provider for the care they needed. But the danger in this situation is that youth may then learn to see criminal punishment and confinement as appropriate or what they need to address their problems. Such was the case with Vincent, a bipolar sixteen-year-old with severe anger problems who became institutionalized after his long stay in JDF. After spending over a year in custody, he now feels uneasy going back to school as a high school student, even longing to go back into detention where he is comfortable.

I find Vincent sitting in time-out in the hallway, and he opens up about his struggles adjusting to the school after being in JDF for over a year. "Honestly I want to go back to juvenile hall right now sir. Just for a few days, just to get my head straight. I just feel better in there."

"You feel safer in there?" I ask him.

"That too." Vincent adds.

"Why do you feel like it's more dangerous out here?"

"Cuz I can't control myself out here," Vincent explains.

"Why do you feel like you like it more in there?" I ask, feeling a bit confused.

"I dunno, I just been in there so long I think I just got used to it. I know how it is in there, I know all the staff, all the rules. . . . It's like my home in there."

The state's ideological emphasis on crime control effectively channels poor people with health and personal problems into punitive institutions. Incarceration becomes a common outcome of such problems for many poor youth of color, as those who have to rely on the juvenile justice system as a source of treatment may subsequently learn to see themselves as belonging inside its facilities. Vincent became so used to being confined in custody that at sixteen, he already feels out of place outside of juvenile detention. This experience combined with the multigenerational criminal status ascribed to poor communities of color leads some young residents to see prison as a likely or even fitting consequence of the problems they see plaguing their families or communities. Students regularly hear the adults in their lives tell them that they are bound for prison, and for some this message is internalized, as I would often hear students say to me or to each other that they will go to prison someday, or be in and out of institutions for most of their lives. For example, when I ask Angel his thoughts on the potential of future incarceration, he explains:

> I don't know, cuz there's the way my family is, I don't know, druggies and all that. I feel like I'm gonna eventually get locked up cuz my dad's been locked up my whole life and everything else. I think that's where I fucked up, [because] I always had a fuckin dickhead stepdad. . . . When I went back I was seventeen and he was tryin' to be like, I'm [going to] tell you what to do, woo woo woo. So I was listenin' just cuz they're cop callers. They'll call my probation officer, so I was just listening, whatever. I turned eighteen and I was just like, "Fuck it, I ain't listenin' to them no more!" They can't tell me what to do.

Angel feels that he has a significant chance of being incarcerated at some point as an adult because of his family—both "the way [his] family is" and his father's long imprisonment, but also because he feels his parents facilitate his criminalization. He describes his family as comprised of "druggies," but through this term[5] he frames this family's history of addiction as a status that explains their incarceration rather than as an ongoing medical issue. He reveals a perspective that understands his as a particular type of family whose members get locked up, and his father's prison term as something that makes it more likely that he himself will be imprisoned by virtue of being from his family. He is describing a multigenerational carceral status, one that not only treats addiction as a criminal offense, but also enables law enforcement to insert itself into his parents' relationship with him.

The carceral social order defines the incarcerated by ascribed and criminalized affiliations, and these resulting identities are subsequently exported back into poor communities of color. This process essentially marks residents of these neighborhoods—particularly their young people—as criminal social subjects, and therefore as imprisonable. The consequence of this constructed status is that, in the context of mass incarceration, many social problems affecting poor youth of color are managed through crime control. Punishment subsequently becomes a default state response for addressing substance abuse, mental illness, or domestic violence survivors, treating youth as criminal even when they are victimized.

CONCLUSIONS

The institutionalization of the carceral social order in punitive facilities constructs and socializes criminalized identities that then spill over into criminalized neighborhoods. But the consequences of this spillover are not limited to the mere expansion of carceral affiliations, as it also entails the extension of a logic that identifies the residents of poor communities of color as the appropriate targets of incarceration within a neoliberal political economy. Part of this identification is accomplished by establishing an expertise that recognizes many of the actions of marginalized youth, particularly forms of creative expression, as examples of gang activity. At the same time, neighborhood police learn to use the carceral social order as an authoritative template for identifying local youth as particular types of gang-involved criminal threats in the communities they patrol. But in the state's neoliberal social order, the marking of poor communities of color as criminal functions to delegitimize the welfare state and facilitate a transition to a globalized economy. Toward this end, the reliance on the carceral social order socializes youth workers to see criminalized Black and Brown teenagers as irresponsible and unemployable socioeconomic burdens, and as coming from communities that strain public resources and consequently require punitive social management and control. Once recognized as criminal threats, crime control then becomes a standard state response to the broad range of social problems that impact poor youth of color, feeding them into the criminal justice system.

# Conclusion

## *"How You Just Gonna Make Up Your Mind About Where We're Gonna Be, When Our Minds Should Be Going Higher?"*

On an afternoon in late Spring I pull Rachel, Monica, and Andrea out of class for the last period of the day so that they can work on their assignments in a small group setting. Shortly after we get started, Monica asks me how long I will be working at San Joaquin Educational Academy (SJEA) for my project. "I'll probably be here through the end of the year" I tell her.

"And after that you'll go back to school? Where do you go?" she asks.

"UCSB."

"Where's that?"

"Santa Barbara, like four hours away."

Rachel is listening in, smiling. "I want to go to a school like that."

Monica looks back to me: "Isn't it expensive to go there? Like don't you have to pay a lot to go to college?"

"Kind of, but when you apply you fill out this thing called a FAFSA. You need your parents' tax information, and depending on your situation the government can help pay for you to go to school."

"Will they help if your parents are on welfare?"

"Yeah, if they're on welfare then you probably qualify for them to pay for most of it."

"Oh OK, cuz my mom's on welfare," she says chuckling.

Rachel becomes curious and has her own questions. "Do they look at your history?"

"For financial aid?" I ask.

"No, when you apply to the school."

"Like a criminal history? No, not really. If anything it might help cuz it shows . . ."

Andrea joins in, "Shows you're trying to do better, huh?"

I nod with enthusiasm, excited that they have so many questions about this. "Yeah, exactly, like you've been through all this and learned all these things and now want to go to school."

Monica continues inquisitively, "What do they have at your school? Like, what's it for?"

"Majors?" I ask. "Pretty much anything. I don't even know how many they have."

"What do you do?"

"Sociology."

"What's that?"

"Study of society," I respond.

Andrea, to whom I have already described the project in greater detail than Rachel or Monica, excitedly elaborates. "He's writing a book about our school! He's gonna put me in it, and I'm gonna buy his book when it comes out!" She asks if I'm going to publish it "like a real book," and I tell her that's my goal if I can do it.

"You should, sir," she responds.

The girls start talking about their own goals and what they want to do with their futures. Rachel says that she wants to go into the military for four years then enroll into college, presumably taking advantage of the GI Bill. Andrea, however, is critical of the military, replying, "I don't like the military, there's enough people dying." Monica understands this sentiment but at the same time says her cousin is "making hella money" in the Navy, so she gets why people enlist. But she says she wants to be a nurse working with kids, or a physical trainer helping people recover from injuries. Andrea agrees, saying she wants to be a nurse herself or a juvenile corrections officer.

"I need to figure out what I want to do quick though, cuz its coming up fast!" Rachel realizes, anxious about her impending adulthood.

"I used to want to be a teacher when I was younger, but fuck that!" exclaims Monica. They all start laughing, imagining themselves as teachers and joking about how hard it would be dealing with kids and how mad they would get, especially at a school like SJEA.

Their laughter ends abruptly as a tall, stiff, and serious probation officer (PO)—an offsite officer I don't recognize—passes through the room. The girls all get quiet until he passes. Once he is gone Andrea tells the others, "Man, I would be scared if that was my PO."

"That's Armando's PO!" Monica explains. "He told him that if he gets another dirty he's gonna hold him 'til he's eighteen." She stops for a moment, writing something on her paper. "Everyone says Armando is going to prison."

Andrea scowls and shakes her head. "That's fucked up. I got into it with this one guy cuz we were arguing and he was all 'I'm going to Wasco and you're going to Chowchilla.' I beat him up and I was like, 'Man, fuck you! How are you gonna say that about me, just plan where I'm gonna end up?' In two years, I'm not gonna be locked up. I'm gonna be in school somewhere. How you just gonna make up your mind about where we're gonna be, when our minds should be going higher?"

In writing out this manuscript, I wanted to avoid ending this work on an upbeat note. There is something a little too comfortable about following up stories about poor and young people suffering with a discussion of how resilient they are. It lends itself too easily to a complacency that assumes the people in this story fight back, and will ultimately be alright.

We should not feel comfortable about anything that has been discussed in this text. We should feel angry. The participants, and particularly the young people, whose stories comprise this manuscript are not alright. Some have died in the time between staring this research and publishing it in this book. Many more face uncertain futures as they wrestle to escape the justice system and try to establish themselves as adults.

However, at the same time, ending on this grim note is not fair to the young people in this story either. They have not resigned themselves to imprisonment, and many rightfully resent the suggestion that they are bound for this fate. Like most adolescents they are uncertain about the directions of their lives, and they have their own ambitions and aspirations they want to pursue. Some like Rachel and Monica dream about attending a university. More than anything, most want to simply make their family proud by graduating from a "normal" school. It is important for me to include these dimensions of who the students are, because if you as readers are to believe that they are not simply criminals, it is necessary for you to hear from them that they do not see themselves as criminals.

Much like the penal facilities that hold many of their relatives, friends, and neighbors, the students at SJEA find themselves caught in an institution that is essentially designed to warehouse them. They are often graded based on how docile they can remain while watching movies, listening to books-on-tape, filling in worksheet packets, sewing pillows, or even just coloring. Through such activities the school emphasizes student control over education, and rather than incorporating youth back into local school districts, the institution instead functions to hold them out. In preparing them for future warehousing rather than incorporation into the labor market or public sphere, it effectively reinforces the multiple voices who have told these youth that they are bound for prison.

But students resist this. When one of my regular tutoring groups received the same packet of worksheets for a third day in a row, they spent less than a minute circling random answers to finish it as quickly as possible. They soon became bored, and with little else to do just put their heads down on the table. Edgar finally writes something onto the front page of his packet and turns it towards me.

"I wrote Mr. Turner a note," he tells me. On the front of his packet it reads, "Mr. Turner give us a new packet!" It makes me laugh, and when JC sees it he grins and writes on his too: "I agree with Edgar, so do it!"

The boys' gesture is small but revealing. Like so many of their peers here, they are young people hungry for engagement and for opportunities to defy what is overwhelmingly expected of them. But as teenagers linked to carceral affiliations, they are regarded as dangers designated for this kind of human storage, contained in spaces that prioritize controlling them over engaging their curiosities. Rather than being warehoused, many explained they wanted to return to public schools where they could be mixed in with "nerdy" or high-achieving students who they said they could learn and benefit from. For these youth, identifying with a criminalized affiliation is not synonymous with identifying as criminal.

The affiliations these students adopt—and the carceral social order in general—are constructed through the sorting policies and institutional segregation that penal authorities use to preserve security in the prison. In efforts to control rivaling prison gangs, correctional staff use the racial identities, hometowns, and peer networks of incoming prisoners to categorize them into gang-associated groups that are then isolated from each other. This establishes a system of racialized collective identities that structures everyday life in the prison, and that inmates use to access protection and support during their incarceration. However, because these identities are based in gang rivalries, the process that ties inmates to these groups also positions them into the conflicts between them.

In high-incarceration neighborhoods, young people learn about these groups and rivalries that their community members are positioned into through the experiences of imprisoned and paroled loved ones. Through this secondary prisonization (Comfort 2008), young residents come to identify with the affiliations of their imprisoned friends and relatives, and despise their rivals for hurting people they care about. The concentration of incarceration into poor communities of color therefore contextualizes this neighborhood familiarity with carceral affiliations. However, many of these youth are also sorted into this social order themselves by juvenile justice institutions that reproduce the categorizing work of the prison. In these spaces, the affiliations that youth hear about from older contacts become important for navigating the juvenile facility, reinforcing the role affiliations play in these adolescents' lives. While these affiliations are constructed, reproduced, and institutionalized through the management practices of punitive facilities, the knowledge of how to use these identities to successfully navigate the carceral institution is organically passed down in the collective strategies that communities employ to adapt to persistent incarceration.

The collective identities created through these institutional processes are distinct from prison and street gangs, but come to contextualize conflicts and violence both inside and outside the penal facility. As residents in high-incarceration neighborhoods become aware of how their neighbors are classified inside the prison, these identities come to contextualize the community's relationship with its incarcerated members. The young people featured in this work understand and make sense of the prison's connections to their neighborhoods through the carceral identities that also shape many of their day-to-day experiences in the juvenile justice system. Passed down from the experiences of incarcerated community residents, these criminalized affiliations function as learned ways of being that serve as important situated identities in the event of imprisonment. Recognizing imprisonment as a common experience for local residents, criminalized youth learn to incorporate these affiliations into their gender, race, and class identity performances, and imagine how they would fit into the prison's divisive social order. But these simultaneously learned and ascribed identities also effectively mark young people as imprisonable subjects requiring future surveillance and punishment. As these identities become more visible in the community, the penal sorting process that created them is likewise established as an authoritative structure for labeling poor youth of color as particular types of criminal gang members. Mirroring the process imposed on those entering the carceral facility, local police learn to identify gang members in the community by racially categorizing poor youth of color, then positioning them into the rivalries between affiliations based on their neighborhood, peers, and appearance.

This extension of prison-based identities, and the presumed criminality that is associated with them, is an important aspect of how the state makes criminal subjects, and how this subsequently keeps the system of mass incarceration going. The broad utilization of the carceral social order as a criminalizing template represents a significant expansion of what Foucault argues is the prison's designed function—producing delinquency by constructing and defining popular understandings of criminality (1977). The categories assigned to incoming prisoners in the sorting process are imagined and treated as criminal gangs in themselves. Consequently, they are recorded in people's files as gang involvement, shape the conditions of one's probation or parole, and become part of a criminal status attached to those circulating through the penal system. But as these spread back to home communities through interpersonal relationships and appropriation by local facilities, the prison's ability to produce this delinquency extends beyond the penal institution itself. The exportation of the sorting process as a labeling technique extends with it a logic that identifies poor communities of color as gang-infested spaces, and within a political economy that relies on the prison to sustain itself, as the fitting targets of mass imprisonment. In this manner, mass incarceration is able to perpetuate itself by making itself seem necessary—it produces the very "criminals" that it then needs to contain.

What is accomplished by this extensive identification of the young residents of poor Black and Brown communities as public threats is an ideological call for their continual criminalization, control, and punishment. This cements the imprisonable status ascribed to poor communities of color, which ensures survival of mass incarceration as a system, but also protects the status quo for the various structures that benefit from this system. The authoritative preoccupation with finding and monitoring gang members ultimately buttresses state efforts to facilitate a globalized economy (Gilmore 2007), one in which the dismantling of the welfare state and the subsequent shift in public resources to crime control is rationalized by the threat criminal gangs are presumed to pose. In addition to legitimizing this channeling of resources into public safety, this community criminalization also contributes to the isolation and divestment of working-class Black and Latina/o neighborhoods. The popular recognition of these spaces as gang neighborhoods depresses residents' home values while inflating those of communities that can highlight their distance from this recognized criminality. In Fresno this plays out as suburban and commercial development pushes further and further north, benefiting from the White and middle-class flight from its southern neighborhoods that is fueled by the official distinction of these residential spaces as "gang areas."

The findings of this ethnography complicate how we should talk about the collateral consequences of mass incarceration. One of the insidious outcomes of cycling so many people from one place through the carceral system is that it establishes the prison as an influential socializing institution in the community. Part of the socializing work accomplished by this "prisonization" is teaching the incarcerated to negotiate and perform the identities that are institutionalized by the prison through racial sorting and seg-regation. But this also has consequences for prisoners' loved ones and home communities, as families and neighborhoods are implicated in the status and conflicts generated by prison sorting. As these practices are also appro-priated by local facilities, probation youth experience this secondary pris-onization by learning to perform the same carceral identities in punitive contexts. This gives us an empirical illustration of how Wacquant's carceral continuum (2001) operates in poor Black and Latina/o communities. But as law enforcement increasingly entrenches itself into additional community institutions (Kupchik 2010; Rios 2011), more and more spaces may conceiv-ably become such "punitive contexts."

Diminishing the prison's influence as a socializing force, as well as the violence and labeling that unfolds from this bridging of prison and neigh-borhood, therefore requires a "downsizing of the carceral state" (Thompson 2011) and its presence in marginalized communities. Minimizing the importance carceral affiliations have in communities of color demands eliminating imprisonment as a common life event for poor Black and Latina/o residents. Reducing the social influence of the prison requires cur-tailing the systems that feed mass incarceration as well as those that actu-ally carry it out. For example, public school districts must protect their most marginalized students by structurally disrupting the school-to-prison pipe-line through curbing expulsions, keeping students enrolled in schools, and restricting the encroachment of law enforcement into educational systems. Additionally, recognizing these consequences of mass incarceration makes a strong argument for decarceration, or reducing the prison system itself. Making the prison a less prominently featured tool of the justice system may make it a less dominant presence in poor communities of color and expose fewer residents to the conflicts and labels institutionalized inside. The recent restructuring of California's prison system, aimed at easing the overpopulation of prison facilities, offers an opportunity to reduce the number of people sorted into carceral rivalries. However, at this point this restructuring has primarily entailed transferring and incarcerating more people at county jails, shifting problems to the local level without question-ing our reliance on incarceration and the impact it has for criminalized communities of color. Curtailing the consequences that mass incarceration has imposed on these communities requires taking the opportunity afforded by realignment to not only keep tens of thousands of state residents out of prison, but to also look to alternatives to imprisonment. Ideally, minimizing the prison's role in the state's management of crime and social problems may spare marginalized Californians from the processes that currently institutionalize carceral rivalries, criminal labels, and an imprisonable status into their daily lives.

This work also has important implications for how we think about the school-to-prison pipeline. While we typically think of this pipeline as working one way—funneling disadvantaged youth into corrections—this research shows that something also comes back down the pipeline from the prison that structures and legitimizes this criminalization of young people. We can see here how understandings of criminality based in penal sorting practices shape the logic and processes by which young people are racially cast as particular types of gang members and associates, and how this facilitates pushing them onto a trajectory that ends in imprisonment. The schools and the juvenile facilities that comprise this pipeline categorize students in the same manner as the prison, effectively marking them as presorted inmates. As a result, the young people targeted by this process learn to look to the experiences of previously or currently incarcerated relatives and neighbors as lessons on how to manage the punitive facility and the carceral social order that structures it. Disrupting the school-to-prison pipeline must therefore be understood as both a structural and ideological project. In addition to terminating the institutional connections between school districts and law enforcement agencies that criminalize students, challenging this pipeline must also entail a resistance against the logic of racial sorting that flows down from the prison and informs the categorization of poor students of color into groups of presumed gang affiliates. This resistance is particularly important for young people who are transferred into alternative or continuation schools, as adolescents who are seen as difficult students are effectively isolated into facilities in which the labels ascribed to them are more difficult to evade or resist.

Similarly, in critiquing the juvenile justice system and school to prison pipeline, it would be shortsighted to blame the struggles of young people in these facilities on mean-spirited teachers or POs who simply don't understand them. The staff members I met in the Juvenile Detention Facility genuinely wanted to help youth, and the faculty at SJEA were very dedicated and caring teachers. Interestingly, many of the youth really looked up to some of them and even wanted to work in juvenile justice facilities themselves when they grew up. But at the same time these staff members are embedded in a system in which helping youth means criminalizing them, locking them up, and assuming that this "tough love" will teach them a lesson rather than simply cement their position within the carceral social order. Changing this pattern is not a matter of finding better teachers or more understanding law enforcement personnel, but about rethinking the dominant logic that guides these institutions—namely, that identifying and controlling gang members is an effective approach to preventing violence.

The findings presented in this work also call for us to rethink the extent to which we rely on policing gang identities as a solution for problems of crime and neighborhood violence more broadly. In detailing the processes by which criminalized affiliations are defined, enforced, and framed as gangs within the punitive institution, this work reveals the extent to which "gangs" function as a legal construct for articulating the criminality collectively ascribed to communities of poor and nonwhite people. Indeed, the criminalization of familial and neighborhood peer networks as gangs directly shapes the perception among many of the youth consulted in this book that their own eventual incarceration is perhaps likely, precisely because it is their relationships with parents, siblings, cousins, uncles, neighbors, and friends that is regarded as criminal. Suspected gang affiliation has become an unquestioned basis for excluding and controlling people as social threats—it serves as a blanket justification for surveilling the street corners of poor neighborhoods, for pulling over and interrogating young people, for pushing students out of public school districts, for arresting and incarcerating teenagers, for keeping adolescents contained within the juvenile justice system through endless probation violations, for sending them to prison as adults, and for then keeping them on parole for much of their adult lives. But as a crime control strategy, policing gangs can be a law enforcement campaign without end, as it essentially targets a threat that can potentially never really be eliminated. Instead, much like the War on Drugs, it focuses on an enemy that can be perpetually and instantly replaced whenever removed. This is because as a constructed and ascribed status, a new "gang member" can always be identified the moment the previous target has been arrested and extracted from the neighborhood. Additionally, emphasizing gangs as a priority for policing also establishes them as a priority in the sorting and management of people after arrest. Here, long periods of confinement and uncertainty in carceral facilities provide ample opportunity to firmly institutionalize the very criminalized group identities that the justice system purports to combat.

If justice system institutions are indeed interested in neutralizing the influence of "gangs" or criminalized affiliations, this has to begin with reducing the emphasis they place on gang membership in the identification and processing of the young people they monitor. This book demonstrates that facilities should hesitate to categorize or segregate young people based on assumed or potential gang ties, as this imposes gang-associated identities onto many otherwise uninvolved youth. Similarly, courts and police must recognize that relying on gang membership as a measure of criminality (through sentencing enhancements or the identification of criminal suspects) is not only imprecise, but also makes these identities and rivalries much more difficult for criminalized populations to avoid. The socialized affiliations described in this work not only push youth towards gang involvement (Lopez-Aguado 2016), but such strong group identities are also correlated with self-reported offending among self-identified gang members (Hennigan and Spanovic 2012). Imposing and perpetuating these identities is then clearly counterproductive for public safety, adding another dimension to Clear's contention that overincarceration increases crime (2007). Recognizing the state's role in naming and imposing gang identity calls for authority figures and youth workers to use extreme caution in assuming gang membership, and for researchers to acknowledge this when operationalizing it in future scholarship.

Finally, in keeping with this deemphasizing of gangs as a priority in policing, we must also deprioritize the importance we place on gang membership as a basis for organizing inmates and probation youth in punitive facilities. This shift would require a dramatic reorganization of how punishment is structured in the state, one that is certainly possible and towards which previous steps have shown considerable promise. The state of Texas used to have problems with racial violence in its prison system similar to those seen in California until a court order demanded the system desegregate its facilities. After Texas integrated 62 percent of the double cells in its prison system in the 1990s, the rate of interracial inmate-on-inmate assaults dropped from 31 incidents per thousand inmates to 14 incidents per thousand, and intraracial inmate-on-inmate assaults went from 43 incidents per thousand inmates to 17 per thousand, despite a near tripling of the inmate population in Texas (Trulson and Marquart 2002). Trulson and Marquart attribute the decline to prison officials improving classification processes in the absence of racial sorting, which allowed them to make more compatible cellmate pairings and more accurately identify and isolate violent inmates. The state court's ruling against segregated prisons forced prison officials to develop a new system for sorting prisoners that took a number of factors into consideration when determining where to house them. This change resulted in dramatically lower rates of violence in the prison, both between races and within racial groups.

A similar pattern unfolded towards the end of my time at SJEA. After the students started fighting each other over who could sit at the tables under the shade, the probation officers decided to change how they grouped the students. Instead of dividing the blacktop by affiliations, the POs decided to simply separate them based on who was responsible for supervising them: all of the students whose PO was at the school were on one side, and all the students with off-campus POs were on the other. This arrangement grouped students across affiliations and basically forced them to sit together.[1] Initially this move led to more frequent fights between active gang members committed to battling with rivals who in some cases were now sitting much closer, but something else happened as well. Organizing students this way made it easier for students who were not gang involved to stay out of these conflicts and not pick a side. Because their tables were now grouped closely together, there was not enough space for a clear divide between differently affiliated students. Gang-involved youth sat on opposite sides of these clusters of tables to maintain their distance, but everyone else now sat at the tables in the middle where it wasn't obvious which side, if any, they were on. In this new setup, unaffiliated students could actually remain neutral.

When I first presented this research, a colleague commented that "if people wanna fight, they're going to find a way to fight. But this is a system that all but forces people to fight." The carceral social order institutionalized inside correctional facilities is not only a system that pits inmates against each other, but even worse it is one that sets in motion a process by which young people learn to position and perceive themselves as carceral subjects. While popular discourse commonly blames criminalized youth of color for getting themselves into trouble, we need to recognize that young people learn to manage the paths that are set before them. The students who informed this research recognized that the path many expected them to follow led directly to the prison. The possibility of this fate became even more real as the survival strategies they learned to appropriate (affiliations that helped them navigate punitive environments) were criminalized and used as evidence of their criminality. This is a lived reality for criminalized communities throughout the state that we must confront, and one that what we, the state, and concerned communities have the capacity to change.

# Notes

1. Parts of this chapter were previously published in Patrick Lopez-Aguado, "The Collateral Consequences of Prisonization: Racial Sorting, Carceral Identity, and Community Criminalization," *Sociology Compass* 10, no. 1(2016): 12–23.

2. Foucault (1977) argues that this is the central accomplishment of the prison because it secures state power by depoliticizing illegality and framing obedience as a moral objective, thus preventing illegality from spreading into broader rebellion against the state.

3. Wacquant (2001) argues that the purpose of this containment has historically been to exploit the labor power of Black communities, and that the contemporary carceral continuum serves this function by forcing Black workers into underpaid and exploitable labor positions on the economic periphery.

4. As of 2004, known as the California Department of Corrections and Rehabilitation (CDCR).

5. In 2005, the Supreme Court ruled in *Johnson v. California* (03–636) that racially segregating inmates, even for the purpose of preventing violence, was unconstitutional and ordered that state prison facilities be desegregated. The CDCR has promised to comply, but thus far little progress has been made and the practice of sorting and segregating inmates by race still continues largely uninterrupted.

6. "Car" is a term used to refer to a sorted racial group in the prison, such as the "White car" or the "Fresno car."

7. There are some exceptions to this geographic distribution. For example, in Northern California being Chicana/o versus Mexican shapes much of the split between Norteña/os and Sureña/os (Mendoza-Denton 2008).

8. Avenal and Pleasant Valley State Prisons are commonly known as "Bulldog pens." These are the two prisons closest to Fresno, but a parole officer in Fresno also informed me that "they send all those guys to Avenal or

Pleasant Valley cuz nobody else wants to deal with them," suggesting this was part of segregation efforts. This statement is consistent with John Irwin's claim that Norteños and Sureños were intentionally sent to different facilities (2005).

9. Twenty-five of the thirty-four census tracts in Fresno (some overlap city limits) with poverty rates of 40 percent or more are found south of McKinley. High-poverty neighborhoods north of McKinley are still generally 60 percent to 70 percent nonwhite.

10. The District Attorney's Office also has positions supported by grant-based funding, giving them almost twice as many attorneys at their disposal compared to the Public Defenders' Office (Benjamin 2015).

11. Many reentry services in the Central Valley are also concentrated in Fresno, leading parolees from surrounding rural counties to relocate to Fresno. Many of the parolees I have met in my preliminary research at local reentry assistance and rehabilitation agencies were originally arrested and incarcerated in neighboring Tulare, Kings, or Madera Counties. It should be noted that at the time of this research, Tulare (158.7% of state average) and Kings (225.3%) Counties had some of the highest incarceration rates in the state of California (California Sentencing Institute 2017). Fresno County's incarceration rate stood at 129.6 percent of the state average.

12. These violations of probation reincarcerate the individual and extend the period of their probation for another year, making it increasingly difficult to leave the system.

13. Receiving tutoring assistance was in no way dependent on students contributing interviews, and many of the youth I worked with throughout my time at SJEA never participated in interviews.

14. Participants were also given $20 gift cards to thank them for their contribution and compensate them for their time. Student subject payments were supported by dissertation research grants from the University of California Institute for Mexico and the United States, and the UC Santa Barbara Chicano Studies Institute.

15. I rarely had to ask about this directly. Most of the time interviewees volunteered this information themselves in the course of telling their life stories, which almost always featured a point where they had to decide if they were going to gangbang or not. While it is possible that some students lied in interviews about gang membership (like one boy who changed his answer after I assured him I was not sharing his interview with his PO), the vast majority of interviewees' self-depictions of gang activity (whether claiming or denying it) were consistent with both how they interacted with other students and how other students generally perceived and described them.

16. These included cliques of Bulldogs, Norteña/os, Sureña/os, Twamp, Murder Squad, Whites, Asians, taggers, and skaters.

17. Participants were given $10 in cash to thank them for their contribution to the research and to compensate them for their time. Adult interviewees received smaller subject payments than the student participants because I

conducted these interviews before I received any research grant support, and therefore had to pay the adults out-of-pocket.

## CHAPTER 1

1. Statement from Wasco State Prison's official website, http://www.cdcr .ca.gov/Facilities_Locator/WSP.html.

2. A reference to the CalGang database, a statewide database of gang members and associates as identified by law enforcement personnel.

3. Quote taken from Parenti 1998. Fresno's Violent Crime Suppression Unit was formed in 1994, but disbanded in 2002 after several wrongful death and sexual harassment lawsuits. It was effectively replaced with the Fresno Police Department's gang suppression campaign Operation Bulldog.

4. Parolees knew that prisoners were often still assaulted in PC units, or in other parts of the prison where they could be exposed to "mainline" inmates. Additionally, some of the parolees who did go into PC were jumped after they were released when local gang youth heard they were a "dropout."

5. The number of Black students enrolled at SJEA steadily rose over the course of the year. As more Black students attended the school, the divides between Twamp and Squad became more apparent. However, at this time there were only a few Black students at the school, and almost all of them affiliated with Twamp.

6. POs usually knew if the youth on their caseloads banged or not, what feuds they were involved in, and who they did or didn't get along with, but did not often know so many details about the other youth at the school. With so many students and so much continual turnover, it seemed easier for staff supervising everyone at one time to organize students into manageable groups.

## CHAPTER 2

1. See Hunt et al. 1993 or Rafael 2009 for examples.

2. Many prison scholars (Phillips 2012; Fleisher and Decker 2001; Skarbek 2011) use Lyman's (1989) definition of prison gangs, which describes them as "a self-perpetuating and criminally-oriented organization that controls the prison environment through intimidation and violence against non-members, operating within a chain of command and code of conduct" (Phillips 2012, 53). Cars are fundamentally defined by institutional sorting, meaning they cannot be self-perpetuating, and do not resemble or operate as such criminal organizations.

3. These groups were heavily racialized in large part because of how racially segregated neighborhoods in Fresno are. Whites and Asians were not explicitly categorized by place but did tend to come from the same neighborhoods, and this became part of their shared identities.

4. Some cars (such as Norteños or Sureños) were explicitly based on regional ties, but within all racial groups the parolees tended to stick with others from the same hometowns or regions while they were in prison, matching

patterns documented in previous prison research (Irwin 2005; Phillips 2012; Cunha 2008).

5. This geographic division was not always so clean. For example, there are also Bulldog neighborhoods in West Fresno, and there are Norteña/o and Bulldog neighborhoods in the surrounding farm towns, but the geographical divisions described here are where these affiliations were most concentrated.

6. Scholars and law enforcement commonly understand the emergence of these umbrella identities as an evolution of street-corner gangs into vertically organized "corporate gangs" focused on controlling local drug trades (Venkatesh 2000). However, Fresno's affiliations do not fit this model.

7. A slang term for someone who is mentally ill.

8. Here James uses "nationality" to talk about race, evident in how he uses it to describe his own status as a Wood, which he later refers to as a "White ethnic group."

9. Whites and Southsiders in particular had very strict rules that enforced racial segregation and forbid sharing food, cell phones, or hygiene supplies outside the car.

10. Although there was some policing among the probation youth about whom they could socialize with, this was not nearly so strict or as detailed as what parolees describe in the prison.

11. The participants in this research, and people present in these sites in general, are predominantly male. The politics that structure violence in men's prisons were also absent in women's facilities. Finally, I frame this section around masculinity because girls I observed also adopted performances they describe as masculine in juvenile institutions.

12. This is of course not to say that criminalized boys and men are irrational or lack technical skills, but that the presence of the carceral social order prioritizes a physically imposing masculinity as the most relevant to adopt in this context. A strong commitment to this carceral masculinity pushed youth to fight, which extended their probation and blocked them from reentering the public school district. For adults, this similarly extended sentences and consequently disrupted career development.

13. Pascoe describes this as part of a "fag discourse" in which teenage boys perform a normative masculinity by using this slur to shame unmasculine boys, although most boys could escape this stigma and reassert their masculinity by identifying another boy as a fag (2007). Several boys at SJEA engaged in this same fag discourse, but here the term "bitch" functioned as the gender-regulating mechanism Pascoe describes more so than "fag"; whereas boys would laugh off being called a "fag," being called a "bitch," even jokingly, would prompt either an immediate deflection to someone else, or a challenge to the accuser to demonstrate that one was in fact not a "bitch."

14. A "wannabe" is a child who "wants to be" a gang member but is too young to be accepted by the current cohort of members. Calling a fifteen- to eighteen-year-old young man a wannabe is essentially infantilizing him as a young boy.

CHAPTER 3

1. *Güero* ['weɾo] is a Spanish term from Mexico used to describe a light-skinned person, although not necessarily someone who is White or mixed race.

2. Cars varied in their use of recognized leadership: some had strict hierarchies while others explicitly avoided any such structure. Among cars that did have reps, gang members tended to have the most authority (Lindsey 2009). For a thorough breakdown of the leadership hierarchies of incarcerated racial groups see Walker (2016).

3. A derisive slang term for Sureña/os.

4. I argue that Ben's use of "cool people" here is not intended to describe these students as popular, but to describe them as peers one can be cool or get along with, primarily Bulldogs, taggers, and other Eastside Latina/os. "Busters" is a derogatory term for Norteña/os.

5. The girls' discussions on this were less accessible to me as a male researcher.

6. Bulldogs and Norteña/os share many similar styles with some subtle differences, as both find themselves on the same side of many of the cultural, linguistic, and national splits between Northern/Central and Southern California Latina/os (Mendoza-Denton 2008).

7. Tattoos served a similar function in the prison, as one Norteño parolee explains: "In some places that's how you identify other people, know what I mean? Cuz you go to places and you want to know if there's any homeboys there. And they don't know if you're there, so you peel your shirt to figure out who's who."

8. See Romo 2011 for more on how California Blaxicans (mixed-race Black/Mexican individuals) are pressured to conform to monoracial identities.

9. Similarly, not sharing sensitive or personal information across racial cars was also one of the most serious rules in the prison's racial politics as well.

CHAPTER 4

1. Parts of this chapter were previously published in Patrick Lopez-Aguado, "'I Would be a Bulldog:' Tracing the Spillover of Carceral Identity," *Social Problems* 63, no. 2(2016): 203–21.

2. In 2005 California Youth Authority was rebranded as the Department of Juvenile Justice (DJJ), perhaps in part as an attempt to distance the system from its own notoriety.

3. Data gathered from infraction tallies reported by YA's Disciplinary Decision Making System, as reported in Krisberg 2003. It is important to note that Krisberg points out that these are very conservative measures that likely undercount the level of institutional violence, as these are only cases in which someone either admitted to wrongdoing or was found guilty by facility authorities. To this point, many instances likely go unreported, or are documented

under lesser charges that may be easier to prove (i.e., as "sexual harassment" as opposed to "sexual assault") Finally, this data is from 2002, when the institutional population was already much smaller than it was in the mid-1990s when Henry was incarcerated.

4. The excerpts sampled in this paragraph can be found at http://www.pris ontalk.com/forums/archive/index.php/t-520057.html.

5. *Paisa* is a term used in some Chicana/o communities to refer to Mexican nationals or first-generation migrants—Mexicana/os rather than Chicana/os. In some prisons, it can also be a category that individuals are sorted into, one composed of Spanish-speaking inmates who are not gang affiliated. This shields them from some of the racial politics or conflicts, but *paisas* are still generally recognized as associated with Sureños.

6. Much like Los Angeles's infamous Skid Row, Tent City is in an old industrial district downtown where the city has concentrated almost all of its homeless shelters and service organizations. Because there are far more homeless people than there are available beds in the shelters, hundreds of people line the streets and crowd in vacant lots and under the freeway overpasses in tents, sleeping bags, and improvised lean-tos every night.

7. Sadly, there are actually considerably more resources available for parolees in Fresno than in many other places, especially the surrounding rural regions.

8. Standard practice for "dropping out" and transferring to protective custody is a debriefing with law enforcement in which recognized gang members must provide any incriminating information they have on other gang members.

9. Gilmore and Wacquant both argue that mass incarceration has emerged as a means of state support for an otherwise unsustainable mode of capitalism, one that is characterized by public divestment and a grossly polarized labor market.

10. Under California's prison realignment, far fewer parole violators are sent back to prison, as they are more likely to be detained in local county jails. They are, however, still retained in the system and confined to institutional settings in which the carceral social order is enforced.

## CHAPTER 5

1. It is important to note here that this should not be taken as evidence that sorting "works" to prevent racial violence in the prison. As a practice it still institutionalizes racial conflicts that regularly erupt into violent encounters, and structures feuds that carry over into inmates' families and home communities. Finally, examinations of the Texas state prison system found that both interracial and intraracial assaults decreased after facilities desegregated their inmate populations (Trulson and Marquart 2002).

2. Neighborhood gang names have been changed here to protect the identities of research participants.

3. See Goodman (2008). Parolees in this research also noted this, as when asked about how they would know what to expect at a new prison, many responded that COs would "tell you how the yard is at the gate."

4. The school used numbered codes to quickly call each other for help using handheld radios. "Code 1" meant somebody needed general assistance, "Code 2" was used when students were arguing and needed to be separated before they started fighting, and "Code 3" meant that students were already actively engaged in a physical fight.

5. Greg is cautious about staff hearing some of these details, particularly the derogatory gangs terms exchanged, because youth knew that such details would be used against them in court. Saying something like "scrap," "dog," or "buster," especially during a fight, was often used against students to validate them as gang members or to justify giving them harsher sentences or stricter probation terms.

6. A less-lethal firearm used to suppress riots, which may fire rubber bullets or beanbag rounds among other forms of ammunition (also known as a "riot gun").

7. Operation Bulldog generated some 12,000 arrests over the next five years, and by 2013 media reports estimated that some 75 percent of county jail inmates were Bulldogs. The irony of course is that if this massive effort to "eliminate Bulldogs" accomplished anything, it was strengthening and spreading this identity by feeding so many residents back through the carceral machinery.

CHAPTER 6

1. Interestingly enough, most taggers were not originally arrested for this. Most got in trouble at school for drugs, fighting, or disrupting class, showing the impact of the criminalizing of school discipline in poor communities of color, as these were youth who would probably be celebrated as artists in other schools.

2. A quick image search of the popular character Garfield is a good example that highlights the range of facial expressions artists create by drawing in such "droopy" eyelids.

3. Fresno is a large secondary media market for Bay Area professional sports teams. Most of these teams' games are broadcast in Fresno, creating a substantial local fan base. The San Francisco Giants even have a minor-league baseball team based in Fresno.

4. At SJEA, this discourse was most common among the classroom/office assistants and probation officers. In my experience the teachers and private security guards were less likely to participate in these conversations or describe students in these terms, many refraining entirely.

5. Similarly, Jill McCorkel (2013) and Reuben Miller (2014) both discuss how the term *addict* is regularly used in penal or reentry institutions to vaguely refer to criminality rather than a condition requiring medical care.

CONCLUSION

1. Students from different gangs and affiliations took classes together the entire time I was at SJEA because the principal felt this was important for them to learn to work alongside those they didn't necessarily get along with. POs seemed to have more authority on how students were arranged outside, but this change made their approaches more consistent.

# Bibliography

Anderson, Elijah. 2000. *Code of the Street: Decency, Violence, and the Moral Life of the Inner City.* New York: W. W. Norton.

Benjamin, Marc. 2015. "ACLU Lawsuit Says Fresno County Public Defense Is Inadequate." *The Fresno Bee.* July 15. www.fresnobee.com/news/local /article27334588.html.

Blatchford, Chris. 2008. *The Black Hand: The Bloody Rise and Redemption of "Boxer" Enriquez, a Mexican Mob Killer.* New York: HarperCollins.

Braman, Donald. 2004. *Doing Time on the Outside: Incarceration and Family Life in Urban America.* Ann Arbor: University of Michigan Press.

Brotherton, David C. 2008. "Beyond Social Reproduction: Bringing Resistance Back in Gang Theory." *Theoretical Criminology* 12(1): 55–77.

California Department of Corrections and Rehabilitation (CDCR). 2014. "Characteristics of Felon New Admissions and Parole Violators Returned with a New Term: Calendar Year 2013." www.cdcr.ca.gov/Reports_Research /Offender_Information_Services_Branch/Annual/ACHAR1/ACHAR 1d2013.pdf.

California Sentencing Institute. 2017. A Project of the Center on Juvenile and Criminal Justice. www.cjcj.org.

Carson, E. Ann, and Daniela Golinelli. 2014. *Prisoners in 2012: Trends in Admissions and Releases, 1991–2012.* Washington, DC: Bureau of Justice Statistics, US Department of Justice.

Cate, Matthew L. 2006. "Special Review: Improper Housing of Maximum Custody Inmates at California State Prison Reception Centers." Office of the Inspector General, State of California. www.oig.ca.gov/media/reports /ARCHIVE/BOA/Reviews/Improper%20Housing%20of%20Maximum %20Custody%20Inmates%20at%20California%20State%20Prison%20 Reception%20Centers,%20Special%20Review.pdf.

Census. 2015. "2009–2013 American Community Survey." http://quickfacts .census.gov/qfd/states/06/0627000.html.

Chambliss, William J. 1973. "The Saints and the Roughnecks." *Society* 11(1): 24–31.

Clear, Todd R. 2007. *Imprisoning Communities: How Mass Incarceration Makes Disadvantaged Neighborhoods Worse.* New York: Oxford University Press.

Clemmer, Donald. 1958. *The Prison Community.* New York: Holt, Rinehart & Winston.

Comfort, Megan. 2008. *Doing Time Together: Love and Family in the Shadow of the Prison.* Chicago: University of Chicago Press.

Comfort, Megan. 2012. "'It Was Basically College to Us': Poverty, Prison, and Emerging Adulthood." *Journal of Poverty* 16(3): 308–22.

Connell, R.W. 1995. *Masculinities.* Berkeley: University of California Press.

da Cunha, Manuela Ivone P. 2008. "Closed Circuits: Kinship, Neighborhood and Incarceration in Urban Portugal." *Ethnography* 9(3): 325–50.

Davis, Mike. 1990. *City of Quartz: Excavating the Future in Los Angeles.* New York: Verso.

Durán, Robert J. 2013. *Gang Life in Two Cities: An Insider's Journey.* New York: Columbia University Press.

Ewick, Patricia, and Susan S. Sibley. 1995. "Subversive Stories and Hegemonic Tales: Toward a Sociology of Narrative." *Law and Society Review* 29(2): 197–226.

Feldman, Allen. 1991. *Formations of Violence: The Narrative of the Body and Political Terror in Northern Ireland.* Chicago: University of Chicago Press.

Fleischer, Mark S., and Scott H. Decker. 2001. "An Overview of the Challenge of Prison Gangs." *Corrections Management Quarterly* 5(1): 1–9.

Flores, Jerry. 2016. *Caught Up: Girls, Surveillance, and Wraparound Incarceration.* Berkeley: University of California Press.

Foucault, Michael. 1977. *Discipline & Punish: The Birth of the Prison.* New York: Vintage Books.

Garfinkel, Harold. 1956. "Conditions of a Successful Degradation Ceremony." *American Journal of Sociology* 61(5): 420–24.

Gilmore, Ruth Wilson. 2007. *Golden Gulag: Prisons, Surplus, Crisis and Opposition in Globalizing California.* Berkeley: University of California Press.

Goffman, Erving. 1961. *Encounters: Two Studies in the Sociology of Interaction.* Indianapolis, IN: Bobbs-Merrill.

Goodman, Philip. 2008. "'It's Just Black, White, or Hispanic': An Observational Study of Racializing Moves in California's Segregated Prison Reception Centers." *Law & Society Review* 42(4): 735–70.

Gordon, Avery F. 2007. "A World Map." In *An Atlas of Radical Cartography,* edited by Lize Mogel and Alexis Bhagat. Los Angeles: Journal of Aesthetics & Protest Press.

Gupta, Akhil, and James Ferguson. 1997. "Culture, Power, Place: Ethnography at the End of an Era." In *Culture, Power, Place: Explorations in Critical Anthropology,* edited by Akhil Gupta and James Ferguson. Durham, NC: Duke University Press.

Hagan, John, and Ronit Dinovitzer. 1999. "Collateral Consequences of Imprisonment for Children, Communities, and Prisoners." *Crime and Justice* 26: 121–62.

Haney, Craig. 2003. "Mental Health Issues in Long-Term Solitary and 'Supermax' Confinement." *Crime & Delinquency* 49(1): 124–56.

Harding, David J. 2010. *Living the Drama: Community, Conflict, and Culture among Inner-City Boys.* Chicago: University of Chicago Press.

Hennigan, Karen, and Marija Spanovic. 2012. "Gang Dynamics through the Lens of Social Identity Theory." In *Youth Gangs in International Perspective: Results from the Eurogang Program of Research*, edited by Finn-Aage Esbenson and Cheryl Maxson, 127–50. New York: Springer.

Hirshfield, Paul J. 2008. "Preparing for Prison?: The Criminalization of School Discipline in the USA." *Theoretical Criminology* 12(1): 79–101.

Hunt, Geoffrey, Stephanie Riegel, Tomas Morales, and Dan Waldorf. 1993. "Changes in Prison Culture: Prison Gangs and the Case of the 'Pepsi Generation.'" *Social Problems* 40(3): 398–409.

Irwin, John. 2005. *The Warehouse Prison: Disposal of the New Dangerous Class.* Los Angeles: Roxbury.

Irwin, John, and Donald Cressey. 1962. "Thieves, Convicts and the Inmate Culture." *Social Problems* 10(2): 142–55.

Jones, Nikki. 2009. *Between Good and Ghetto: African American Girls and Inner-City Violence.* New Brunswick, NJ: Rutgers University Press.

Katz, Susan Roberta. 1996. "Where the Streets Cross the Classroom: A Study of Latino Students' Perspectives on Cultural Identity in City Schools and Neighborhood Gangs." *Bilingual Research Journal* 20(3–4): 603–31.

Kneebone, Elizabeth. 2014. "The Growth and Spread of Concentrated Poverty, 2000 to 2008–2012." Brookings Institution. www.brookings.edu /interactives/the-growth-and-spread-of-concentrated-poverty-2000-to -2008–2012/.

Krier, Dan, C. Richard Stockner, and Paul Lasley. 2011. "The Economic and Cultural Impacts of Veterans on Rural America: The Case of Iowa." *Journal of Rural Social Sciences* 26(3): 57–82.

Krisberg, Barry. 2003. *General Corrections Review of the California Youth Authority.* Sacramento: California Department of Justice, Office of the Attorney General.

Krisberg, Barry, Linh Vuong, Christopher Hartney, and Susan Marchionna. 2010. *A New Era in California Juvenile Justice: Downsizing the State Youth Corrections System.* Berkeley, CA: Berkeley Center for Criminal Justice.

Kupchik, Aaron. 2010. *Homeroom Security: School Discipline in an Age of Fear.* New York: New York University Press.

Lindsey, Tonya D. 2009. "'It'll Never Happen': Racial Integration in California Men's Prisons." *Justice Research and Policy* 11: 78–103.

Lipsitz, George. 2012. "In an Avalanche Every Snowflake Pleads Not Guilty: The Collateral Consequences of Mass Incarceration and Impediments to Women's Fair Housing Rights." *UCLA Law Review* 59: 1746–809.

Lopez-Aguado, Patrick. 2016. "'I Would be a Bulldog': Tracing the Spillover of Carceral Identity." *Social Problems* 63(2): 203–21.

Lyman, Michael D. 1989. *Gangland: Drug Trafficking by Organized Criminals.* Springfield, IL: Charles C. Thomas.

Lynch, James P., and William J. Sabol. 2004. "Assessing the Effects of Mass Incarceration on Informal Social Control in Communities." *Criminology & Public Policy* 3(2): 267–94.

Marza, Jeff, and Christopher Uggen. 2006. *Locked Out: Felon Disenfranchisement and American Democracy*. New York: Oxford University Press.

Massey, Douglas S., Andrew B. Gross, and Kumiko Shibuya. 1994. "Migration, Segregation, and the Geographic Concentration of Poverty." *American Sociological Review* 59(3): 425–45.

Mauer, Marc. 2006. *Race to Incarcerate*. New York: New Press.

Mauer, Marc, and Meda Chesney-Lind. 2002. "Introduction." In *Invisible Punishment. The Collateral Consequences of Mass Imprisonment*, edited by Marc Mauer and Meda Chesney-Lind. New York: New Press.

Mauer, Marc, and Ryan S. King. 2007. *Uneven Justice: State Rates of Incarceration By Race and Ethnicity*. Washington, DC: The Sentencing Project.

McCorkel, Jill A. 2013. *Breaking Women: Gender, Race, and the New Politics of Imprisonment*. New York: New York University Press.

Mendoza-Denton, Norma. 2008. *Homegirls: Language and Cultural Practice among Latina Youth Gangs*. Malden, MA: Blackwell.

Miller, Reuben Jonathan. 2014. "Devolving the Carceral State: Race, Prisoner Reentry, and the Micro-Politics of Urban Poverty Management." *Punishment & Society* 16(3): 305–35.

Moore, Joan W. 1978. *Homeboys: Gangs, Drugs, and Prison in the Barrios of Los Angeles*. Philadelphia: Temple University Press.

Nolan, Kathleen, and Jean Anyon. 2004. "Learning to Do Time: Willis's Model of Cultural Reproduction in an Era of Postindustrialism, Globalization, and Mass Incarceration." In *Learning to Labor in New Times*, edited by Nadine Dolby, Greg Dimitriadis, and Paul Willis. New York: Routledge.

Pager, Devah. 2007. *Marked: Race, Crime, and Finding Work in an Era of Mass Incarceration*. Chicago: University of Chicago Press.

Parenti, Christian. 1998. "War on Crime." *San Francisco Bay Guardian*, November 18.

Parenti, Christian. 2000. *Lockdown America: Police and Prisons in the Age of Crisis*. New York: Verso.

Pascoe, C. J. 2007. *Dude, You're a Fag: Masculinity and Sexuality in High School*. Berkeley: University of California Press

Petersilia, Joan. 2003. *When Prisoners Come Home: Parole and Prisoner Reentry*. New York: Oxford University Press.

Petersilia, Joan, and Jessica Greenlick Snyder. 2013. "Looking Past the Hype: 10 Questions Everyone Should Ask about California's Prison Realignment." *California Journal of Politics and Policy* 5(2): 266–306.

Pettit, Becky, and Bruce Western. 2004. "Mass Imprisonment and the Life Course: Race and Class Inequality in US Incarceration." *American Sociological Review* 69: 151–69.

Phillips, Coretta. 2012. "'It Ain't Nothing like America with the Bloods and the Crips': Gang Narratives inside Two English Prisons." *Punishment & Society* 14(1): 51–68.

Rafael, Tony. 2009. *The Mexican Mafia*. New York: Encounter Books.

Rios, Victor. 2011. *Punished: Policing the Lives of Black and Latino Boys*. New York: New York University Press.

Rios, Victor, and Patrick Lopez-Aguado. 2012. "Pelones y Matones: Chicano Cholos Perform for a Punitive Audience." In *Performing the US Latina and Latino Borderlands*, edited by Arturo J. Aldama, Chela Sandoval, and Peter J. García. Bloomington: Indiana University Press.

Robertson, James E. 2006. "Foreword: 'Separate but Equal' in Prison: *Johnson v. California* and Common Sense Racism." *Journal of Criminal Law and Criminology* 96(3): 795–848.

Romero, Mary. 2001. "State Violence, and the Social and Legal Construction of Latino Criminality: From El Bandido to Gang Member." *Denver University Law Review* 78: 1081–112.

Romo, Rebecca. 2011. "Between Black and Brown: Blaxican (Black-Mexican) Multiracial Identity in California." *Journal of Black Studies* 42(3): 402–26.

Sampson, Robert J. 2012. *Great American City: Chicago and the Enduring Neighborhood Effect*. Chicago: University of Chicago Press.

Sampson, Robert J., Stephen W. Raudenbush, and Felton Earls. 1997. "Neighborhoods and Violent Crime: A Multilevel Study of Collective Efficacy." *Science* 277: 918–24.

Sharkey, Patrick. 2013. *Stuck in Place: Urban Neighborhoods and the End of Progress toward Racial Equality*. Chicago: University of Chicago Press.

Simon, Jonathan. 2007. "Rise of the Carceral State." *Social Research: An International Quarterly* 74(2): 471–508.

Skarbek, David. 2011. "Governance and Prison Gangs." *American Political Science Review* 105(4): 702–16.

Skarbek, David. 2014. *The Social Order of the Underworld: How Prison Gangs Govern the American Penal System*. New York: Oxford University Press.

Spatial Information Design Lab. 2008. "The Pattern." Report prepared for the Million Dollar Blocks Project, Columbia University, New York. http://spatial informationdesignlab.org/sites/default/files/publication_pdfs/ThePattern .pdf.

Spiegel, Sarah. 2007. "Prison 'Race Riots': An Easy Case for Segregation?" *California Law Review* 95(6): 2261–293.

Sykes, Gresham M. 1958. *The Society of Captives: A Study of a Maximum Security Prison*. Princeton, NJ: Princeton University Press

Thompson, Heather Ann. 2011. "Downsizing the Carceral State: The Policy Implications of Prison Guard Unions." *Criminology & Public Policy* 10(3): 771–79.

Torrey, E. Fuller, Aaron D. Kennard, Don Eslinger, Richard Lamb, and James Pavle. 2010. "More Mentally Ill Patients Are in Jails and Prisons Than Hospitals: A Survey of the States." Arlington, VA: Treatment Advocacy Center.

Travis, Jeremy. 2004. "Reentry and Reintegration: New Perspectives on the Challenges of Mass Incarceration." In *Imprisoning America: The Social Effects of Mass Incarceration*, edited by Mary Patillo, David Weiman, and Bruce Western. New York: Russell Sage Foundation.

Trulson, Chad R., and James W. Marquart. 2002. "The Caged Melting Pot: Toward an Understanding of the Consequences of Desegregation in Prisons." *Law and Society Review* 36(4): 743–82.

Van Cleve, Nicole Gonzalez. 2016. *Crook County: Racism and Injustice in America's Largest Criminal Court.* Palo Alto, CA: Stanford University Press.

Venkatesh, Sudhir Alladi. 2000. *American Project: The Rise and Fall of a Modern Ghetto.* Cambridge, MA: Harvard University Press.

Venkatesh, Sudhir Alladi, Eva Rosen, Cynthia Golembeski, Grace June Kim, Sarah Williams, Laura Kurgan, James Connelly, and Ann Foss. 2007. *A Research Note: The Socio-Spatial Consequences of Inmate Release in New York City.* A report prepared for the Center of Urban Research and Policy, Columbia University, New York

Wacquant, Loic. 2001. "Deadly Symbiosis: When Ghetto and Prison Meet and Mesh." *Punishment & Society* 3(1): 95–133.

Wacquant, Loic. 2009. *Punishing the Poor: The Neoliberal Government of Social Insecurity.* Durham, NC: Duke University Press.

Wald, Johanna, and Daniel F. Losen. 2003. "Defining and Redirecting a School-to-Prison Pipeline." *New Directions for Youth Development* 99: 9–15.

Walker, Michael L. 2016. "Race Making in a Penal Institution." *American Journal of Sociology* 121(4): 1051–78.

Weider, D. Lawrence. 1974. *Language and Social Reality: The Case of Telling the Convict Code.* The Hague: Mouton.

Western, Bruce. 2006. *Punishment and Inequality in America.* New York: Russel Sage.

Woodward, Rachel. 2000. "Warrior Heroes and Little Green Men: Soldiers, Military Training, and the Construction of Rural Masculinities." *Rural Sociology* 65(4): 640–57.

# Index

Black Guerilla Family, 3
Blacks
affiliations of, 33, 207n5
bullying by Whites, 55
criminalization of poor, 133–137
exploitation of, 205n3
mixed-race, 101
Brandon (student), 57–58, 62
Bulldogs
as affiliation, 2, 60–64
formation of, 9, 14, 118–120
identity through familiarity, 97–98
policing of, 13, 211n7
prison facilities for, 205–206n8
style associated with, 178–180

California Department of Corrections
and Rehabilitation (CDCR), 9, 14,
30. See also specific facilities by
name
California Youth Authority (YA), 115–
116, 144–145, 209n2(ch4). See
also specific facilities by name
Cameron (student), 134–135
carceral social order
adoption as survival strategy, 53–60,
116–117, 130–133
categorization of inmates, 29–39, 41,
53–54, 117–118, 151–152, 205n5
conflict protocols, 141–144
criminalization of communities,
133–137, 167–175
defensive violence, 144–153
defining affiliations, 60–64, 207n3
finding safety in numbers, 39–40,
54–56, 82, 140
gang identity shifts, 64–67
impact on families, 11–13
institutional construction of, 21–22,
52–53, 80–81, 192
learning rules of, 64–67
mixed-race categorization, 82–83,
95–101
neighborhood youth understanding
of, 121–128, 144–146, 158–161
peer sorting, 81–84
physical space and, 39–40, 43–48,
84–88, 146–150, 202–203

policing methods, 175–180
refusal of affiliations, 2, 83–84, 102–
109, 159–160
reinforcement of, 22
resistance to, 2–4, 102–109, 126–127,
156–157, 159–160
shaping of identities by, 22, 27–29,
48–50
socialization of, 9, 39–43, 198–200
suspension of outside rivalries for
stability, 143–145
systemic reforms, 201–203
transmission into outside
communities, 6, 7–8, 23, 205n3
Carla (parolee), 128–130
Carlos (student), 59
cars (group identity)
advantages of, 60–61, 141–142
definition, 205n6
leadership, 209n2(ch3)
rules of, 66–67, 86–87, 207–208n4
Mr. Castro (teacher), 173–174
Celia (staff member), 183
Central California. See Bulldogs
Chicana/os. See also Latina/os;
Mexicana/os
affiliations, 62–63, 102–105
criminalization of poor, 133–137
cultural divisions, 68, 69–70, 100,
210n5
personal style, 88, 89–94, 177–178
Chris (student), 70–71
Christian (student), 152–153
Clayton (police officer), 175–176
Clear, Todd, 5
cliquing up. See carceral social order
clothing, 88, 89–93, 177–178, 177–180
college, 193–195
Colton (student), 173–174
Comfort, Megan, 11
communities. See also youth
concentrated incarceration, 4–6
criminalization, 5–9, 14, 167–175,
205n2
disinvestment of public funds, 15,
128–133, 136–137
impressions of prison life, 121–128,
144–146